Theodore T. Munger

The Freedom of Faith

Theodore T. Munger

The Freedom of Faith

ISBN/EAN: 9783337284770

Printed in Europe, USA, Canada, Australia, Japan

Cover: Foto ©Lupo / pixelio.de

More available books at **www.hansebooks.com**

ON THE THRESHOLD.

By T. T. MUNGER. 16mo, gilt top, $1.00.

Talks to young people on Purpose, Friends and Companions, Manners, Thrift, Self-Reliance and Courage, Health, Reading and Intellectual Life, Amusements, and Faith.

This book touches acts, habits, character, destiny; it deals with the present and vital thought in literature, society, life; it stimulates one with the idea that life is worth living. . . . The production of a book of this sort is not an every-day occurrence: it is an event: it will work a revolution among young men who read it; it has the manly ring from cover to cover. — *New York Times.*

The spirit in which the book is written is neither narrow nor unduly critical, but sympathetic rather, and healthful and manly. The work is a plea, not for asceticism or rigidity of any kind, but for self-respect, open-mindedness, and right-living; for good faith and earnestness of life; for cheerful courage, honesty, and good health alike of body and mind. It is such a plea as all manly young men will listen to with interest and profit. — *New York Evening Post.*

It is a book calculated to do a great deal of good wherever it is attentively read, as it can hardly help being by any one who dips into it at all. We wish especially that every young man on the threshold of life might have such a wholesome introduction to its struggles and prizes as this book furnishes. — *Christian Register* (Boston).

There is a finished, not to say eloquent brightness in these chapters, which carries the reader on with kindling interest from page to page. . . . At once wise and winning, and free from anything *common.* — *The Independent* (New York).

It is sensible, earnest, candid, and discriminating, and, withal, thoroughly interesting. — *The Congregationalist* (Boston).

*** *For sale by Booksellers. Sent, post-paid, on receipt of price by the Publishers,*

HOUGHTON, MIFFLIN & CO., BOSTON, MASS.

THE

FREEDOM OF FAITH.

BY

THEODORE T. MUNGER,
AUTHOR OF "ON THE THRESHOLD."

"Peace settles where the intellect is meek;
The faith Heaven strengthens where He moulds the creed."
WORDSWORTH

NINTH EDITION.

BOSTON:
HOUGHTON, MIFFLIN AND COMPANY.
New York: 11 East Seventeenth Street.
The Riverside Press, Cambridge.
1884.

CONTENTS.

	PAGE.
PREFATORY ESSAY: "THE NEW THEOLOGY"	1

SERMONS.

I.
On Reception of New Truth 45

II.
God our Shield. I. 71

III.
God our Reward. II. 91

IV.
Love to the Christ as a Person 107

V.
The Christ's Pity 129

VI.
The Christ as a Preacher 149

VII.
Land Tenure 169

VIII.
Moral Environment 191

IX.
Immortality and Science 215

X.
IMMORTALITY AND NATURE 235

XI.
IMMORTALITY AS TAUGHT BY THE CHRIST 255

XII.
THE CHRIST'S TREATMENT OF DEATH 271

XIII.
THE RESURRECTION FROM THE DEAD 293

XIV.
THE METHOD OF PENALTY 315

XV.
THE JUDGMENT 337

XVI.
LIFE A GAIN 357

XVII
THINGS TO BE AWAITED 377

"THE NEW THEOLOGY."

"Man's chief and highest end is to glorify God, and fully to enjoy Him forever." — *Westminster Catechism.*

"I shall merely enumerate a few of the most common of these feelings that present obstacles to the pursuit or propagation of truth: Aversion to *doubt;* desire of a supposed happy medium; the love of system; the dread of the character of inconsistency; the love of novelty; the dread of innovation; undue deference to human authority; the love of approbation, and the dread of censure; regard to seeming expediency." — *Whately's Annotations on Bacon's Essay on Truth,* page 10.

"The principles on which I have taught: First. The establishment of positive truth, instead of the negative destruction of error. Secondly. That truth is made up of two opposite propositions, and not found in a *viâ media* between the two. Thirdly. That spiritual truth is discerned by the spirit, instead of intellectually in propositions; and, therefore, Truth should be taught suggestively, not dogmatically. Fourthly. That belief in the Human character of Christ's Humanity must be antecedent to belief in His Divine origin. Fifthly. That Christianity, as its teachers should, works from the inward to the outward, and not *vice versâ.* Sixthly. The soul of goodness in things evil." — *Life of F. W. Robertson,* Vol. ii. p. 160.

PREFATORY ESSAY.

"THE NEW THEOLOGY."

The purpose of this Essay is to state, so far as is now possible, some of the main features of that phase of present thought popularly known as " The New Theology : " to indicate the lines on which it is moving, to express something of its spirit, and to give it so much of definite form that it shall no longer suffer from the charge of vagueness.

I use, however, the phrase New Theology simply as one of convenience, disclaiming for it any real propriety, and even denying its appropriateness. For the thing that it represents is not new nor yet old. It might better be described — as it has been — as a Renaissance: for the conceptions of Christian doctrine that are now floating in the minds of men, with promise of crystallizing into form, are not of recent origin; they prevailed in the first centuries of the church, while the stream ran clear from the near fountain, and they have appeared all along in individual minds and schools, as the higher peaks of a mountain range catch the sunshine, while the base is enveloped in mist and shadow, — not many, and often far separate, but enough to show the trend, and to bear witness to the light. Neither is this phrase used to designate a class, nor to separate one set of men from another. The distinguishing line does not run between different minds, but rather runs through all minds. Every calm, reflecting person now interested in theology may detect in himself a line of demarkation between sympathies that cling to the old and that reach out after the new. With the noisy, thoughtless shouters for the new because it seems to be new, and with the sullen, obstinate sticklers for the old because it is the old, these pages have little to do. There is, however, a large class of earnest, reflecting minds who recognize a certain development of doctrine, a transfer of emphasis, a change of temper, a widened habit of thought, a broader research, that justify the use of some term by which to designate it. This class need little teaching, save that of their own trained intelligence; they know the age and its requirements; they know the Scriptures, the spirit of their teachings and the law of their interpretation; they know how to hold themselves before the philosophies in whose court the main questions are decided; they have open eyes before the growing knowledge of the world and the unfolding manifestations of God. But while this class have been quietly passing from one phase of thought to another, without shock to their minds or detriment to their characters, there is a far larger class who are thrown into confusion by the change it has observed in the other. Only the trained intellect passes easily through changes of thought and belief: others see in change only a loss; they regard modification of view as abandonment; they cannot readily adjust their eyes to the increasing light. Hence there is at present a sad state of popular confusion as to religious belief. The people hear new statements in regard to inspiration, atonement, retribution, and the war of words that follows in councils and from the press and pulpit and platform intensifies their confusion, — stormy assertion, passionate denial, retreats into the past on one side, and blind rushing into the jaws of a material philosophy on the other side, Calvin or Herbert Spencer, the old creed or no Bible, blind fear offset by blind audacity. Meanwhile, "the hungry sheep look up and are not fed;" "the people perish for lack of knowledge;" they know not what to believe. They cannot be fed or quieted by exhortations to believe what they have always believed, nor are they fed or content when assured that every-day morality is all they need to concern themselves about, or that all theology is to be reconstructed, in due time, on a basis of physical evolution. For, while there is, without doubt, a strong popular drift towards materialism, there is also a counter, protesting drift that flows out of the inextinguishable spiritual instincts. When religion is presented to men enveloped in a material philosophy, they scent danger, and turn from it "blindly wise," driven by an instinctive fear lest they be "canceled in the world of sense." But the people cannot themselves formulate these instincts and reduce them to their rational equivalents; they cannot make the transition from that which no longer feeds and satisfies to the fresher conceptions that can. Hence it is largely an age of arrested belief, dangerous to all, fatal to many. The blame is thickly and widely scattered about, — on pulpit and pew, on science and philosophy, on theologians and editors, on the orthodox and the heterodox; let us each take our share, for there is a certain deep homogeneity of the age that renders it accountable for its condition. There is, however, this sure ground of hope: that the great body of mankind will not long live without a faith.

While what is called the New Theology is, in part, the cause of this condition, it also finds in it the reason of its being. It is not a disturber of the peace in the realm of belief, but comes forward to meet the unconscious thought and the conscious need of the people, and, if possible, do something towards quelling the anarchy of fear and doubt that now prevails. It is not a vague thing,

> "Wandering between two worlds, one dead,
> The other powerless to be born,"

but a definite movement, that attempts to link the truth of the past with the truth of the present in the interest of the Christian faith. It justifies itself by the belief that it can minister to faith, and by a conviction that the total thought of an age ought to have the greatest possible unity, or, in plainer phrase, that its creed ought not to antagonize its knowledge.

In attempting to give some expression of the New Theology, I wish to state with the utmost emphasis that I do not speak for any party, but only describe things as I see them. And especially would I disclaim any *ex-cathedra* tone that may seem to issue from any form of words. I speak from the stand-point of the sharpest and even most isolated individuality, — for myself alone.

I will first refer to certain negative features, indicating what it is *not;* and then more fully to its positive character.

1. It does not propose to do without a theology.

It seeks no such transformation of method or form that it can no longer claim the name of a science. It does not resolve belief into sentiment, nor etherealize it into mysticism, nor lower it into mere altruism; yet it does not deny an element of sentiment, it acknowledges an element of mysticism, and it insists on a firm basis in ethics. It is the determined foe of agnosticism, yet it recognizes a limitation of human knowledge. While it insists that theology is a science, and that therefore its parts should be coördinate and mutually supporting, and an induction from all the facts known to it, it realizes that it deals with eternal realities that cannot be wholly compassed, and also with the mysteries and contradictions of a world involved in mystery and beset by contradictory forces. If it finds itself driven into impenetrable mystery, as it inevitably must, it prefers to take counsel of the higher sentiments and better hopes of our nature, rather than project into it the frame-work of a formal logic, and insist on its conclusion. It does not abjure logic, but it refuses to be held by what is often deemed logic. While it believes in a harmony of doctrines, it regards with suspicion what have been known as systems of theology, on the ground that it rejects the methods by which they are constructed. It will not shape a doctrine in order that it may fit another which has been shaped in the same fashion, — a merely mechanical interplay, and seeking a mechanical harmony. Instead, it regards theology as an induction from the revelations of God — in the Bible, in history, in the nation, in the family, in the material creation, and in the whole length and breadth of human life. It will have, therefore, all the definiteness and harmony it can find in these revelations, but it will have no more, since it regards these revelations as under a process still enacting, and not as under a finality. The modern authors whom it most consults must be regarded as holding a theology worthy of the name, — Erskine, Campbell, McLeod, Maurice, Stanley, Robertson, the Hare brothers, Bushnell; and if we enumerate its representatives among the living, we must recite the names of those who are eminent in every form of thought and in every work of holy charity.

2. The New Theology does not part with the historic faith of the church, but rather seeks to put itself in its line while recognizing a process of development. It does not propose to commit " retrospective suicide " at every fresh stage of advance. It holds to progress by slow and cosmic growth rather than by cataclysmal leaps. It allies itself even with the older rather than the later theologies, and finds in the early Greek theology conceptions more harmonious with itself than those in the theology shaped by Augustine.[1]

[1] See the very able and suggestive article, by Prof. A. V. G. Allen, on

3. It does not reject the specific doctrines of the church of the past. It holds to the Trinity, though indifferent to the use of the word, but not to a formal and psychologically impossible Trinity; to the divine sovereignty, but it does not make it the corner-stone of its system, preferring for that place the divine righteousness, *i. e.*, a moral rather than a dynamic basis; to the Incarnation, not as a mere physical event, for that has entered into many religions, but as the entrance into the world through a person of a moulding and redeeming force in humanity,—the central and broadest fact of theology; to the Atonement as a divine act and process of ethical and practical import—not as a mystery of the distant heavens and isolated from the struggle of the world, but a comprehensible force in the actual redemption of the world from its evil; to the Resurrection as covering the whole essential nature of man; to Judgment as involved in the development of a moral nature; to the eternal awards of conduct considered as laws and principles of character, but not necessarily set in time-relations; to human sinfulness under a conception of moral freedom; to Justification by faith in the sense of a faith that, by its law, induces an actual righteousness—a simple, rational process realized in human experience; to Regeneration and Sanctification by the Spirit as most imperative operations based on the utmost need, and on the actual presence and power of the Spirit in the life of humanity. It does not explain

"The Theological Renaissance of the Nineteenth Century," in the *Princeton Review*, November, 1882, and January, 1883.

away from these doctrines their substance, nor minimize them, nor aim to do else than present them as revealed in the Scriptures and as developed in history and in the life of the church and of the world.

4. It is not iconoclastic in its temper; it is not pervaded by a spirit of denial, but is constructive — taking away nothing without supplying its place; it does not, indeed, find so much occasion to take away and replace as to uncover and bring to light. Believing that revelation is not so much *from* God as *of* God, its logical attitude is that of seeing and interpreting.

5. It is not disposed to find a field and organization outside of existing churches, conscious that it is building on that Eternal Foundation which alone has given strength to the church in every age. It claims only that liberty whereunto all are called in the church of Christ. It asserts that the real ground of membership in the church is fidelity to the faith, and that this ground is not forfeited because it refuses to assent to human and formal conditions that the church has taken on, and which are not of the substance of the faith. Emphasizing as it does the headship of Christ in the visible as well as invisible church, it would retain its place in the church on the basis of its loyalty to Christ and as its all-sufficient warrant, paying small heed to a narrow, ecclesiastical logic that now confounds, and now distinguishes between, the bounds of the visible body and the breadth and freedom of Christ's church.

I pass now to the positive features of the New Theology.

1. It claims for itself a somewhat larger and broader use of the reason than has been accorded to theology.

And by reason we do not mean mere speculation nor a formal logic, but that full exercise of our nature which embraces the intuitions, the conscience, the susceptibilities, and the judgment, *i. e.*, man's whole inner being. Especially it makes much of the intuitions — the universal and spontaneous verdicts of the soul; and in this it deems that it allies itself with the Mind through which the Christian revelation is made.

The fault of the theology now passing is that it insists on a presentation of doctrines in such a way as perpetually to challenge the reason. By a logic of its own — a logic created for its own ends, and not a logic drawn from the depth and breadth of human life — it frets and antagonizes the fundamental action of human nature. If Christianity has any human basis it is its entire reasonableness. It must not only sit easily on the mind, but it must ally itself with it in all its normal action. If it chafes it, if it is a burden, if it antagonizes, it detracts from itself; the human mind cannot be detracted from. Man is a knower; the reason never ceases to be less than itself without losing all right to use itself as reason. Consequently a full adjustment between reason and Christianity is steadily to be sought. If there is conflict, uneasiness, burdensomeness, the cause is to be looked for in interpretation rather than in the human reason. For, in the last analysis, revelation — so far as its acceptance is concerned — rests on reason, and not reason on revelation. The logical order is, first reason, and then revelation — the eye before sight. It is just here that a narrow and formal theology inserts its hurtful fallacy; it says, Use your reason for ascertaining that a revelation is probable, and has been made, after which the only office of the mind is to accept the contents of the revelation without question, *i. e.*, without other use of the reason than some small office of collating texts and drawing inferences. But this is formal and arbitrary. The mind accepts revelation because it accepts the *substance* of revelation. It does not stand outside upon some structure of logical inference that a revelation has been made, and therefore is to be accepted, but instead it enters into the material of the revelation, and plants its feet there. The reason believes the revelation because *in itself* it is reasonable. Human nature — so far as it acts by itself — accepts Christianity because it establishes a thorough *consensus* with human nature; it is agreeable in its nature to human nature in its normal action. It wins its way on the man-ward side by winning the assent of the whole reasonable nature of man. The largest play must be allowed to this principle. It is thus that the light of thought enters into and guides all spiritual processes, and discloses their reality. It is thus, and thus only, that the reason of man meets and recognizes the reason of God that is wrought into the revelation. Otherwise, belief is a mechanical thing, and spiritual processes become blind acts of the will. It is arbitrary and unscientific to use the reason up to a certain point, and then hood it with blinding restrictions; to think and weigh and feel up to the point of the discovery of a revelation, and then remand thought and feeling to the background, and so reduce the whole action of the mind to an acceptance of texts. Thought and feeling are as necessary for interpretation as for acceptance, and it is as legitimate for the reason to pass judgment upon the *contents* of revelation as upon the grounds of receiving it; they are, in fact, identical. In brief, we accept the Christian faith because of the reasonableness of its entire substance, and not because we have somehow become persuaded that a revelation has been made. It is impossible to conceive of it as gaining foothold in the mind and heart in any other way, nor can faith in it be otherwise secured. And the revelation will be forever appealing to the reason; playing into it as flame mingles with flame, and drawing from it that which is kindred with itself. The inmost principle of revelation is that the mind of God reveals itself to the mind of man; and the basis of this principle is that one mind is made in the image of the other, and therefore capable of similar processes of thought and feeling. Revelation is not a disclosure of things to be done, or of bare facts pertaining to eternity, but is rather an unveiling of the thought and feeling of God to men, in response to which they become sons of the Most High. This is the hold that it has on humanity, and this is the method of its acting. Hence, in simple phrase, it must be on friendly terms with the human reason and heart. It is on such terms; it is only through misinterpretation that it antagonizes the sober conclusions of universal reason and evokes the protest of the universal human heart.

If it be said that human nature is weakened and perverted by evil, and therefore cannot be relied on for just estimates of the contents of revelation, we answer that it is then equally unfit to form a judgment on the question of having or not having a revelation. If reason can determine the universal point, it can determine the particular points; if it can cover the whole, it can cover the parts. But, what is of greater moment, to attribute inability to the reason is to pave the way to Pyrrhonism. If I cannot know in such a way as to satisfy my reason, I must forever doubt. Here is where Pascal fails as a defender of the faith, holding that because the reason is corrupted it can be sure of nothing, yet asserting the duty of belief, — a very monstrosity of inconsistency; yet he bravely accepts it, and has, at last, but one word for the questioner: "Do as I do: go to mass and use holy water." The impotence of his conclusion is the condemnation of his premise.

There are indeed limits to reason, and it has in it an element of faith, but so far as it goes, it goes surely and firmly; it is not a rotten foundation, it is not a broken reed, it is not a false light. It may be so sure that it can justly protest in the face of Heaven, "Shall not the Judge of all the earth do right?" It will be humble and docile and trustful, but these qualities are not abrogations of itself. It does not claim for itself the ability to measure the whole breadth and reach of truth; it does not say, I will not believe what I cannot understand, for it knows full well that human reason is not commensurate with eternal truth. But this is quite different from silencing reason before questions that have been cast upon human nature, yet are so interpreted as to violate every principle of human nature; *e. g.*, it is not called to hold its belief in God as a reasonable belief, and to accept a conception of God that throws it into a chaos of moral confusion and contradiction. To trust is a great duty; but as reason has an element of faith, so faith has an element of reason, and that element requires that the fundamental verdicts of human nature shall not be set aside. The lines on which trusting reason, or reasoning trust, proceed do not run straight into impenetrable mystery, and come back from that mystery to slay reason and well-nigh slay faith.

The familiar illustration, drawn from the duty of the child to obey the parent without understanding why, is a partial fallacy. The highest relation between child and parent is that in which there is sympathetic obedience because the child understands why. "No longer do I call you servants; for the servant knoweth not what his lord doeth: but I have called you friends; for all things that I heard from my Father I have made known unto you." "Mine own know me, even as the Father knoweth me:" when the Revised Version thus tells us that believers know Christ even as the Father knows him, there is not much room for mystery in the revelations of the Christ.

This blind acceptance of revelation as something with which the reason has little to do, in respect to which the New Theology parts company with the Old, is based on the conception that revelation is grounded on miracle, *i. e.*, on sense, — a principle that Christ condemned over and over: "Blessed are they that have not seen, and yet have believed."

2. The New Theology seeks to interpret the Scriptures in what may be called a more natural way, and in opposition to a hard, formal, unsympathetic, and unimaginative way.

Its strongest denial and its widest divergence from the Old Theology lie here. It holds profoundly to inspiration, but it also holds that the Scriptures were written by living men, whose life entered into their writings; it finds the color and temper of the writer's mind in his work; it finds also the temper and habit of the age; it penetrates the forms of Oriental speech; it seeks to read out of the mind and conception and custom of the writer instead of reading present conceptions into his words. In brief, it reads the Scriptures as literature, yet with no derogation from their inspiration. It refuses to regard the writers as automatic organs of the Spirit, — "moved," indeed, but not carried outside of themselves nor separated from their own ways and conceptions. It is thus that it regards the Bible as a *living* book; it is warm and vital with the life of a divine humanity, and thus it speaks to humanity. But as it was written by men in other ages and of other habits of speech, it needs to be interpreted; it is necessary to get back into the mind of the writer in order to get at the inspiration of his utterance; for before there is an inspired writing there is an inspired man, through whom only its meaning can be reached. This is a very different process from picking out texts here and there, and putting them together to form a doctrine; yet it is by such a process that systems of theology have been formed, and cast on society for acceptance. The New Theology does not proceed in such a way. The Old Theology reads the Scriptures with a lexicon, and weighs words as men weigh iron; it sees no medium between the form of words and their first or preconceived meaning. It looks into the Bible as one looks through space, beyond the atmosphere, upon the sun, — seeing one point of glowing light, but darkness on every side; one text of burning sense, but no atmosphere of context, or age, or custom, or temper of mind, or end in view. The New Theology does not tolerate the inconsistency of the Old, as it slowly gives up the theory of verbal inspiration, but retains views based on verbal inspiration. It will not remove foundations and prop up the superstructure with assertions.

Again, it does not regard the Bible as a magical book; it is not a diviner's rod; it is not a charmed thing of intrinsic power, representing a far-off God. The New Theology remembers that the mass, the confessional, the priestly office, the intercession of saints, were the product of a theology that held to a mechanical, outside God, and that these superstitions sprang from the demand of the human heart for a God near at hand. It remembers that when these superstitions were cast off and the theology retained the Bible was put in their place, and with something of the same superstitious regard. Hence, it was not read naturally and in a free, off-hand way, as it was inspired and written, but in hard and artificial ways, and was used much as men use charms. The New Theology does not reduce to something less the inspiration of the Bible, nor does it yield to any theology in its sense of its supreme value in the redemption of the world; but it holds it as purely instrumental, and not as magical in its power or method. It is a history of the highest form in which God is manifesting himself in the world, but it is not the manifestation itself; it is not a revelation, but is a history of a revelation; it is a chosen and indispensable means of the redemption of the world, but it is not the absolute means, — that is in the Spirit. It is necessary to make this distinction in order to read it, otherwise it cannot be interpreted; it lies outside the sphere of our rational nature, — a charmed mystery, before which we may sit in awe, but not a voice speaking to our thinking minds.

Again: the New Theology is not disposed to limit its interpretation of the Scriptures by the principle contained in the phrase "the plain meaning of the words." This is a true principle, but it may be used in a narrow and untrue way. It is one of those phrases that wins immediate assent because it flatters the popular mind, like the appeals to "common sense,"—a trick under which a vast amount of error and slipshod belief has crept into the world. It is by an undue and exclusive use of this principle that a theology has been created intolerable to human nature. Now a theology cannot be forced on the human mind. Men may be required to believe what they do not *like* to believe, but they cannot be forced to believe what they cannot believe, *i. e.*, to believe against the universal voice of reason and heart and knowledge. There will first be silence, then denial and rejection, and all along inefficiency or abnormal results. To escape from a theology so created, there must be a broader principle of interpretation than this of "the plain meaning of the words;" or, rather, this principle must be enlarged, until it becomes something quite different. There must be recognized the principle of moral evolution or development,— a principle that removes whatever difficulties some may feel as to Hebrew anthropomorphism; it must be allowed that every writer of the Bible wrote under human limitations, and that it is within the province of the reason to discover the limitations and so get at the meaning, as it does with any other book, with only this difference, that when it thus reaches the meaning it is wholly trustworthy.

Another principle is that the Bible, like the order of history, is a continually unfolding revelation of God; it is a book of eternal laws and facts that are evolving their truth and reality in the process of history. Its full meaning is not yet disclosed; it is an ever-opening book. It is always leading man in the right direction, but it does not show him at once, in clear light, the whole domain of truth. It is therefore a book to be constantly and freshly interpreted; it may mean to-morrow more than it means to-day. This principle of "the plain meaning of the words" is to be used under other principles and in connection with all possible knowledge.

The point has recently been made by a critic of the Unitarian school that "the Bible is an orthodox book." With profound respect for the honesty and ability of the critic, the New Theology regards with indifference a criticism that encourages the Old Theology to foster theories that the critic plainly sees can lead only to its final and utter collapse, provoking the instant and necessarily expected inference that "we must revise our Bible or keep our creed." The New Theology agrees neither with the critic nor with the comment; it holds principles of interpretation that bind it neither to the school represented by the one nor by the other. To assert an identity between the Bible and the theology of New England as it was sixty years ago is to ignore previous ages of church history, and scores of years since; it is to ignore all other theology, — the early Greek, the Arminian, the Mystical, and the Romish. Yet upon such a summons, some are induced either to "revise the Bible or keep the creed." The New Theology will do neither; it refuses to be deceived by an " undistributed middle" of a syllogism; it chooses instead to reinterpret the Bible, *i. e.*, find out what it actually means, and revise the creed if it is necessary.

By what rule, under what impulse, for what reason, shall it do the former? The answer is brief: When it must; *i. e.*, when there is such an accumulation of knowledge and of evidence against the apparent meaning that the mind cannot tolerate the inconsistency, it must search the text to see if it will not bear a meaning, or rather does not contain a meaning, — indeed, was intended to convey a meaning that we have failed to catch, — consistent with ascertained facts. It is already a familiar process, as illustrated in the treatment of the first chapters of Genesis. The Bible receives no detriment from being interpreted under such a principle; how much larger, in their truth, are these chapters than they were a century ago! This is not a chameleon process; it does not reduce the Bible to a pliant mass, to be shaped anew by every restless critic; it does not deprive it of positive meaning and character. It regards it rather as a revelation of God, the full meaning of which is to be evolved in the history of the world, — a light that simply burns brighter as time goes on. It is this very characteristic that makes it a miraculous book, if we care so to name it. It is to be remembered, also, that the Bible generates the light in which it is to be interpreted, — "the master light of all our seeing;" it were well if that light were more used! There is no denial of the fact that doctrines now regarded as parts of orthodoxy are the reflections of the social condition in which they were formulated. The doctrines of divine sovereignty, of total depravity, and of the atonement are shot through with colors drawn from the corruption of Roman society, from the Roman sense of authority and the Roman forms of justice. The Bible furnished isolated texts for holding these conceptions, but the Bible, as a whole, did not furnish the conceptions; had it been used to furnish conceptions of doctrines, we would not now have what goes for orthodoxy. But Rome passes, and the Bible endures; the leaven of heathen society is eliminated, and the leaven of the Gospel works its slow transformation in the world. It generates a sense of freedom and humanity that renders impossible a belief in divine sovereignty, and human depravity, and legal atonement, and future retribution, as they were first formulated, and are still retained, in the Old Theology. The present universal protest against the old conception of retribution is due simply to the fact that the Gospel itself has trained the mind to such a point of tender, humane, and just feeling that it necessarily repudiates it. The defenders of the old view hurl the Bible, as though it were a missile, at doubters and deniers; the New Theology says, Let us open it again, and read it in the light that it has kindled in our minds and in society, not despising the tenderness and humanity which are its offspring. Whatever the Bible may be, it is not a Saturn, devouring its own children.

3. The New Theology seeks to replace an excessive individuality by a truer view of the solidarity of the race.

It does not deny a real individuality, it does not

predicate an absolute solidarity, but simply removes the emphasis from one to the other. It holds that every man must live a life of his own, build himself up into a full personality, and give an account of himself to God: but it also recognizes the blurred truth that man's life lies in its relations; that it is a derived and shared life; that it is carried on and perfected under laws of heredity and of the family and the nation; that while he is "himself alone" he is also a son, a parent, a citizen, and an inseparable part of the human race; that in origin and character and destiny he cannot be regarded as standing in a sharp and utter individuality. It differs from the Old Theology in a more thorough and consistent application of this distinction. That holds to an absolute solidarity in evil, relieved by a doctrine of election of individuals; this holds to a solidarity running throughout the whole life of humanity in the world, — not an absolute solidarity, but one modified by human freedom. It is not disposed wholly to part company with the Old in respect to the "fall in Adam" (when the Scriptures, on this point, are properly interpreted), and hereditary evil, and the like; it sees in these conceptions substantial truths, when freed from their excessiveness and their formal and categorical shapes, but it carries this solidarity into the whole life of man. If it is a fallen world, it is also a redeemed world; if it is a lost world, it is a saved world; the Christ is no less to it than Adam; the divine humanity is no smaller than the Adamic humanity; the Spirit is as powerful and as universal as sin; the links that bind the race to evil are correlated by links equally strong binding it to righteousness. It goes, in a certain manner, with the Old Theology in its views of common evil, but it diverges from it in its conceptions of the redemptive and delivering forces by ascribing to them corresponding sweep. To repeat: it does not admit that Christ is less to the race than Adam, that the Gospel is smaller than evil; it does not consign mankind as a mass to a pit of common depravity, and leave it to emerge as individuals under some notion of election, or by solitary choice, each one escaping as he can and according to his "chance," but the greater part not escaping at all. It does not so read revelation and history and life, finding in them all a corporate element, "a moving altogether when it moves at all," — an interweaving of life with life that renders it impossible wholly to extricate the individual. It allies itself with the thought of the present age and the best thought of all ages, that mankind is moved by common forces, and follows common tendencies falling and rising together, partakers together in all good and ill desert, verifying the phrase, "the life of humanity." It believes that the Spirit broods over the "evil world" as it brooded upon the chaos of old; that humanity is charged with redemptive forces, wrought into the soul and into the divine institutions of the family and the nation, and whatever other relation binds man to man; and it believes that these forces are not in vain.

Still, it does not submerge the individual in the

common life, nor free him from personal ill desert, nor take from him the crown of personal achievement and victory. It simply strives to recognize the duality of truth, and hold it well poised. It turns our attention to the corporate life of man here in the world, — an individual life, indeed, but springing from common roots, fed by a common life, watched over by one Father, inspired by one Spirit, and growing to one end ; no man, no generation, being "made perfect" by itself. Hence its ethical emphasis ; hence its recognition of the nation, and of the family, and of social and commercial life, as fields of the manifestation of God and of the operation of the Spirit ; hence its readiness to ally itself with all movements for bettering the condition of mankind, — holding that human society itself is to be redeemed, and that the world itself, in its corporate capacity, is being reconciled to God ; hence also an apparently secular tone, which is, however, but a widening of the field of the divine and spiritual.

4. This theology recognizes a new relation to natural science ; but only in the respect that it ignores the long apparent antagonism between the kingdoms of faith and of natural law, — an antagonism that cannot, from the nature of things, have a basis in reality. But while it looks on the external world as a revelation of God and values the truth it may reveal ; while even it recognizes in it analogies to the spiritual world and a typical similarity of method, it does not merge itself in natural science. It is not yet ready, and it shows no signs that it

ever will be ready, to gather up its beliefs, and go over into the camp of natural science, and sit down under the manipulations of a doctrine of evolution, with its one category of matter and one invariable force. It is not ready to commit itself to a finite system, a merely phenomenal section of the universe and of time, with no *whence,* or *whither,* or *why,* — a system that simply supplies man with a certain kind of knowledge, but solves no problem that weighs on his heart, answers no question that he much cares to ask, and throws not one glimmer of additional light on his origin, his nature, or his destiny. It accepts gratefully the knowledge it discloses of the material universe, its laws and its processes; it admits that science has anticipated theology in formulating the method of creation known as evolution, that it has corrected modern theology by suggesting a closer and more vital relation between God and creation, and so has helped it throw off a mechanical theory and regain its forgotten theory of the divine immanence in creation. But farther than this it does not propose to go, for the simple reason that it is the end of its journey in that direction. The New Theology, like the old, refuses to merge itself in a system that is both material and finite, and therefore incapable of a moral and spiritual conception. It denies that the universe can be put into one category, that matter is inclusive of the spiritual, or what is deemed spiritual; it denies that the material world is the only field of knowledge, and that its force is the only force acting in the world. It asserts the reality of the spiritual as above the material, of force that is other than that lodged in matter, of truth realized in another way than by induction from material facts, however fine their gradation, of an eternal existence and a human self-consciousness correlated in mutual knowledge and freedom and power. It makes these assertions on scientific grounds and as inductions from phenomena, and therefore claims for itself the possession of knowledge that is such in reality.

It is the more careful to make these assertions that involve an infinite and eternal Will and a human consciousness of God in free and eternal relations to God, because it has witnessed the experiment of those who have attempted to preserve faith without a theosophy. "Step by step, the theological is supplanted by the scientific, the divine by the human view,"— a process that finally brings "eternal things" within a finite system, or retains them as mere sentiments that will surely fade away, and so leave man at the mercy of a system of necessity under which all nobility and freedom will die out, or linger but as contradictory instincts.

The New Theology accepts the phrase "a religion of humanity," but it holds that it is more than an adjustment of the facts of humanity, and more than a reduction of the forces of humanity to harmony. It accepts the theory of physical evolution as the probable method of physical creation, and as having an analogy in morals; but it accepts it under the fact of a personal God who is revealing himself, and of human freedom,— facts not to be ascertained within the limits of a material philosophy. It holds that the main relations of humanity are to God, and that these relations constitute a theology, a science of God; for in Him we live, and move, and have our being.

5. The New Theology offers a contrast to the Old in claiming for itself a wider study of man.

It chooses for its field the actual life of men in the world in all their varying conditions, rather than as massed in a few ideal conditions. It finds its methods in the every-day processes of humanity, rather than in a formal logic. It deals with human life as do the poets and dramatists: it views humanity by a direct light, looks straight at it, and into it, and across its whole breadth. A recognition of human nature and life,— this is a first principle with the New Theology. To illustrate: take a sermon of Robertson's, that on "The Principle of the Spiritual Harvest;" see how every sentence rests squarely on human life, touching it at every point, the sermon and human experience meeting as if cast in a mould. Compare with this some of the recent utterances on everlasting punishment,— able, and wrought out with great exactitude of thought, yet touching human life at not a single point; eliciting no response from consciousness or experience, from moral sense or common sense; deftly constructed things, built outside of the world, and as if shaped by another order and for other beings than those we know; resting on nothing but a formal logic, built out of definitions that anticipate the conclusions, through which they antagonize every natural operation of the human mind.

The Old Theology took for itself small foothold on humanity. Theology is, indeed, the science of God, but it is not that alone; it is also the science of the relations between God and man, which, though not the main, is as real a factor as God. The Old Theology stands on a structure of logic outside of humanity; it selects a fact like the divine sovereignty or sin, and inflates it till it fills the whole space about man, seeing in him only the subject of a government against which he is a sinner; it has nothing to say of him as he plays with his babe, or freely marches in battle to sure death for his country, or transacts, in honest ways, the honest business of the world. It lifts him out of his manifold and real relations, out of the wide and rich complexity of actual life, and carries him over into a mechanically constructed and ideal world, — a world made up of five propositions, like Calvinism or some other such system, — and views him only in the light of that world; requires him to think and feel and act only in the light of that world; teaches him that there is no other world for him to consider, and that his life and destiny are bounded by it, that there is no truth, no reality, no duty, no proper field for the play of his powers, no operation of the Spirit of God, no revelation of God, outside of this sharply-defined theological world.

We have but to name the matter in this way to understand the subtle isolation that invests the clergy of this theology, men apart from the world, out of practical sympathy with it, having no place for it in their theory, thinking on different lines, and making small use of its wisdom or its material. It explains the subtle antagonism that runs through all literature. There is no poet, nor novelist, nor dramatist, no profound student of human nature, no mind with the gift of genius and insight and broad, free sympathy with humanity, no great interpreter of human life, but in one way or another indicates his dissent from this theology. Nowhere has it had greater sway than in Scotland. It is not denied that it develops certain sides of character into almost ideal perfection; but why is it that nearly every great mind in Scotland, for more than a hundred years, has rejected its theology wholly or in part? Hume, Burns, Scott, Carlyle, Irving, Erskine, Campbell, McLeod, McDonald, — the defection of such minds from a faith so thoroughly inwrought into the texture of the national mind is a problem not to be explained by the vagaries of genius. It is to be explained rather by the fact that these great minds either felt or saw — some one and some the other — that the bounds of the theology were not commensurate with the bounds of human life. Hume was repelled into infidelity; Burns satirized it, Scott turned his back on it, Carlyle kept silence, McDonald protests against it, Erskine and Campbell and McLeod sought to modify it. The present restlessness in the world of theological thought is due largely to the fact that the teachings of literature have prevailed over the teachings of the systems of theology. One covers the breadth of human life, the others travel a dull round in a small world of their own creation; they no longer interest men.

The protest is hardly stronger in literature than in the pulpit, where it shows itself in two forms: first, in an unthinking sensationalism, that throws all theology aside and preaches from the newspaper, retaining only a few theological catch-words for a seeming foothold, while it discourses of duty and conduct with more or less wisdom, as happens, but without a philosophy or any other basis for meeting the questions that invariably rise in the mind when summoned to think on eternal truths; again, it shows itself in quiet and persistent efforts to modify and enlarge the definitions of the Faith, to widen the field from which truth is drawn, to broaden the domain of theology till it shall embrace the breadth of human nature and the knowledge of the world, — recognizing the fact that God is revealing himself in the whole life of the world, in the processes of history, in the course of nations, in all the ordained relations of life, in the play of every man's mind. It thus multiplies the relations in which man stands to God; it brings God and man face to face, the full nature of One covering the whole nature and life of the other. It is the characteristic fault of the Old Theology that it touches human life as a sphere touches a plane, — at one point only; as in the doctrine of divine sovereignty, the whole being of God resting on man in that one truth. The New Theology would present them rather as plane resting on plane, — the whole of God in contact with the whole of man. It thus allies itself not only with the Scriptures, and with philosophy and science and human consciousness, but it awakens a sense of *reality*, the securing of which lies at the basis of the Incarnation, — the divine life made a human life, the Son of man eating and drinking, a *living* way, that is, a way lived out in very fact in all the processes of human life, and so leading to eternal life.

The pulpit of the New Theology, in its efforts to broaden its field, encounters the criticism that it secularizes itself. It may be its temptation and its danger, but only because it is not true to itself. It was the criticism brought against the Son of man, but the fact that He was the Son of man was its refutation. The New Theology does indeed regard with question the line often drawn between the sacred and the secular, — a line not to be found in Jewish or Christian Scriptures, nor in man's nature, a line that, by its distinction, ignores the very process by which the kingdoms of this world are becoming the kingdom of the Lord Jesus Christ. It is one thing for the pulpit to go over into the unredeemed world and use its spirit and methods and morality, to fail to distinguish between good and evil; it is quite another thing to recognize in the composition and on-going of human society a divine revelation and process. Hence, it draws its theology from the Bible, indeed, but because it finds in the Bible the whole body of truth pertaining to humanity. And if there is any truth, any fact of science, any law of society, outside of the Bible, it "thinks on these things."

This full and direct look at humanity induces what may be called the ethical habit of thought.

The New Theology seeks to recover spiritual processes from a magical to a moral conception. It insists that these processes and facts are governed and shaped by the eternal laws of morality. It would have a moral God, a divine government truly moral, a moral atonement, and not one involving essential injustice, nor clouded with mysteries that put it outside of human use; an atonement resting on God's heart, and calling into play the known laws and sentiments of human nature, and not one constructed out of a mechanical legality; an atonement that saves men by a traceable process, and not one that is contrived to explain problems that may safely be left with God; an atonement that secures oneness with the Christ, and not one framed to buttress some scheme of divine government constructed out of human elements. It regards faith as a moral act, a direct acceptance and laying hold of God in trusting obedience, a simple and rational process; and it opposes the view which regards it as simply a belief that an atonement has been made, a holy life being merely its proper adjunct. It would make faith an actual entering into and fellowship with the life of the Christ, and the individual's justification by faith the actual realization and consequent of this oneness. It does not differ essentially from the Old Theology in its treatment of regeneration, but it broadens the ground of it, finding its necessity not only in sin, but in the undeveloped nature of man, or in the flesh. It is disposed also to regard it as a process, involving known laws and analogies, and to divest it of that air of magical mystery in which it has been held; a plain and simple matter, by which one gets out of the lower world into the higher by the Spirit of God.

It is said of this Theology that, leaning so heavily on human life in all its complexity and contradiction, it necessarily lacks logical precision and coherence, and that its parts are not mutually self-supporting. It accepts the criticism, and confesses that it does not first and mainly aim at these features; it does not strive to compass itself with definitions, nor to bring the whole truth of the Faith within the bounds of a system. It does not, for example, make it a prime object to shape one doctrine in order that it may fit in with another, or so shape all that they shall present a harmonious structure. It is not its first object to build a system, and it does not proceed in that fashion because it does not regard it as a *living* way, that is, a real way. To illustrate: it does not make future retribution an inference from some governmental scheme, or the complement of a doctrine of decrees and election. It is thus aside from the ordinary thought of men; nor can they ever be brought to believe that their destiny is contained in the conclusion of a formal logic. Whatever the destiny of men may be, the New Theology will not assert it in either direction in order to perfect a system. Indeed, it does not greatly care for systems as they have been hitherto constructed. It seeks rather to observe the logic of life, the premises and sequences, the syllogisms and conclusions, that are involved in daily existence, in the struggles and conflicts and contradictions of this struggling and contradictory world. It takes for its own that logic which is found in Macbeth, and Hamlet, and the Scarlet Letter, in the Prometheus and Job, in the parables of the Sheep and the Goats, and the Prodigal Son, and the Lost Sheep, — a logic not easily wrought into a system, but as systematic as human life. It aims simply at a larger logic, the logic wrought into the order of the world as it is daily evolved under the inspiration of Eternal Wisdom and Love.

6. The New Theology recognizes the necessity of a restatement of belief in Eschatology, or the doctrine of Last Things.

It is not alone in this respect; it is the position of nearly every school and organ of theological thought. The New Version compels it, the thought of the age demands it. But while there are enough who urge the necessity, whenever a champion appears in the lists he receives but a cold welcome from those who summoned him. The New Theology recognizes the necessity, but its work is not summed up in meeting this need. In the popular conception it is identified with mere criticism of existing views of everlasting punishment. No mistake could be greater; still, seeing the necessity in common with others, it does not withhold itself from the subject, and if its essays, though largely negative and tentative, are met by contradiction and ecclesiastical censure, it does not stay its hand nor heed the clamor. "Truth hath a quiet breast."

First, and broadly, the New Theology does not propound any new doctrine relative to future eternal salvation or eternal punishment. It is popularly supposed to concern itself chiefly with the future condition of men, but it rather draws away from such a field. It is less assertive here than in any other region of theological thought. It is, however, critical of the Old Theology, deeming it to be wise above what is written and out of line with the logic of the Faith; but it does not follow it into the future existence, with denials that imply a statement of the contrary, nor with positive assertions of its own. And the reason is that it transfers, to a large extent, the scene of the action of the truths pertaining to the subject from the future world conceived as a world of time and space to a world above time and not set in dimensions of space. In briefer phrase, it does not regard the *future* world as identical with the *eternal* world. Hence, its constructions on the subject turn largely on the word "eternal," which it does not regard wholly as a time-word, but as a word of moral and spiritual significance; it has little to do with time, but rather has to do with things that are above time; there is no more and no other relation between time and eternity in the future world than there is in the present world. This conception of the word does not necessarily imply that eternal punishment will not be everlasting; only, if that belief is entertained, it does not rest on this word, but is to be based on other grounds. And the battle waged over it is due simply to the mistaken anxiety of one side lest it shall be robbed of a text. But this rendering of the word does not antagonize the doctrine it has been held to teach; it simply separates it from the doctrine.

The New Theology emphasizes this use of "eternal" as a word of moral and spiritual import, because it puts in their right place and relation the action of all the great processes of the Faith. The Faith is not a finite thing, but an infinite; its truths are not conditional, but absolute; the play of its laws is not within time, but above time; its processes are not hedged about by temporal limits, — *in* time it may be, but not bounded by it; its facts have an eternal significance, which is other than that measured by "the cycles of the sun." Thus the Christ is the eternally begotten Son of God, and He is the Lamb that hath been slain from the foundation of the world. This conception carries the interpretation of the Faith into the region of God, and allies it in its processes to his existence and his thought, which are above time. It proceeds on the specific belief that the Christ spoke and acted as in the eternal world. He would not otherwise have been a manifestation of God, nor would He have spoken eternal truth. It holds this logic with stern cogency, for it sees that only thus the historic life of the Christ becomes an ever-present and ever-enduring reality; only thus can it regard the Faith as free from the chance and mischance of time, as larger than the confines of Judea, as broader than the stretch of centuries, as independent of the incidents and accidents of a changing world. Only thus can a correlation be established between the life and words of the Christ and the action of the Spirit.

They do not mean the same, the One is not a carrying out of the Other, the One does not take the things of the Other and show them unto us, except as there is accorded to One the same absolute and eternal method that confessedly belongs to the Other.

But the New Theology does not plant its entire conception of the subject upon one word. It seeks rather to enlighten itself by the general light of the entire revelation of God; and thus it finds itself driven to such conclusions as these: namely, that every human being will have the fullest opportunity for attaining to the end of his creation as a child of God; that every human being will receive from the Spirit of God all the influence impelling to salvation that his nature can endure and retain its moral integrity; that no human being will be given over to perish while there is a possibility of his salvation. These are the very truisms of the faith, its trend, its drift, its logic, its spirit, and its letter, when the letter is interpreted under the spirit; and they are equally the demand of the human reason. It might also be added as a truism that if the Gospel is intended for the world it is a Gospel for the world in very fact; if there is " a true light which lighteth every man coming into the world," it will surely lighten every man. If, in its present action, the faith is conditioned by time and proceeds under a law of development, we need not conclude that its application to the world of mankind is limited to time, or is bounded by periods or stages of development; this may involve essential injustice and other equally improbable elements. And so we are told that the Old Testament worthies are lifted by their faith out of their age and stage of development, and, by waiting, are "made perfect" with those of a later age, and under "some better thing" that God had provided; that is, the final condition of character for these ancient believers was not gained in their own age. But in what sphere did they await a perfection not to be gained except in connection with future generations? The specific truth involves the general one, namely, that character is not necessarily determined in any given stage of development. There is reason in this: man is an eternal being, and the great processes that affect his destiny take eternity for their field. It is thus that the seeming injustice and inequality that are incidental to his life under time are met by a transfer to the eternal world. The first fact pertaining to man is that he is eternal by virtue of the image in which he is created; the second fact is that he is temporal: his destiny takes its rise in one and is greatly affected by it, but its completion and adjustment must be through the other. Only thus is he properly coördinated; only thus can he be justly treated.

If it be said that these truisms conflict with certain texts, we waive yet do not grant the point, and answer that it is on the basis of these truisms there is such a *consensus* between Reason and Revelation that we accept it and hail it as a Gospel. If it be said that this makes Reason the judge of Revelation, we dissent, and yet assert that Revelation is not loaded with characteristics that shut it off from appeals to reasonable belief. It is not denied by any that the Gospel, in its inmost spirit and in its largest expression and purpose, means *salvation*. As such, it invests and presides over all other truths that may be connected with it. The key-note of the Old Testament is deliverance, and the Christ is the Lamb of God which taketh away the sin of the world. It is not in accord with nature in the limited field in which we observe and feel it. The Gospel is not within the category of sensible nature; if it were we would not need it. Nor is it in accord with a legal system; it is the antagonist of such a system. We may find in nature, and in human law and custom, analogies to processes in the Gospel, but we do not find in them the measure and total method and scope of the Gospel.

The immediate form under which the subject is now engaging attention is that of "probation," — with the question whether there is one or more. An immense advance has been made in rational thought and scriptural interpretation in regard to it; concessions are made on every side which, if not new, are unfamiliar. Still, the feeling cannot be avoided that the process of clearing is attended by a certain hardness of treatment not properly belonging to it, and under terms that are foreign to its meaning, and with limitations that are not justified by generous thought. It is largely associated with the phrase "a chance," — a poor word in itself, an unscientific, a chaotic word. To interpret probation as the equivalent of "a chance," and only insisting that it shall be fair, puts human life in a false relation to God, who has revealed himself as the Father of men. Probation may be involved in the idea of a family, but it is not the spirit or end of it; it is simply incidental. The father, indeed, educates his children for future use and responsibility; but only in some indirect sense are they under probation; they are not reared in an atmosphere of "chance," even though fair, or of an overhanging doom to be averted, but are children in the father's house, reared in hope and love and freedom. We are not here in the world to be tested, but to be trained under God's lessons. Tested we are, but what father puts his household under a test? The question of probation comes to the front only when the proper elements of household life have been eclipsed. And what, then, is probation? A "chance," and one at that? Not in such terms is the history of a lost child of God's family described, but as a sheep that the shepherd seeks till he finds. This is paternal, this is God-like, and it is far removed in spirit from the conception involved in such a phrase as "chance," whether fair or not, whether one or many. That man is under probation is, indeed, true; it is involved in the possession of a moral nature, and it is to be regarded as such rather than as a condition springing out of sin. Man is under probation, not because he is a sinner, but because he is a moral being, undergoing a formative process. It should, therefore, not be treated in a harsh, doom-like way, but as a gracious feature of a gracious system. No father says to his children, " You have a chance; it shall be fair; I will not be hard with you; it will last just so long; if you do not meet the test you may go your own way." It is, indeed, possible that in a desperate exigency of family-life a father might be forced to say this, but it is not in such guise that a wise and tender parent presents himself to his children. As little is it the aspect of the Heavenly Father before men. Probation is a fact, but it is not a fact to be treated as though it were already a semi-doom.

Whether there be one probation or more, there is an immense gain to theological thought in getting the subject out of physical and temporal bounds into the region of morals. But is it not plain that when this is done the question whether there is one or more vanishes? Probation is a continuous state or process till it ends by its own nature. It is one or many, as we choose to regard it, just as education may be regarded as a single or sub-divided process. All discussion of this sort is a mere logomachy. Probation may be divided into as many days, or hours, or distinct moral experiences as one undergoes. It is simpler and more scientific to say that man has but one probation, but, by its nature, it cannot have any bounds of time, whether of earthly life or world-age. It may, indeed, synchronize with the world-age, but only because that goal of time is postponed till the problem of existence has been solved by every human being. But probation will not be determined by the world-age, but by its own laws. It ends when character is fixed, — if indeed we have any right to use a word so out of keeping with moral freedom, — and it is not possible to attach any other bound or limit to it. And character is fixed in evil when all the possibilities of the universe are exhausted that would alter the character. The shepherd in the parable seeks the lost sheep till he finds it; shall we add to the parable, and say, " or till he cannot find it " ? If we do so, it is in view of the fact that the will of man, made in the image of God, is a mystery deep as the mystery of God himself.

Such are some of the features of this fresh movement in the realm of theology, for it can scarcely be called more than a movement, an advance to meet the unfolding revelation of God. It is not an organization, it is little aggressive, it does not herald itself with any Lo here or Lo there, it does not crowd itself upon the thought of the age, it is not keyed to such methods. It has no word of contempt for those who linger in ways it has ceased to walk in; it has no sympathy with those who have forsaken the one way. It does not destroy foundations, nor sap faith, nor weaken motives; it does not reduce the proportions of evil nor dim the glory of righteousness; it does not chill the enthusiasm of faith, nor hold it back from its mightiest effort of sacrifice. It seeks no conquest represented in outward form, but is content to add its thought to the growing thought of the world, and, if it speaks, content to speak to those who have ears to hear. It makes no haste, it seeks no revolution, but simply holds itself open and receptive under the breathing of the Spirit that has come, and is ever coming, into the world; passive, yet quick to respond to the heavenly visions that do not cease to break upon the darkened eyes of humanity.

ON THE RECEPTION OF NEW TRUTH.

"Never forget to tell the young people frankly that they are to expect more light and larger developments of the truth which you give them. Oh, the souls which have been made skeptical by the mere clamoring of new truth to add itself to that which they have been taught to think finished and final!" — REV. PHILLIPS BROOKS, *Yale Lectures.*

"Infidelity is the ultimate result of checking the desire for expanded knowledge." — EDWARDS A. PARK, D. D.

"In the Bible there is more that *finds* me than I have experienced in all other books put together; the words of the Bible find me at greater depths of my being; and whatever finds me brings with it an irresistible evidence of its having proceeded from the Holy Spirit." — COLERIDGE.

"The soul once brought into inner and immediate contact with a divine power and life is never left to itself." — J. LEWIS DIMAN, D. D., *Sermon No. VI.*

ON THE RECEPTION OF NEW TRUTH.

"And Peter opened his mouth, and said, Of a truth I perceive that God is no respecter of persons: but in every nation, he that feareth him and worketh righteousness, is acceptable to him." — THE ACTS x. 34, 35.

IF we were to take this book of the Acts, and put it off at a little distance, so as to get its outline as a whole, and its trend, we should find that its main purpose is to unfold the broadening spirit and form of the church of God.

It is a history of transition. On its first page the Christ ascends, and is no more contained in Judea. As the heavens, into which He rises, overarch the whole world, so his gospel begins to spread its wings for its world-wide flight. Soon the Spirit — universal as the "casing air" — breathes upon the Apostles, and they begin to act under an inspiration as free and wide as the wind that typifies it. On every page some barrier gives way; with every line the horizon broadens; one province after another is brought within the circle of the expanding faith, till at last Corinth and Athens and Rome are found playing their parts in this divine, world-wide drama. There is in this book of the Acts, as in Homer, and in all great histories, a wonderful sense of motion. One feels as if sailing in a great ship, under a bounding breeze, out of a narrow harbor into the wide sea; every moment the shores withdraw, and the waters broaden, and the winds blow freer, till at last we get room to turn our prow whichever way we will. So in reading this history, it is no longer Judea, but the world; no longer Jerusalem, but Rome and Spain also; no more one chosen people, but all nations. Everywhere the Spirit is seeking worshipers; the bud of divine promise has opened, and its perfume fills the world.

With this change of scene there is corresponding change of personal attitude; conversions not only in character, but in opinion; it is a record not only of repenting and turning, but of broadening. For conversion does not necessarily enlarge a man; it may simply turn him in another direction. It is possible to come out of evil into good, and yet remain under intellectual conceptions that dwarf and restrain one. There is a broad world-wisdom that often runs along with a worldly life, that may be lost if the better life is held under narrow conceptions, so that while the change may be a gain morally it is a loss intellectually; a process that has had illustration from the first until now,—in the proselytes whom St. Paul found it so hard to teach the distinction between the letter and the spirit, and in those of to-day who fail to distinguish between conduct and character, between dogma and life, between the form and the substance of the Faith. Valuable as this book of the Acts is as a record of events, and as the *nexus* between the Dispensations, it is more valuable as introducing the life of the Spirit, and as showing how the faith of ages develops into liberty and the full life and thought of humanity. Here we have the full revelation of God evoking the full life of man.

The incident before us is a happy illustration of this, — a minute and graphic history of the experience of a Roman centurion; a history priceless in its assurance of possible sainthood outside of the church, yet showing its hard conditions: telling us how his devout aspirations carried him into the realm of vision, and drew him towards the faith that was more than his, and brought upon him an inspiration greater than any that came upon his blind yearnings after righteousness. Here also is a somewhat similar experience of Peter, matching and rounding that of Cornelius; for God is teaching them both, drawing them off into the realm of vision, where they can be more effectually moulded to the divine uses. Sleep is not vacant of spiritual impression. God giveth his beloved, not sleep, but "*in* sleep." Into that mystery of physical repose that unbars the doors of the mind and withdraws the sentry of the will, the Spirit may come as unto its own, and say what it could not when the man is hedged about with wakeful and watchful powers. Shakespeare puts the deepest moral experiences of evil men into their dreams; why not also into those of the good? And so Peter introduces into the world a truth, often foreshadowed, and long in course of preparation, but not yet realized, that God is no respecter of persons, has no partialities, hears the prayers of all men, and is pleased with their good deeds. This history, with these dovetailing incidents, is mainly a lesson in breadth and largeness of view. In closer phrase, it is a full expression of a gradually developing revelation of God. Cornelius is led out of his small world of simple devoutness, a world where the light and the darkness contended, and brought into the full light and harmonies of divine knowledge. And Peter is led out of his still clinging Judaism, with its imperfect conceptions of God, and distinctions of food exalted into religion, and is made to know that God, having created all men and all things, has no partialities; and that because God has none, he is to have none, — his first effectual lesson in the requirement he had before heard, to be perfect, as the Father in heaven is perfect.

Notice how God not only enlarges and broadens the views of these men, but does this in the direction of himself. Peter is taught to think as God thinks, to look on men as God looks on them. He is enlarged upward, heightened as well as broadened in his knowledge. For there is an enlargement of view that is mere breadth without height; it keeps along the level of the earth, grows wise over matter and force, pierces to the centre in its search, weighs and measures all it finds, creeps but never soars, deeming the heights above to be empty. It is the direction knowledge is now taking. The science and a great part of the literature of the day and of what is called "culture," and the vast crowd that claims for some reason to "know the world," the average man in society and business, all tend to a mental largeness that has extent without height. It is always difficult to maintain the equilibrium of truth. In preceding centuries the mind shot upward, but within narrow limits; the gaze of thought was heavenward, as in the pictures of the saints. There was no look abroad, almost none upon the earth; nature was simply to be used as found, not studied for further uses. Hence, there was great familiarity with the lore of religion, but dense ignorance of the laws of matter and of human society; there were no mysteries in heaven, but the earth did not even suggest a problem. Knowledge was high, but it was not broad. To-day the reverse is true: thought runs earthward and along the level of material things, but hesitates to ascend into the region of the spirit. It is interesting to note how this tendency pervades classes that apparently do not influence one another: thus the scientific class, and the lighter literary class; neither reads the works of the other, nor are there any natural avenues of sympathy between them, yet in each we find the same close study of matter and man, and the same ignoring of God and the spiritual nature. Or, compare the man of universal culture with the average man of the world, who reads the newspaper, and keeps his eyes open on the street: the latter knows little of the former, never reads his books, nor even dilutions of them, yet we find them holding nearly the same opinions about God and the Faith, vague, misty, and indifferent; but both are very observant of what is about them. Such a fact seems to indicate that, instead of one class leading the way, or one set of minds dominating the rest, all are swept along by currents that flow out of some unseen source. It seems to controvert the familiar saying that philosophy shapes the thought of the world. Never were the demonstrations of ethical and spiritual philosophy clearer or stronger than at present, but the age is materialistic. Never were the evils of materialism and the necessity of the spiritual so keenly felt, yet the tide of the former sweeps on without abatement. It seems to indicate the presence of other forces than those found in chance habits of thought, or in the brain of the strongest thinker. Aquinas and Hume, Bacon and Spencer, are not so much originators as exponents of currents of thought; they represent a force which they themselves seem to be. There are ages of faith and ages of doubt; it is not easy to doubt in one or to believe in the other. None of us are exempt from these prevailing tendencies, however much we may contend against them. Nor is it well that we should be wholly exempt; it is doubtless better that an age should have homogeneousness, else it will work at cross-purpose, and unduly chafe and fret at itself. It is for some wise end that the gaze of men is for a time diverted from the heavens and turned to what is about them. It had become necessary that man should have a somewhat better knowledge of the world, and of his relations to it and to society. Hence his attention is directed thither by a divine and guiding inspiration, and no thinking man can be exempt from it. The only danger is lest the tendency become excessive, and we forget to look upward in our eagerness to see what is about us. It is the office of Christian thought to temper and restrain these monopolizing tendencies and secure a proper balance between them, to hold and enforce the twofold fact, that while our eyes are made to look into the heavens, our feet are planted in the soil of this world. Tennyson has no wiser lines than these: —

> "God fulfills himself in many ways,
> Lest *one* good custom should corrupt the world."

The thing we are apt to fail of to-day is not breadth and thoroughness of knowledge of what is about us, but of what is above and within us.

I have fallen into this train of thought by reflecting how God led Peter away from his small notions of religion, the doing or not doing this or that, and brought him into a higher and larger conception of Himself.

As we read the story we wonder at the readiness and ease with which Peter gave up old habits of thought and entered into new ones. It is not easy for us to realize how great and violent a change he thus made in a moment. We have our convictions, strong enough they seem; but we have little conception of the power of an Oriental's convictions in respect to religion. Our strongest convictions pertain to liberty and social order; the Oriental's pertain to religion. He is easily enslaved, but not easily converted. The western mind will not brook tyranny, but it readily modifies its faith. Still, it is not easy for any one suddenly to lay down one's life-long convictions and take up new ones. Change of opinion is naturally slow and partial. But here is Peter, with the traditional spirit of an Oriental, and the added inflexibility of the Jew, violating this apparently natural order, and passing at once under a new set of ideas. What is the explanation?

1. It seems to be in the nature of religious changes that they shall occur suddenly. There may be, there must be, long seasons of preparation for any moral change, but the transition is instantaneous. It is the law of revelation. Its way is prepared by the slow processes of reason and education, but the revelation itself is quick, immediate, and not to be traced. Divine truth comes by flashes. The heavens open, and the Spirit descends as on the swift wings of a dove. Saul goes a-persecuting, and a light above the sun's dazzles him into instant submission. The Holy Spirit comes like a rushing wind upon the disciples, and in an hour they are new men. The jailer hears and believes in a night. Luther, while toiling up the holy stairs of the Lateran, holding to salvation by works, drops that scheme on the way, and lays hold of the higher one of salvation by faith. Ignatius Loyola in a dream has sight of the Mother of Christ, and awakes a soldier of Jesus. It is often so. We do not so much grow into the possession of new spiritual truths as we awake to them. Their coming

is not like the sunrise that slowly discloses the shapes and relations of things, but is like the lightning that illuminates earth and sky in one quick flash, and so imprints them forever on the vision, like the coming of the Son of man, if indeed there be any other coming of Him than in fresh revelations of truth. Intensity makes up for time; the subtler agency engraves a deeper impression. Character is of slow and steady growth, but the revelations of truth that inspire character are sudden. A new outlook is gained and the man is changed, as, in climbing a mountain, it is some sharp turn in the path that reveals the new prospect which inspires the onward march. Some can affirm that it was in a moment that the charm of poetry, the pleasurable consciousness of thought, the passion of love, the dignity of manhood, the obligation of service, the sense of the divine goodness, came upon them. These experiences are not so much growths as revelations, and because they come quick they move us; we take up their motion; we are inspired by their energy. To provide us with such experiences, the element of unexpectedness, of surprise and catastrophe, is put into life. An uneventful life is apt to be poor and barren, unless one has the rare gift, like Wordsworth, of turning every sunrise and sunset, every storm, every changing phase of the old landscape, every fresh day of uneventful household life, into newness. It is the events of life — marriage, births, sickness, travel, new scenes and relations, the changes that drop from fortune's wheel, the thunderbolts out of clear skies, the sudden lift of dark clouds — that bring new visions of truth. It was through a wonderful dream that Peter got that conception of God, new to himself and to the world, which so instantly mastered him.

2. His ready change was also due to the fact that he got sight of larger and more spiritual truths than he had been holding.

When truths, or what claim to be such, are of equal proportion, we balance them, or try one and then the other; but as soon as one asserts itself as larger and finer we accept it instantly. Peter had been used to believing that God was a respecter of persons, but when he caught sight of the fact that God has no partialities, but accepts all men who work righteousness, his truth-loving nature rushed at once toward the greater truth. We have an appetence for new spiritual truth, and take to it readily. Hence every new notion or device that calls itself religious gets certain and quick following, but it only shows how insatiable is the demand for the new. This does not imply that we are to go about peering into the corners of the universe to find new truths, nor that we are to sit down and manufacture them. Truth already exists; there is now all there ever will be. All we have to do is to take it; to hold ourselves open to it; to do God's will, and we shall know it; to read it as Providence writes it before our eyes; to listen to the still voice of the Spirit; to keep a single eye, an open ear, and an obedient will. It is of the nature of spiritual truth that it reveals itself. The fundamental Christian idea is God seeking man, not man seeking God;

the latter phrase represents a subordinate idea. We make but a poor figure when we attempt to think out a religion, or even to think our way through one. It is not a search *after* God, but a revelation *of* God. The grand movement and impulse are on the divine side. We ourselves can find nothing; we can only take what comes, watch the unveiling of divinity, careful only lest anything revealed escape our notice. The main thing for us to do is to get out of the caves of sin and self-conceit into the open air, where the sun shines and the Spirit breathes. An upturned face, an honest heart, space about us for the Spirit to get access, — these are the conditions of a continually fresh feast of eternal truth.

There is also in such truth a self-attesting power that tends to secure instant reception. When one comes to me with a new machine, or a new theory of government, or of the material universe, or of physical life, I hesitate; but when I see a new disclosure of the divine love, or a fresh exhibition of the value of humility and patience, or of some new adaptation of Christianity to human society, or of the superiority of spirit over matter, or indication that it is other than matter and inclusive of it, I at once believe. It is simply another candle brought into a lighted room.

This self-attesting quality goes farther and becomes commanding. Truth so seen allies itself with God and takes on divine authority. Peter says, "*God* hath showed me that I should not call any man common or unclean." It is one of the subtle workings of all high truth that it vests itself, as by some instinct, with the divine attributes. No one would call a doctrine of expediency an *eternal* truth, even if he believed it; a sense of language, running deeper than he knows, would forbid. But this same subtle sense of language almost requires us to put the epithet before love and duty and sacrifice. So vested, truth becomes authoritative and shuts out all hesitation; with Peter, we rise and eat.

I have had in mind thus far not any new laws of conduct or mysteries pertaining to God, or man, or destiny, but rather fresh and expanding vision of old truths, other sides of many-sided truth. Strictly speaking, there is no such thing as new truth; truth is not a creatable thing, being simply the reality of existing things; but there is such a thing as fresh sight of the truth that now is and always has been and ever will be. To keep ourselves in the way of it is a clear and vital duty. We can hardly do anything worse for our moral growth than to hold it in such a way that it may not change its form, or proportion, or aspect, to us. When we bind it up in a form of words, or let it lie quiet in unthinking minds, or wear it as a sort of charm while we go about our work or pleasure, we have made a very poor and meagre thing of it. Not that one is to hold his faith as in a constant flux, or suffer himself to be blown about by every new wind of doctrine, but rather that he should attain the twofold attitude of alertness and passivity: passive to the Spirit that is ever breathing upon us, and alert to note and follow the unfolding revelation of God in the world.

It is, I doubt not, a matter of conscious experience with many, this fresh insight into truth, the germ or heart remaining the same, but taking on new forms and displaying new powers. It is such a relation to truth that keeps the mind delighted with it, exciting it by sweet surprises and inspiring it by new prospects. Thus it becomes living water, springing up into eternal life.

It is a mistake to regard the truths of the Christian faith, even those that are called leading and fundamental, as having a fixed form. Were they revelations *from* God, they might perhaps be so regarded; but being revelations *of* God, they imply a process of unfolding. Truth is not something handed down from heaven, a moral parcel of known size and weight, but is a disclosure of God through the order of the world and of the Spirit. This is the key to the history of the Old Testament, the central element of the revelation by the Christ, the method of the Spirit. It is allied to the highest assertions of science, the other side of the arch that springs to meet that which rises out of the visible creation, the keystone of which is God, creator of the world and redeemer of humanity.

Having spoken generally, I shall now speak more particularly of some of these truths, with a view to calling attention to this intermingling of permanent and changing qualities. The aim will be to inspire and aid belief rather than to challenge it, and to touch the themes in a broad and inclusive way, and by no means in the opposite way.

Take first the truth known as the Trinity,

though one could wish, with Calvin, "that the word itself were buried in oblivion." It has another look to-day from that it wore a hundred years ago. That view, if urged still, makes a very dry, formal, unnourishing thing of it. If, however, we suffer it to be transformed, under the expanding conception of God that has come in with the age, it grows vital and inspiring. It is the characteristic thought of God at present that He is immanent in all created things, — immanent yet personal, the life of all lives, the power of all powers, the soul of the universe; that He is most present where there is the most perfection : —

> "He is more present unto every creature He hath made
> Than anything unto itself can be."

With such a conception of God, it becomes easy to see how there should be a Son of man who is also the Son of God, and a Spirit everywhere present and acting. Revelation and thought so nearly meet that there is no chasm between, and no stress is laid on faith as it passes from one to the other. The formal trinity and the formal unity, the more barren conception of the two, pass away, and God in Christ, filling the mould of humanity to the full, becomes a great, illuminating truth. We may or may not pronounce the ancient phrases, but we need no longer hesitate to say, " Father, Son, and Holy Spirit;" meaning a paternal heart and will at the centre, a sonship that stands for humanity, a spiritual energy that is the life of men, and through which they come into freedom and righteousness. This conception of God may be brought into the category of science, and even be required by it. It allies itself with its great postulates and demonstrations, and not only falls in with its analogies, but is needed for their application to humanity and its history.

So of the atonement: it contains a truth that mankind has never been willing to live without, and yet it has always been putting on new forms and yielding a richer life. It is the most elastic of the doctrines, capable of very low and very high expression. The conception of it that prevailed two hundred years ago shocks us of to-day. And more recent views of it as a matter of penal satisfaction and substitution, and as a mere contrivance for the expression of the divine feeling, no longer feed spiritual life; and so we are struggling towards St. Paul's and the Christ's own statement of it as containing the law and method of life for every man: "He that loseth his life for my sake shall find it." We are getting to read this truth as meaning Christ formed in us, a law and way of life. And just as the older conceptions fade out, and the greater ones dawn, is there not only a deeper spiritual life, but a plainer coördination between the life they beget and the necessities of human nature.

So also of regeneration: the foundations of this stringent doctrine are broadening and deepening with advancing thought. It has been held simply as a moral necessity, having its basis in sin; but we are beginning to see that the Christ taught it also as a psychological necessity. We must be born again, not merely because we are wicked, not because of a lapse, but because we are flesh, and need to be carried forward and lifted up into the realm of the spirit, — a constructive rather than a reconstructive process. Thus presented, it appears at once as a universal necessity, and allies itself with the thought of the age.

In the same way, the much and justly criticised doctrine of divine sovereignty and decrees is resolving into the universality of law, the favorite conception of the age. Science, with its doctrine of an original, ultimate force, advances more than half-way towards this assaulted truth, while the larger conception to which it has helped us has taken its debatable features out of the hands of both contending schools.

Or take the doctrine of sin, its inheritance and its relation to the personal will: the old-time presentations of it were crude and harsh, but as we interpret it in the light of experience and history, we affirm it with increased emphasis. The keenest thought of the world is overtaking the thought of revelation. The doctrine of heredity as found in the pages of science, the doctrine of freedom as found in the pages of philosophy and the observation of life, yield nearly all we care to claim.

So, too, of the miracles. I do not think the best thought is now stumbling over miracle, as it was a few years ago. Modern intelligence has grown so wide that it embraces both law and miracle in one harmony, and cares little to find any line of demarkation between them. Law fades out into miracle, and miracle runs up into law. No one now defines one as the violation of the other. An assertion of "the reign of law" does not disturb us so long as we are conscious of the hourly miracles wrought by personality. The point of contact and union may not be seen, but we trace their converging lines into the mystery that surrounds God's throne, believing that they meet in Him, who is both a will and a force to the universe,—a force in it, and a will over it.

Take next retribution, the most controverted of doctrines: the subject has merely fallen into the crucible of modern thought, and is emerging in new shape. It will never be denied so long as men have eyes to trace cause and effect, and it will never cease to have power so long as it is kept in that category, where only it belongs, and where it becomes simply a matter of intelligence. Just now we are shifting our point of view, and stripping the subject of certain arbitrary and dogmatic coverings that had come upon it. We are putting it in the light of law and daily experience and Christ's word. We are finding out that it is not a matter of future time, but of all time; or rather, not a matter of time at all, but an eternally acting principle. But it is undergoing no greater modification at present than it has undergone in the past. It has fallen into an atmosphere of hope, and so allied itself with the spirit and logic of revelation, and is thus becoming a genuine motive to conduct and ceasing to be an incubus of despair. The true preacher of retribution is not one who tones it down to mere remorse and separation from God, — things that no evil-doer takes into account, — carefully separating from it all physical suffering and every other conception of pain calculated to move men; a retribution eliminated of all motive, and simply drawn out into infinity. Instead, he sets the subject in the practical light of cause and effect in the external world, and in the more searching light of the same law working in the moral nature, where it binds hand and foot and casts into the outer darkness; he points out the horrible consequences of crime and ignorance and low pleasure; he unfolds the wretchedness that follows avarice and self-seeking and indolence and low-thoughtedness; he makes it clear that the wages of sin is death; in short, he emphasizes the two features of retribution that alone are effective, namely, its nearness and its certainty, and lifts it into the timeless ranges of eternity, where alone its true emphasis is found. Like the kingdom of heaven, of which it is the dark shadow, it is not to be defined by any Lo here or Lo there, or shut within any time-phrases. Dogmatism on either side is no longer regarded with favor. So long as we cannot explain evil, we have no right to claim definite knowledge of its consequences. So long as we cannot sound the depths of our own nature, we cannot predicate with certainty what that nature will do or become in any direction. The most reverent and profound thought of the day merely seeks to rescue the subject from a dogmatism that reflected immorality upon God, and made it a burden too heavy for the human spirit to endure; provoking thus an instinctive rejection that paved the way to total unbelief. The new thought is in the interest of faith; the old was fast ministering to doubt and denial and fierce contempt. Meanwhile the Christ's words grow luminous under the tenderer thought of humanity, and are seen to uphold the human heart and reason, while they also hold the conscience steadily to the contemplation of the immeasurable evil of sin.

Take last the inspiration of the Bible. The theories of a generation ago are fast disappearing, verbal, dynamic, plenary, an inspiration covering all historical and scientific reference; none of them are any longer insisted on. There is not now, and probably never will be, any generally accepted theory of inspiration, simply because it cannot be so compassed; as the Christ said, "Thou canst not tell whence it cometh and whither it goeth." It is the breathing of God upon the soul; who can put that into a theory? So far as it shall have form or method of statement, it will be found in the larger truth of the Holy Spirit in all the scope of its action. We are getting to speak less of the inspired *book*, and more of the inspired *men* who wrote it; the quality or force of inspiration lying not so much in the form, or even matter, of the thing written, as in the writer himself,—his relation to his age, the clearness of his thought, the pitch of his emotions, the purity of his spirit, the intensity of his purpose. We do not so much look into a book to find an infallible assertion as into the inspired author, expecting to find trustworthy guidance and reflected inspiration; remembering, however, that, though inspired by the Spirit, he is but an inspired *man*, knit to his age and race and condition. The revelation, therefore, will have a twofold character: it will be divine and human, the one conditioning the other; not an imperfection, but rather the only kind of revelation that could serve our needs, for the line of revelation from God to man must run through the human heart. If it takes color and form on the way, it is no less divine and trustworthy.

But without a theory, we are reading the Bible with fuller faith than ever before. The more light we bring to it from nature and study and experience, the clearer its truths stand out; in such light it is becoming its own evidence, and no more needs an apologetic theory than a candle needs an argument for illumination. We are not even careful to dispute about this or that seeming inaccuracy; instead, we are confident that here is a book that keeps ahead of all thought, and constantly furnishes new light and fresh inspiration to mankind.

These illustrations might be increased till they comprehended the entire range of Christian doctrines. And when we had gone through them all, we should find, on review, one feature attaching to them severally and collectively, namely, that each one has a permanent essence and a shifting form; the essence unquestioned, the form always under debate. To see and make this distinction is in itself of utmost value; it is enough to save one to the Faith. But a thoughtful mind will go farther, and ask, How happens it that Christianity has this twofold feature of a permanent essence and a shifting form? The answer will take him into that world of thought recently opened, the main feature of which is the law of development or evolution. Into this world the Faith must go. The timid may linger on the threshold, but the time has come to enter in and set the Faith face to face with this principle that now colors and dominates all thought. Once in, the atmosphere is found friendly. It is not something to be quelled, but an ally to be pressed into service. What it does for every other department of thought it may do for the Faith, — open another door between the mystery of the external order and the human reason. It not only thus finds itself in friendly relations with other realms of thought and knowledge, a state that the mind imperatively demands, being made to seek a harmony of all truth, but it is now able to understand and vindicate itself. When it contemplates itself as under development, it has the key of its interpretation; it can account for its changes; it can defend its history; it can separate its substance from its forms; it can go free and unburdened of past forms which were never of its essence; it can once more take its place at the head of the sciences, and demand the loyalty of all, not because it recognizes their method, but because it alone offers a solution of the method, and is the solvent of all sciences. Recognizing this principle, we can read the Old Testament, and need no other explanation or apology than it affords. The sayings of the Christ no longer wear a simply personal or half-explicable meaning, a somewhat wiser Oriental ethic, but become principles and revelations of eternal truth. The mustard-seed, the leaven, the seed cast into the ground, and the earth bringing forth fruit of herself, — these parables not only fall in with the principle, but attest Christ's absolute knowledge of it. It accords with that prime feature of revelation before referred to, as *of* and not *from* God; a coming of God into the world by a process parallel with human development, and the source of it.

It is not meant, however, that Christianity is to take its place under any school of scientists or philosophers, using their data and binding itself to their conclusions. Evolution is not to be identified with any school of thought or department of knowledge; it is a principle pertaining to the order of the world. Christianity has its own data and phenomena, and they are not to be classed in any other category.

It will be noticed that the reception of new truth has been spoken of in two ways that are apparently contradictory: one as quick and as by instant revelation; the other gradual, a growth or development. They are not inconsistent, but represent the two methods of revelation: the twofold nature of truth as having a divine source and element and a human ground and element, and the twofold nature of man as spirit and mind. These methods play into each other. One prepares the way for the other. One is slow, and keeps pace with the gradual advance of society and a like development of the individual. The other is quick, is allied to the mysterious action of the Spirit, which knows not time nor space, and accords with the loftiest action of our nature. I gain knowledge slowly; I gain the meaning of knowledge instantly; it is a revelation of the Spirit that acts when knowledge has done its work. There were ages of civil and ethical training, of progress and lapse and recovery and growth, but the meaning of it flashed upon the consciousness of the world in a day. And so a man thinks, studies, undergoes life, gropes now in dark ways, or stands still, in despair of truth; but finding this intolerable, presses on, and at last, in some better moment, some hour of spiritual yearning or tender sympathy or bitter need, the heavens open to his willing eyes, and in one swift glance he sees the meaning of all he has known, and feels the breath of the descending Spirit. Now he knows, indeed. Now there is meaning in the world and in life. The sense of vanity that invariably clouds existence and oppresses thought, when not so illumined, passes away. Now he begins to live to some purpose. Death is swallowed up in life. The material is merged in the spiritual. The eternal order takes the place of this shadowy and elusive order of nature that once held him, and he tastes the satisfactions of the Spirit.

GOD OUR SHIELD.

"Man is conscious of the being of God, and lives and acts in this consciousness, and the reality of the being of God so comes to him." — MULFORD, *Republic of God*, page 1.

> " Thus God has will'd
> That man, when fully skill'd,
>   Still gropes in twilight dim;
> Encompass'd all his hours
> By fearfullest powers
>   Inflexible to him:
> That so he may discern
>   His feebleness ;
> And e'en for earth's success
>   To Him in wisdom turn,
> Who holds for us the keys of either home,
> Earth and the world to come."
>
> JOHN HENRY NEWMAN, *The Elements*.

"Turn, Fortune, turn thy wheel with smile or frown:
With that wild wheel we go not up or down."

TENNYSON'S *Geraint and Enid*.

"We exist here in a double connection: first, with the transitory on one side, and, secondly, with the untransitory on the other; and we fare as many other creatures do that are made for two distinct elements, coming into distress in one element the moment they lose connection with the other." — DR. BUSHNELL, *Moral Uses*, page 383, English ed.

"There is throughout nature something mocking, something that leads us on and on, but arrives nowhere, keeps no faith with us. All promise outruns the performance. We live in a system of approximations. Every end is prospective of some other end, which is also temporary; a round and final success nowhere. We are encamped in nature, not domesticated." — EMERSON.

GOD OUR SHIELD.

"After these things the word of the Lord came unto Abram in a vision, saying: I am thy shield, and thy exceeding great reward." — GENESIS xv. 1.

THERE are two main things that man needs in this world: he needs protection and the fulfillment of his desires and labors, a negative and a positive, a shield and a reward, something to protect him while in the battle, something to reward him when it is over.

This promise is silently keyed to the note of struggle as underlying life, the conception of life that the wise have always taken. It is the condition of the highest virtue; it is the aspect that every earnest life takes on. It is as a conflict that existence begins in Eden, it is a victory that crowns it in the new Jerusalem; the first word in Scripture is of trial, the last is of overcoming. Life is not mere continuance or development; it is not a harmony, but a struggle. It continues, it develops, it may reach a harmony, but these are not now its main aspects.

It is this element of struggle that separates us from other creations. A tree grows, a brute develops what was lodged within it; but man chooses, and choice by its nature involves struggle. It is through choice and its conflicts that man makes his world, himself, and his destiny; for in the last analysis character is choice ultimated. The animals live on in their vast variety and generations without changing the surface of the earth, or varying the sequences wrought into their being; but man transforms the earth, and works out for himself diverse histories and destinies. One is perfectly coördinated to nature; the other is but partially so, and is man-like just in the degree in which he gets out of the formal categories of nature into the freedom of his own spiritual and eternal order; great just in the degree in which he rises above instincts, and gets to living out of moral choices.

This is a matter well worth thinking of while the tendency is so strong to identify man with nature, and make him wholly the creature of physical environment; a habit of thought which, if not checked at the proper point, leads to some doctrine of necessity by which the moral sense is paralyzed, and thence to atheism, a path straight, swift, and sloping to the hells of unbridled desire. For when you attempt to account for man as a product of nature, and to shut him up in natural processes, you shut out the heavens and the God who sits on their circle, and make him but another of the beasts "that tear each other in their slime." I do not deny that man is in nature, and that her processes are wrought into him, and even are features of his whole history, but only that he is summed up in nature. The strong tendencies of thought just now are towards such identification of nature and man, with complimentary phrase of him as her crown or flower, the product of her forces lifted to the highest, the final outcome of her order working to its finest issue, and the like. This tendency is in the air and haunts all minds, an evil miasm exhaled from the low fens and primal depths of matter, poisoning faith and breeding diseases that slay all nobility and glory of life. How far it will go cannot be told, but it will go far enough to show that it leads to confusion and despair. But when these sure ends are reached, man will reëxamine himself, and find out that he is divine as well as physical, and that he cannot, even in the light of his own phenomena, be classed with the perishing orders of the external world. Happy is he who now sees the intellectual fallacy in such a conception of man! Happier still is he who has entered into the Christ-idea of sonship in God, and with swift and easy logic reasons that the child must share the life and destiny of the Father! Meanwhile, however pressed by the accuracies of science, and while waiting for its highest conclusions, let us cherish the nobler conception. Anything that even seems to wear the look of descent in thought is to be regarded with suspicion, or passed by.

It is this nobler view of man, as choosing and struggling, that makes it needful he should have protection in the world. If he were only an animal he might be left to nature, for nature is adequate to the needs of all within her category; but transcending, and therefore lacking full adjustment to nature, he needs care and help beyond what she can render. He finds himself here set to do battle, life based and turning on struggle; but nature offers him no shield fit to protect him, nor can nature reward him when the struggle is over. She has no gifts that he much cares for, she can weave no crown that endures, and her hand is too short to reach his brow.

There is a better philosophy back here in the beginnings of history, the beginnings also of true, full life. Abram is the first man who had a full religious equipment. He had open relations to God; he had gained the secret of worship; he had a clear sense of duty, and a governing principle, namely, faith or trust in God. It starts out of and is based on this promise of God to be his Shield and Reward. His sense of God put his life before him in all its terrible reality; it is not going to be an easy matter to live it. Mighty covenants are to be made; how shall he have strength to keep them? He is to become the head of a separate nation; how can he endure the isolation necessary to the beginning? He is to undergo heavy trials and disappointments; how shall he bear them? He is promised a country for his own, but he is to wander a citizen of the desert all his days, and die in a land not yet possessed; how can he still believe with a faith that mounts up to righteousness? Only through this heralding promise: "I am thy shield, and thy exceeding great reward." When you are in trouble I will protect you. When you fail of earthly rewards I will be your reward. But Abram's life, in its essential features, was not exceptional. I do not know that it was harder to live than yours or mine. I do not know that his duties were more imperative, his doubts more perplexing, his disappointments and checks severer than those encountered by us all to-day. He needed and we need two things to carry us through, protection and fulfillment of desires, shield and reward.

Let us now look at the first of these two things with something more of detail.

1. We need protection against the forces of nature.

In certain aspects nature is kind to us and helps us; she strives to repair any injury she may do to us; she is often submissive and serves us with docility. But in other aspects she is cruel and unsparing, and her general aspect is that of a power over us rather than under us. We play with the fringes of her garment; we turn some little of her forces to our use, shut up a little of her steam and gather a little of her electricity and yoke them to our service; we turn aside a rill of falling water here and there and hold up our sails of a hand's breadth to her wide winds, but how little have we trenched on the mighty powers that infold us! How far off are we from any subjugation of nature, how feeble still are we before its greater forces. It may be the function of civilization to turn these forces to use and to get men into friendly relations with them, but when the farthest progress is made in this direction, the general character and aspect of nature will not have greatly changed. Water will still drown, gravitation will still dash in pieces, heat will still slay, gases will still poison. There will be no more pliancy in natural laws to favor the finite condition that man will never escape here. No degree of obedience that we may render to them will prevent oxygen from consuming tissue, or strengthen the walls of the jugular vein, or take away the wasting power from the years. Nature remains in her most comprehensive laws and largest processes, a power over man, alien in temper to his freedom, not correlated in its absolute methods to his conditioned powers, making exactions that he never can meet or evade. A system that has for its largest feature a doom and that leads to a doom, cannot be other than a terror to man until he is provided with some other conception than it affords. I confess that I should be filled with an unspeakable dread if I were forced to feel that I was wholly shut up in nature. We are constantly brought face to face with its overpowering and destroying forces and we find them relentless. We may outwit or outmaster them up to a certain point, but beyond that we are swept helpless along their fixed and fatal current.

But how does God become a shield against them? Only by the assurance that we belong to Himself rather than to nature. When that assurance is received, I put myself into his larger order; I join the stronger power and link myself to its fortunes. I cannot of myself contend against this terrible order of nature as it drives me to wreck on stormy seas, or consumes my body with its relentless tooth, but I can say, " I do not belong to your order." I am speaking here in the line of philosophic thought as well as of religious trust, for faith must have some foothold on the rock of truth. The question pressing hardest to-day is, to which order do we belong, to the material or to the spiritual? Does the one or the other compass us? Is mind a gradation of matter? Is spirit the essence of matter, or is it something *other* than matter, over it and inclusive of it? We talk of Waterloos and Gettysburgs; they were petty conflicts in comparison with this battle now going on in the realm of thought, one side claiming that the material world includes man, the other side claiming that he cannot be summed up in its category and is but partially adjusted to its methods, that its highest principle, which is unvarying law, is opposed to his highest principle, which is freedom, thus preventing full correlation between them and inducing relations that are painful and destructive to him. It makes a great difference practically, which side we take. If the material world includes me, then I have no shield against its relentless forces, its less than brute indiscrimination, its sure finiteness or impersonal and shifting continuance. Then I am no more than one of its grains of dust and must at last meet the fate of a grain of dust. But if spirit has an existence of its own, if there is a spiritual order with God at its head and with freedom for its method, then I belong to that order, there is my destiny, there is my daily life. My faith in that order and its Head is my shield when the forces of nature assault me and its finiteness threatens to destroy me. I say to it, "You may slay my body with your laws, and you will at last, but you will not slay me, nor can you greatly hurt me; nay, you can only bless me in a sort of servile way; I do not belong to you, I belong to God." [1]

2. We need a shield against the inevitable evils of existence.

Sooner or later there comes a time to every one of us when we are made to feel not only that we are weaker than nature, but that there is an element of real or apparent evil in our lot. It does not often come early. Happily the larger half of life is spent before we awake to the fact that a process of decay and loss is going on within us. For fifty or more years there is a triumphant sense of strength and adequacy. We ride on the crest of the waves of life, and have no sense that we can be engulfed in its waters. Out of this strong, divinely-wise ignorance come the great achievements, for it is a certain simplicity in men that leads them to undertake great things. But by and by there comes over us a new sense of ourselves. We detect the working of a law of weakness and decay. Our bodies gradually lose their elasticity, our heritage of strength slowly wastes away, the step grows slower, the feet feel their way along the earth instead of touching it with firm rebound, the eyes lose their keenness, the skin shrivels, the frame shrinks together, the voice loses its soft and

---

[1] I hardly need to say that I do not intend to assert any doctrine of dualism, or to array God and nature as opposing forces. God is inclusive of nature, and the relations of nature to man are benevolent, but it is still true that because man is not throughout coördinated to nature, the relation involves pain from which there is no deliverance except by an alliance with God who is more and other than nature.

clear vibration, the recovery from illness is slow and partial. And thus there dawns on us a sense of mortality peculiarly real. The tables are turned with us. Heretofore life, the world, the body, — all have been for us; now they are against us, they are failing us; the shadow of our doom begins to creep upon us.

How real this experience is every thoughtful person of years well knows. It has in it, I verily believe, more bitterness than death itself. It is the secret of the sadness of age. And there is every reason why this experience should be sad. It is necessarily so until we can meet it with some larger truth and fact. No philosophy can meet, no force of will can outmaster it, no mere habit of cheer can hold its own against it. It is a fact, and cannot be reasoned away, and as the stern law of decay holds on its course, the force of will and the smile of cheer die out by slow or rapid degrees.

> "Whatever poet, orator, or sage
> May say of it, old age is still old age."

It is a horrible fact, and it cannot be anything less, as this cheerful poet is forced to say, — this fact of loss and decay. It may be unmanly not to endure it, but it is not unmanly to see and feel it as it is. But even manly endurance itself fails as the process goes on, and the powers of body and mind shrink towards nothingness. We are not now dealing with sentiment, but with the hardest of facts. The common appeal is to a spirit of cheer, to force of will, for courage to the last, to go down with the flag flying, and the like. This is indeed sentiment, but no philosopher, no physiologist, will use it; they know that the will and courage are involved in this process. The mind stands with one foot on the body. However it may be with it as an entity, its working energies flow out in the same wasting current as those of the body. As this stage of existence draws on, the question is forced upon us,— Is there no shield against this evil? Is there nothing left for us but brute-like endurance, or some phantom-show of cheer and will, nothing but sentiments that are bound up in the dissolving process, and that necessarily come to an end when most needed?

Along with this decadence of powers comes a greater evil, — an apprehension of finiteness. In our years of wholeness and strength there is no such apprehension. Life carries with it a mighty affirmation of continuance, but when life weakens it begins to doubt itself. But the idea of coming to an end is intolerable; it does not suit our nature or feelings; it throws us into confusion; we become a puzzle to ourselves; we cannot get our life into any order or find for it any sufficient motive or end, and so it turns into a horrible jest, unless we can ground ourselves on some other conception. But the sense of finiteness presses on us with increasing force; it seems to outmaster the infinite, and even to assert its mastery in the process at work within us. This process has come to wear a scientific cast, and seems to claim the endorsement of science. We are kept alive by the action of two laws, — the vital and the chemical. Physical life is the result of the struggle between the two, — the vital building up, the chemical tearing down, — constant waste, constant repair. Were the latter to cease, death would shortly follow. Silently, ceaselessly the two forces work in perpetual antagonism, — life weaving in its mysterious loom the cell-tissue that makes up the human fabric, — how we cannot tell, science cannot unravel the process. All we can say is, that it must be the hand of creative Life himself that holds the threads, and throws the shuttle. Over against it is the busy destroyer — oxygen — burning up the life-woven tissue steadily, relentlessly. For years the vital force is stronger and weaves faster than its enemy can destroy. But at last, somewhere in mid-life, the forces are equal. Then the chemical gains on the vital, and pulls down faster than the other builds up. We die simply because chemical force triumphs over vital force, because the law of destruction is stronger than the law of life, because the finite outmasters what seemed infinite. Does it outmaster it or not? That is the question. It is here that we need a shield to interpose against the horrible suggestions of this last battle of life. And it is just here that God offers himself as such a shield, — God himself in all the personality of his being, — the I Am, — *Existence*. The name itself is an argument; existence is in question, and here is Existence itself saying to a mortal man, "I am your shield." Must not the protection bear a relation to the Being who protects? God is behind and in this battle that seems won by death. One side is plain enough.

The chemist can tell us all about it, — how oxygen tears down, — but he can tell us nothing of how life builds up. The Sphinx, staring upon the Nubian sands, is not more dumb than he when he stands before life weaving its tissue. There is a power and a principle present that he cannot detect or measure, and never will; the mystery of being is insolvable; eternity will not give us the key. If he is logical he will not attempt to draw conclusions as to the destiny of man when there is an unknown element in the problem. If this unseen Power sees fit to weave the fleshly fabric in a finite way, we need not conclude that the life itself shares the fate of the apparent web. With an omnipotent Weaver weaving a fabric made up of finite threads, and also of incomprehensible threads, spun and drawn out of his own being, it is not necessary to believe that when the finite are dissolved, the others also are dissolved. Their entire relation is that of antagonism, — may they not be diverse in their destiny? They were originally brought together, — how we do not know, — may they not be separated, — how we cannot understand; but one mystery is not greater than the other. One is a fact, the other may be and has its analogy to support it. We may rest in the conclusion that if God has had a hand in the making of us, his work will endure. Between ourselves longing for life, and this devouring sense of finiteness, stands God — a shield. "I made you," He says, "but you shall not perish because I put you into a perishing body. Because I made you you cannot perish. Because I am the ever-living God you shall live also."

3. God is a shield against the calamities of life.

It is rarely that one gets far on in life without seeing many times when it is too hard to be borne. Take ordinary, average life, I hardly see how men stand up under it. Take a life like that of so many around us, where only one pair of hands is all there is between the family and starvation, with the chances of sickness or no work. Ah! "the simple annals of the poor" are not cheerful reading. Or, take the every-day catastrophes, loss of property, little children, or wife, or husband, swept away by death; take the life-long sorrows, the drunken son, the daughter gone to shame, the marriage that has turned into disgust,— it is not easy to walk steady through the years with such burdens on one. Consider, also, how hopes die out, how life with most settles into a dull ache of disappointment, what multitudes carry about secret sorrows, and how, for most of us, the life that was to be so free, and glad, and prosperous, has turned into a treadmill of toil or dull routine of trifles. I confess I see little life that is of itself rewarding, little life that pays as it goes. There are few who can say with Walter Scott, "*sat est vixisse*," it is enough to have lived. For vast multitudes life is unutterably sad and bitter, for many others it is dull and insipid, for others one long disappointment, for none is it its own reward. It will always wear this aspect to the sensitive and the thoughtful unless some other element or power is brought in. Man cannot well face life without some shield between. He may fight ever so bravely, but the spears of life will be too many and too sharp for him. And no shield will thoroughly defend him but God. The lowest, by its very condition, demands the highest; the weakest calls out for the strongest, — none but the strongest can succor the weakest; the saddest can be comforted only by the most blessed; the finite can get deliverance from its binding and torturing condition only in the eternal one. When Hamlet caught sight of life, and saw what he had got to do and bear, he said, "I'll go pray." You have but to name God before sorrow and it changes color; name Him before burdens and they grow less; name Him before the vanity of life and it disappears. The whole sphere and scene of life is changed, lifted into a realm of power and wisdom and gladness. With the incoming of God there is a sense of reversal, everything that is sad and poor and dark and wrong is turned about and gathers meaning and purpose. A prophetic sense enters into us, and these wandering, disorderly, fragmentary features and experiences of life, are built up into a city that hath foundations in which we repose by faith.

4. God is a shield against ourselves.

It is, in a certain sense, true of us all that we are our own worst enemies. One may have no fatal appetite or habit, and this still be true. There is a wide difference between a development of personality, and that growth and condition known as self-consciousness. One is the highest achievement of life, the other is its curse and failure. The difference springs from the motive or principle of conduct, for in all things the seed determines the shape and character. If this seed is self-love, self-care, self-exaltation, it ends in the creation of a world in which self is the only citizen. It cuts the man off from external inspirations and motives. Humanity ceases to move him. The world breathes upon him no inspiring motive. Human love loses its tender force and appeal. His own instincts and faculties cease to work well. There are no longer sweet influences in the Pleiades. The spirit departs from all things, and nature, instead of a radiating source of influence and thought, becomes a show or vain form that passes dully before his eyes. Whatever he looks upon becomes a mirror that reflects himself, and ceases to be the sign and medium of truth. It is the last and worst result of selfishness that it leaves one alone with self, out of all external relations, sealed up within self-built enclosures. A very fair and seemly life may end in this way. If self be the central thought, it ends in nothing but self, and when this comes about we find that self is a poor companion. It matters not what form it takes, — intellectual conceit, personal vanity, pride of dress, self-pampering, ambition, avarice, or even that commonest of mental habits, the thoughts playing about self in fond and idle ways, — the tendency is to an exclusion of all but self, and so to a fixed state of self-consciousness. And this is misery, this is perdition, to be shut up with self, to walk up and down self and find out at last how small self is, to measure and weigh self and find out how light self is, to feed on self, to dwell, to sleep and wake and converse with self alone, there is nothing worse than this.

If you would see this truth put into its highest expression, read Tennyson's "Palace of Art." The greater poets never mistake when they touch themes like this. The æsthetic school of the day strives to use this poet for enforcing its small fancies and uncertain morality; but this poem, written long ago as if by prophetic inspiration, is the denial and refutation of its main current, and contains its final history; at last —

> "No voice breaks thro' the stillness of this world:
> One deep, deep silence all."

He built its palace, more gorgeous than its weaker fancy can devise, but he left it empty on the simple ground of a lack of that morality which it passes by, or but lightly names. A weak and false representative of this earnest age is this school with its brooding parade of self at the front, reminding one of the curtain of a theatre whereon is painted a careless youth touching the strings of a lute for listless girls amongst flowers and fountains, while behind it is Hamlet rehearsing his great question, "To be, or not to be," or Lear struggling with the tempest and his own heart.

One of the main uses of God, so to speak, is to give us another consciousness than that of self, — a *God-consciousness*. It was this that Christ made the world's salvation, not breaking the Roman yoke, not instituting a new government or a new religion, not revealing any formal law or secret of material prosperity, or any theory of education or reform, but simply making plain a fact, assuring the world that God is, and that He is the Father, and breathing a consciousness of it into men, opening it up to the world's view, and writing it upon its heart as in letters of his own blood; thus he brought in a God-consciousness in place of a world-consciousness and a self-consciousness, this only, but who shall measure its redeeming power! And there is no more gracious, shield-like interposing of God than when He comes in between us and self as a delivering presence. It is the joy of friendship that we are conscious of our friend, and that he draws us away from ourselves. It is the joy of the home that each one is conscious of the other; home-life reaches its perfection when parents and children not only love, but pass on to the highest form of love, — a steady and all-informing consciousness of one another. It shadows forth the largest form of the truth, God dwelling, not amongst but in men, a shield against themselves. It is God Himself who fills this relation. I, the ever-living God, am your shield; not some truth about me, not some "stream of tendency," not some blind or unknown force working towards righteousness, but I who made you in my image, and whom therefore you know, I am your shield!

Thanks for this old and ever new promise flaming its glorious assurance in the front of history! It is the personal God who stands between us and the dread forces of nature, his ministers and ours and no more, between us and our finiteness, between us and calamity, between us and self, with its vanity, its meagreness, and the dread conclusion to which it points.

GOD OUR REWARD.

"O Thou whose power o'er moving worlds presides,
Whose voice created and whose wisdom guides,
On darkling man in pure effulgence shine,
And cheer the clouded mind with light divine.

'Tis thine alone to calm the pious breast
With silent confidence and holy rest;
From Thee, great God, we spring, to Thee we tend,
Path, Motive, Guide, Original and End."
Boethius, translated by D<small>R</small> J<small>OHNSON</small>.

"There entertain him all the saints above,
  In solemn troops and sweet societies,
That sing, and singing in their glory move,
  And wipe the tears forever from his eyes."
Lycidas.

"With God, the human soul not merely interprets the secret of the universe; it comprehends, and is at peace with itself. For God is the satisfaction of its thirst." — C<small>ANON</small> L<small>IDDON</small>, *Elements of Religion*, page 80.

GOD OUR REWARD.

We now take up man's other main need, the positive one, namely, the fulfillment of desires and labors.

It is the characteristic of man that he plans and remembers; he plans to gain an object, he remembers his plan and looks for its fulfillment. Life is based on this idea of a return or reward to be gained; that is, it is not its own reward. It is not enough for man simply to live. The ox lies down in the shade and chews his cud in utter content. There is, doubtless, a vast joy, an immeasurable, blissful content in the animal creation that seems to mock the inseparable woe of humanity. Their almost perfect health, their harmonious adjustment to their surroundings, their entire oneness with their world and their kind, must yield a joy nearly perfect in its kind. A bird's song, a child's laughter, are simply the expression of joy in bare existence. But a man soon gets beyond the state when he can say, "It is enough to live, to eat and drink and sleep and dwell at peace with my kind." There are indeed moments when the cup of life overflows; days in June when heaven and earth draw so near together that the rapture of both fills the heart, and one is forced to cry with the poet: "O God, I thank thee that I live." There are moments also when love so overwhelms the other faculties that we think not of yesterday or to-morrow, but only of our present perfect bliss, as when words of plighting troth have been uttered, or, in some tenderer moment, a father takes his prattling child on his knee, and in the unutterable outgoing of his love, catches a glimpse of how God loves, and why, loving so, He dwells in infinite repose. But such moments are transient, bits of eternity unduly realized, chance foretastes of what shall be when that which is perfect is come. The law of our condition soon reasserts itself; the ecstasy of eternity passes, and time resumes its sway over us, time that gives us nothing because it has itself no existence, and can only promise us something in the future, crying as it flies past on its swift wings: "to-morrow and to-morrow!"

This great figure standing in front of the mists of antiquity, the first man with clear heavens above him, outlined our leading relations to life and to God. He had in some way, it matters not how, got a clear sight of God, and it worked upon him in a legitimate way: it awed and commanded him, and drew him out of himself toward God, so that God was more to him than his child; for it is in the nature of God and of man, that God should be more to man than his child, even his only child. And having such sight of God, he has like faith in Him, a vast, all mastering, all possessing faith answering all the ends of righteousness, nay, it *is* righteousness. What is external righteousness, — the petty details of doing, or not doing, — to this passionate, immeasurable loyalty of faith? The faith itself sweeps to the outermost skirts of conduct and infuses its devotion into every act and feeling. Here, in such a faith as this, not in any legal posturings and formal coming and going, is found the true philosophy of life. Now, what shall God do for a man, how deal with one who trusts him in this way? He will be his shield, will protect him against the world and mischance and his own finiteness. And he will see to it that this other great necessity, this looking for a fulfillment of labors and desires, is met; and he will see to it in a personal way, and, in a sense, become the reward itself: "I will be thine exceeding great reward."

And so Abram lived his life of solitary obedience, waiting but never doubting, patiently enduring, looking for the promised country but never finding it, and at last died without its sight. But all along God was rewarding him, making life tolerable if not triumphant, calm if not joyful, while the great, main desire of his life, the dream and aspiration of his years, is carried over into the world to come. He found a country, but it was beyond the Jordan of death. It was not a land flowing with the milk and honey of earth, of heavy clusters of grapes and abundance of corn, but was a heavenly country: its riches were the fruits of his own patient endurance, its valleys were the depths of his own humility, its mountains were the exaltations of his own faith, all wrought into some fit expression amongst the realities of eternity.

I like to draw water from these ancient wells, especially from this dug by our father Abraham, because its waters are so sweet and wholesome. They spring up from the central depths of our common nature, they quench the strong thirsts of our immortal being. There is a sublime naturalness and simplicity in the way in which Abram is led through life. God deals with him and he deals with God, in lofty, natural, and direct ways. He needed very nearly the same things that we need, and God led him very nearly as he leads us.

We will break up this divine rewarding into some of its particulars, with the question, How does God become our reward?

It is a striking fact that God's leading representations of true and righteous life are that it is not in vain, that it will be rewarded. This is the truth that underlies that commonest of all religious words, *bless*, a word used with such iteration that its meaning has well-nigh dropped out of it. That God will *bless*, is the sum of our prayers. We mean, if we mean anything, that God will prosper us, that success may attend our labors, that we may reach happy consummations, that we may get good things, that we may receive benefits of some kind. Thus our commonest and deepest feeling in religion is keyed to a divine reward; it shows that we were made to have it, clear proof that we are the heirs in God's kingdom, that the ascetic idea of going without is not in his plan. The little child believes that all things belong to it and claims everything it can touch, book, or toy, or picture, stretching out its hands for the moon with a divine sense of ownership. And the child is not wrong; the child is never wrong in its spontaneous conduct, acting out what God put into it, reflecting the thought of the face that its spirit beholds. All things do belong to it, and are withheld only while it is in its spiritual minority, for purposes of discipline, and until it learns to distinguish between the good and the evil. But at last God's children, being heirs, inherit, and all things become theirs. These are not idle words, nor a dream of conceited religionists. Down equally deep with the truth, that man, like God, is a giver, is the other truth, that he is a receiver, like God in this also for whom are all things. The largest generic truth from which we think, is that God made man in his own image, a truth not so much to be restricted as spread out and applied in the whole field of human speculation. If it opens abysmal depths and heights in God, from which we shrink as not for us, it is still God who summons us towards Himself, even to a seat in his throne. This ceaseless cry and strife for something we have not got, this outstretched hand of humanity, is not a caprice, nor yet an act of selfishness, but rests on this divine, inborn sense of heirship to all things; only, we forget that we must inherit through God, that only the meek possess the earth, the pure in heart see God. But what a truth! What transforming power is wrapt up in it! What a light it throws on toil, and narrow circumstance, and all these restraints and bonds that tie us down to this place and that task! I take it that a great part of this earthly tuition and discipline is not more to work out the evil that is in us, than to prepare us to receive what God has in readiness to give us. I cannot otherwise interpret the great and terrible withholding seen in the vast majority of lives; this fearful negative must mean a gracious positive. I know that we are often summoned to think of all worlds from the conditions of this, to reason that because they are hard here they will be hard elsewhere, but the logic is meagre. I grant that if present and known conditions are the only factors in the argument we have a very dreary outlook, almost worse than none. But when God is introduced into the argument, it changes its drift and conclusion, for He is just and good, and He is also eternal, and hence his plans are not to be judged by their appearance in any section of time. I know not how else to put any meaning on life. Here is a widow, alas, how many such! poor and all but friendless, suffers perhaps for food, shivers with cold, no past but suffering, no future with any hope or light, life a simple struggle to keep her soul alive as God would have her, but she reads, "all things are yours," and carries the promise up to God in faith. What will you do with such a life? What, but say that the withholding is but a preparation for, and pledge of, a corresponding giving. Or, take some finer spirit, a mind athirst for knowledge, burning to see the world and the works of men, to look on art, to hear music, to know history and literature, eager to push out into this great world of thought and fact, filled with a passion truly divine to see and know and realize; but here he is, poor, fettered to some given place and task, perhaps watching a shuttle to earn the bread of dependent ones. What a mal-adjustment! What a blindness of fate! What a cruelty of providence! Yes, unless sometime and somewhere this sublime hunger is satisfied. There is running through all Christ's teachings a subtle thread of *reversal;* it seems to cover circumstance as well as character; it is not always based on the moral; Lazarus passes before our eyes without character; the poor have their blessing on the ground of poverty. The scales of allotment and condition will be evened, the lack here will find its fullness there, whatever it be. We reason far more truly from the character of God than from his acts. One we know, the other is partial, in process; one is absolute, the other is phenomenal; one is eternal, the other is for the time being. So, I do not build my expectations of the future on the processes and conditions now going on, but rather on the absolute nature of God, which is love; it is the nature of love to meet wants, and will omnipotent love leave any wants unmet? I do not forget that life is largely made up of duties and responsibilities, but these are simply forerunners, having no value in themselves, and but the drill and education necessary for a reception of God's measureless gifts. Hence, as soon as we begin to believe in God, to see, obey, and trust Him (the sum and definition of faith), God begins to feed us with promises as He did Abram. Everything is for the believer; but he does not now want, nor could he now receive, everything, but only certain things, and so God promises and gives these, varying the form to suit his expanding nature. Abram longed to become the head of a nation, and God made him the father of all believers; he desired a country, and God gave him an eternal possession. And so it is with all who have turned their faces trustingly towards the great Giver; it were well to know and feel it! God is an imposer of duties; yes, but beyond that He is the Rewarder of those who diligently seek Him. God says, "Thou shalt and thou shalt not," and scourges the disobedient; yes, but above and beneath all this He is the giver of eternal life to all who will, and this must contain all things.

Such a thought is wholesome and heartening; it is intended to give tone and color to life. Hence, it should enter fundamentally, and in its true order, into theology. First of all, God is a giver. Hence, away back in the dawn of history, God said to the first man worthy to hear it: "Now that you believe, I would have you begin by thinking of me as one who will be your shield and reward: I will take care of you, I will give you unspeakable blessings." God began with Abram in this way; it was not hard duty first and the joy of reward finally, but the great, glad hope and promise came first. It is a common thing to mistake the key-note of our faith; we trust Providence as though it were a last resort, and think of duty as perhaps a noble yet rather heavy thing to do. But not to such a key is the psalm of believing life to be sung; it is to be caught rather from these ancient words of God: "Fear not: I am thy shield and thy exceeding great reward."

It may be felt by some that this matter of divine reward is, after all, a vague thing. What is it? Where is it? How does it come about? Is it a direct gift, or is it wrought out through laws? It is vague because it is a matter of trust and gradual realization. What God has in reserve for those who believe on Him, cannot now be measured. Nor do we know through what new conduits the rewarding joys of eternity may flow into us, nor what fresh fountains of bliss may be unsealed within us. The spirit of man is an unsounded, perhaps fathomless depth, a store-house of measureless possibilities. To assert what man will do or not do, what he will become or cannot become, is to assert a knowledge of the infinite; we have no knowledge of man that wholly defines and compasses him. Here all the beauty of the earth and the majesty of the sky come to us through one sense, all the sweetness of melody through one sense, all the lusciousness of fruits through one sense, all the fragrance of odors through one sense,—small inlets and few for things so many and vast. But as we know through science that there are sounds we do not hear, and colors that we do not see, and odors that we do not smell, it is not improbable that we shall be opened wider, and at more points, to the wonders and delights of the universe; for it were unreasonable to suppose that the head of creation does not at last comprehend creation, making gains as we go hence like that of the embryo, which, when born into the world, finds its one sense of feeling supplemented by sight and hearing. So, also, the few faculties through which we now receive pleasure, intellectual, social, physical, may be increased, so that, instead of touching the external world at these few points, we may touch it at a thousand, and every point of contact be an inlet of joy. Or these present faculties may be enlarged to an immeasurable capacity. But these things are matters neither of knowledge or faith ;.they are the wise dreams of the "prophetic soul" that may turn to reality.

It is as far as we can go in this matter to say that God rewards in two ways: by the results of obedience, and, in a less clear but no less real way, by the direct gift or impartation of Himself. They are not distinct, but stand in the relation of process and end, or condition and result.

Forever and forever is it true that reward follows obedience, tritest yet truest of all words. It is the one all embracing, unfaltering truth, the gravitation of the moral universe, — Obey and be blest!

Obedience does not merely avoid the suffering of broken law, but it yields a positive reward. Every act of obedience, if consciously rendered and so becoming an act of faith, has a reward commensurate with the act. It might have been otherwise, and obedience had for its only end the cold result of suffering avoided. But we are made on a more generous plan. Whenever, anywhere in this universe, any soul hears the divine voice saying, "Thou shalt" and reverently obeys, it finds, however it be with other results, this unfailing one, a deep and peaceful satisfaction in having obeyed. And so it is that a life of humble, honest labor may have overspreading it a steady sense of reward. The man goes to his daily toil and comes home at night, with small returns perhaps that are quickly spent, a somewhat weary and rather hopeless tread-mill it seems, but he says, "I have at least the reward of doing my duty." Without it he would despair; without it humanity would not tolerate the burden of existence. This reward can be greatly heightened by getting clear sight of such duties as they are related to God's will. The unconscious reward is real and large; no little child ever returned from a wearying errand without it; no savage in Africa ever obeyed the inward voice whispering in his dull brain, "thou oughtest," but God dropped the reward of peace into his heart. The inner life of heathendom has not yet been presented to our thought. When will missionaries tell us of the good they find as well as the evil? It is the struggling and overborne goodness that would most appeal to our sympathy; it is the smouldering embers of not yet burnt out virtues that would stimulate us to add the gospel flame. One has recently spoken: "Call them heathen who will; but from what I know of their hearts, they do not seem to be forsaken by the Divine Spirit."[1] As deep calls unto deep, so every loyal heart, touched by God's Spirit, goes

---

[1] See letter from a missionary in India to the Rev. Newman Smyth, D. D., in *The Independent*, Jan. 18, 1883.

out in yearning, helpful love towards these heathen who pray as they best know, and not wholly in vain.

But a clear view of life as reflecting God's will, lifts the obedience into the consciousness where all the faculties play upon it.

The reward of simple, daily duty is sometimes best seen in the dark contrast of disobedience, as the stars shine fairest upon the blackness of empty space. We often grow dull to the value of our virtues, we forget the rewarding power of our habitual obedience. We are temperate, industrious, thrifty, patient, kind, true, faithful, wise, reverent, but forget that home, love, respect, peace, health, strength, property, and perhaps honors are their rewards, paid at the counter of God's daily reckoning. Hence, when duty grows dull, it is well to look off into the black regions of disobedience. Alas! we seldom have need to look far. Lust, with its satiety or disgrace or corruption; drunkenness with its tyranny, and waste and poverty and disease; selfishness come at last to despairing solitude; dishonesty breeding suspicion and alienation; avarice with its heart of ashes; folly with its harvest of bewilderment and blindness; impiety standing on the border of life, nothing behind or before and despair within;—in the gleams of such black flames we read again the lesson of obedience and shudder at the thought of ever having doubted its rewards.

Still the positive view is the better one, for we must learn to value goodness in its own light and by its own weight. There will thus come about at last, as in the Christ, a joy that is independent of the on-going world, that is not heightened by the sense of external evil, but is the straight outcome of a heart entranced with goodness. When one thus fills every mould of duty with sympathetic obedience, he is doing more than pleasing God and blessing man, he is unsealing hidden depths within himself that are stored with God's own eternal joy. I beg you to think of this; it is not so trite as you may suppose. In our iterated appeals for duty we commonly base them upon pleasing God and blessing man, that is, on its inherent rightfulness and its beneficence, leaving out the profounder argument that it sets one's own nature in order so that by its very law it evolves joy, for no harp was ever strung capable of uttering such music as the soul of man attuned to righteous obedience. It is hearing such music that makes men willing to die for a cause, to live patiently under wrong, to plead for the reform for which the age is not ripe, to stand true while evil corrupts the world. The New Jerusalem lieth four-square; so stands he who has learned to render a trustful obedience to his God; he stands true to the world, true to himself, true to the eternity about him, and true to God.

If there were not such a reward as this, there would be no motive sufficient to propel man on this long voyage of existence. For the reward or motive must be within and have its play within the circle of his own being simply because he has no permanent relations to anything without. There are but two abiding realities, God and self; all else is phenomenal, transient. The earth whereon we stand, the air we breathe, the firmament that inspheres us, will pass away; the goodly fellowship of humanity will yield before the separating years; the hands clasped in tenderest love will part; the child, the friend, the whole encircling life of the world, will be lost to us for a while at least, as we go "to the land of darkness and the shadow of death." The present complexity of life and relation settles surely into a simplicity in which only self and God remain — self alone with God! Hence life in its full sense, ideal life, is simply a true adjustment and interplay between these two, self living unto and in God, and God returning upon self with joy, — a process more stable than the universe and as enduring as God himself. The final word of the soul is: "And now I come to Thee." After one has entered on such an obedience as this, he soon begins to find that he is mainly acting in the sphere of two personalities, — himself and God. I mean this: he is not acting under certain laws and principles, — these conceptions grow dim and become mere phrases and conveniences of speech; but he comes to realize that he is living unto, and as it were, *in* God. And as he goes on, all things at last resolve themselves into this complection; it is God whom he serves, and God is his reward; he wants no other; he lives and dies with one all-satisfying word in his heart and on his lips: —

"Whom have I in heaven but Thee?

And there is none upon earth that I desire besides Thee."

LOVE TO THE CHRIST AS A PERSON.

"Love is inexorable as justice, and involves duty as the sum of the commandments of the law." — MULFORD, *Republic of God*, page 190.

"My heart's subdued
Even to the very quality of my lord."

Othello, I. 3.

"The love of Jesus is noble, and spurs us on to do great things, and excites us to desire always things more perfect." — *The Imitation of Christ*, Chap. V.

"The hold which Christianity has depends on Christ, and the hold which Christ has is chiefly dependent on those personal affections and reverential regard which souls that receive Christ entertain towards Him." — PRES. WOOLSEY, *Sermons*, page 355.

LOVE TO THE CHRIST AS A PERSON.

"And verily I say unto you, wheresoever the gospel shall be preached throughout the whole world, that also which this woman hath done shall be spoken of for a memorial of her." — ST. MARK xiv. 9.

THE fact that three of the New Testament writers rehearse this story shows how fully they entered into Christ's purpose to perpetuate it. They have different plans, and omit or include events and words accordingly, but they do not omit this event and Christ's comment upon it. Evidently it is a marked thing. It is the only intimation made by Christ that any record was to be made concerning Him. Here is something, He says, that shall have a universal record. Yet these faithful historians tell the story somewhat differently, not in a contradictory way, but as each felt it; as a poet, a historian, and a moralist might describe a battle, harmonizing in the main points, but each coloring his account with the hue of his own mind. This variation is a great help in getting at its meaning. St. Matthew and St. Mark adhere to the express purpose of Christ to set the deed of this woman before all the world, and so put their emphasis upon its *memorial* feature, but St. John seems to forget this, and can only remember that the anointing was for the burial of his Lord. His love blinds him to the main point enjoined by Christ; but the omission itself is significant, as it shows how the central idea had already been accomplished in him; he does not think of the woman, but of the service done to his Master. And the event has been used by a great preacher of the age, kindred in spirit to this disciple, to show how keen is "the insight of love" in detecting the true uses and ends of service. The apostle and the preacher were held by a feature of the event, but how beautiful and profound the attraction!

The beauty and pathos of the incident is apt to shut us off from any critical thoughts about it. The passion and humility of the love, the *abandon* of its expression, the fine symbolism of its minuter features, anointing not the head only but the feet, and gathering from thence to the flowing honors of her head the now sacred ointment; these points catch and hold the eye till we are inclined to think its main use is to adorn the sacred page as a picture. But it is more than a picture. If events are grouped and colored in such a way as to excite our sense of the beautiful, we may, indeed, pause a moment to reflect how inevitably divine things are beautiful, how surely a true act has a grace of its own; how, as we come into the higher ranges of conduct, truth and beauty and goodness melt into each other. But such thoughts must be transient, the delicious recreation of a moment only, after which we pass on to the substantial truth behind the picture. When we approach it with analysis, we are struck with the fact that in certain respects it has features exceptional and somewhat contradictory to any others found in the history of Christ. A woman deeply moved breaks a box of costly ointment upon his head and feet. In rescuing her from the criticism provoked by this act, He exalts her and her deed into world-wide fame. There is no parallel to this in all these histories. It is not only exceptional, but it is not plain why it is so. The pledged honor seems inordinate. The woman, in a beautiful and touching way, sacrificed a cherished treasure upon the person of Christ, — certainly not a great act unless it were great in some unusual way. It involved but expense, and no personal danger. It had in it no element of self-denial, no great force of will, nothing of the stalwart graces of endurance or heroic purpose. Outwardly it fell far short of what men have always been doing and enduring for Christ. The catacombs of Rome are full of the ashes of believers who were persecuted for his sake, and the crumbling tablets are fast refusing to reveal their names. For centuries a great army of martyrs marched to prison, to the arena, to the stake, but leaders and host are now nameless. There are multitudes to-day whose service seems far more valuable, and is rendered at far greater cost, than the one deed of this woman, but no provision is made for their special remembrance. It seems inconsistent also with Christ's method, for it was this sort of honor and praise that He rigidly excluded. It was a fundamental point in his kingdom that personal exaltation had no place in it; the exact reverse was fundamental.

Something else must be meant than that this woman was to be heralded wherever the Gospel might go. Indeed, when we look carefully at the story, we find that it does not provide the requisite elements of such a fame. The two writers who alone give the laudatory promise, withhold the *name* of the woman, so that if personal fame be meant by Christ, it is not connected with any person; while John, who omits the laudatory promise, alone indicates the name. It is as though a monument were built to some hero and his name omitted from the inscription. There is indeed such a monument in the Public Garden of Boston, that celebrates the discovery of ether, — nameless of all except the mercy thus achieved, — a monument prophetic of the age when there shall be "no pain any more," but equally Christian in the unwitting exaltation of *good* above the *doer* of good. It hints the way to a true reading of the incident before us. Christ evidently had some other purpose than to bestow personal fame on this woman; this were out of keeping with true womanly desire, with the nature and method of his kingdom, with his personal principles, and with the whole tenor of his teaching. But why does He use words that seem to imply it? Reading the story more carefully we find that it is not the *woman* who is to have world-wide mention, but her *deed*, this that she hath done, and herself as some nameless one who rendered it. The *deed* is the centre of significance; there is something in this little act of reverent affection so peculiar and so valuable as to justify the honor put upon it. Let us search it out.

I think we are near the truth when we say that the deed happened to be the exact type of that feeling and relation to himself which Christ regarded as necessary, and so he seized it as a perpetual example; that is, He takes it for use. There is here no sentimentalizing, no lapsing into unusual methods. Instead He takes the act — a personal act indeed, but still the act only, — and makes it a part of his gospel. It memorializes not a person but a temper of mind, yet in and through an environment of personality. This explains why the woman is made so prominent, while the central thought rests on the action; it explains why the world-wide memorial is nameless. It has in it an element forever essential to a true reception of the gospel; hence Christ connects it with preaching, it is to go wherever the gospel goes, and to become a part of it.

Looking at it more closely, we find as its main characteristic that it was the expression of a feeling, and that it was intensely personal. This woman had come under a great sense of gratitude to Christ; she had found in him a response to every better feeling, an insight into her heart that was like self-knowledge, or deeper still, a revelation of self to herself, a sympathy that was as a new life. The thought of Him drew her to goodness, and made evil no longer possible. And so He became enshrined in her soul almost as God; nay, all her thoughts of Him were like her thoughts of God, except that their dread was softened by a human grace. He was inspiration, guidance, strength, everything to her; hence the tribute. She does not, with long and careful thought, consider how she may forward his cause or do some good work that may please Him, — that may come after; now there is but one thing for her to do; it must be something for Jesus himself, upon his person, so that it shall express how personal and vital is his influence upon her. It is not truth, it is not an idea that inspires her, but this Jesus himself, and so upon Jesus himself she lavishes her tribute of reverent love.

But this is a gospel to be preached in all the world: How shall it preach to us? We have no seen and present Lord to receive the raptures and gifts of our love. We can lay no golden or odorous gifts by his cradle, we have no ointment for his wearied feet, no spices for his burial. Such service, were it possible, would seem somewhat apart from even our warmest thought of Christ. We cannot conceive ourselves as acting or as required to act in quite that way. The outward parallel is not for us, but the inward parallel sets forth an unending relation and an unfaltering duty. Christ asked from men nothing of an external nature, but He steadily required their personal love and loyalty. He did not ask of any a place to lay his head, it mattered little if Simon asked Him to his feasts, but, once there, it did matter whether Simon loved Him or not. Waiving all personal ministration, He yet claims personal love. Strange spectacle! Here is a man indifferent to what is done for him or to him, but demanding love! a human contradiction, but hiding a divine truth. It is not truth or purity or wisdom you are to love, but me. You are to be faithful, not so much to your convictions as faithful to me. Nay, what you do is of secondary importance if you first love me.

Thus Christ presented Himself before the world, drawing it off from its speculations, its ritualized dogmas, its traditional ethics, and fixed its thought upon Himself, a new centre of truth and inspiration. His position is without parallel. The philosophers had said, "Accept our ideas, adopt our systems," but Christ said, "Accept *me.*" No religionists have ever made a similar claim. Gautama said, "This is the way, by renunciation." Mohammed said, "There is heaven." They sunk themselves in their theories, and, while claiming leadership, put the centre of their systems in some idea or external end, but Christ merges all ideas and methods in devotion to Himself, and the devotion is summed up in love. A most strange thing; — here is one whose main thesis is abnegation of self, and is himself its prime illustration, and at the same time sets himself up as the centre of the world's love! It is out of such contradiction that we are to look for the issue of the finest truth, as vision is born of darkness and light.

There is in this attitude no final abjuring of philosophy and system and doctrine, but only the adoption of a higher and surer method of reaching them, a vitalizing and humanizing of them. In its last analysis the idea is this: Truth entering human society through a person, and making love its vehicle. For personality is the secret of both the Christian and Judaic systems, — *revelation by a person.* The peculiarity of these systems is not their truth; there is not much question about truth. Men are sure to find it out first or last. And ethical truth is almost the first to clear itself in the human understanding. The old philosophies and mythologies are packed with undoubted truth; enough for all social and personal need if that were all that was necessary. It was inevitable that the precepts of love as the sum of duty should have early utterance; the human mind could not go amiss of them. But to connect them with a person for authority and inspiration was another matter; the efficacy of the precepts lies in the Person that utters them, and in the relation of this Person to man. The fault of Matthew Arnold's definition of God, " a power not ourselves that works for righteousness," is, that it blurs the personality behind the righteousness, and so deprives it of motive. Whatever significance there is in the Jewish Scriptures lies in the personality emblazoned on every page, a God who is not a power only, but also a person, and a power because He is a person, not a "stream of tendency" flowing in free or hindered currents, destined perhaps to flow, but capable also of resistance, with some question of ultimate success, but the *I am*, the Personal Being! Cast this out, and they might have been burned with the books of Alexandria with little loss. But because they contain this uniform and self-attesting assertion of a personal God, as personal as man is, and the basis of his personality, they have lain warm and nourishing at the roots of that civilization which is dominating the world.

There is reason in this. A relation of duty cannot be fully established and sustained except between persons. I owe no duty to force or to "a stream of tendency," I merely fall in with, or resist it, without any play of my faculties except some sense of prudence. This would seem axiomatic, yet it is in the face of such axiomatic truth that we are asked to accept the theories of an unknowable God, theories that annihilate duty by rendering impossible a relation of duty. The Hebrew and Christian Scriptures have presented duty to the world, not only in a rational but in a commanding way, because they assert in the loftiest way the two correlative elements in duty, namely, the personality of man and the thorough personality of God. It is Christ's revelation of this personality, on each side, that constitutes Christianity. It was long before its facts crystallized into systems. The church sprang up about the revealing person of Christ; love to him was the bond that held it together; and so it continued to be till the image of Christ grew dim, and the Master was buried first beneath his church, and then under formal renderings of his truth, and to-day Christendom puts its churches and its theologies before its Lord.

There are those who contend that what we need is not the Christ himself but the truth of Christ; that if we accept the principles He taught, there need be no special enthusiasm or even thought about their author. And thus Christianity is gradually reduced to a philosophy, and thence into mere maxims about good and evil, as though even in Christ's day they were not the lumber of the world.

But let us see if Christ was mistaken in planting his system upon personal love and devotion to Himself. Or, more broadly, why does this Faith, that claims to be the world's salvation, wear this guise of personal relations? Simply because in no other way can man be delivered from his evil. There may be exceptions here and there in whom natural dispositions are so happily blended that they have attained to a stainless if cold virtue. But take men as they are, the bulk and mass of humanity, they are too blind to find their way by the light of precepts, too firmly wedded to evil to be moved by theories of virtue, too solidly imbedded in the custom of an "evil world" to be extricated by any play of reason. And as to experience, the fancied teacher of wisdom, with its "hoard of maxims," it is the weakest of all. Polonius is but "a tedious old fool" to the Hamlets who are struggling with their own weakness in the hard play of human life. It is the subtlest thought in the profoundest drama, that Hamlet is searching for a human love to upstay and inspire him; it is the key to all his wild, testing talk with Ophelia; the love he found, but there was no strength in it; it could not draw together his scattered and faltering energies and set them to some definite end, and so his life sweeps on to its tragic close. There is in all these simply lack of motive-power. Men need instead something of the nature of a passion to dislodge them, some deep swelling current of feeling to sweep them away from evil towards goodness, from self towards God. Suppose Christ had simply depicted the miseries of sin and the inherent fitness and excellence of the virtues, what would He have done? What become? Simply another Rabbi with a few followers for a generation. He began instead by forming personal relations with a few men, captivating them by his divine charms, making them feel at last that his love was more than a human love, even God's own love. Ideas, truths, principles, these are not lacking, but the essence of his power is not in them, for they have no power. The great, reflective novelist has well stated it in her earlier and wiser pages: "Ideas are often poor ghosts; our sun-filled eyes cannot discern them; they pass athwart us in their vapor, and cannot make themselves felt. But sometimes they are made flesh; they breathe upon us with warm breath, they touch us with soft responsive hands, they look at us with sad, sincere eyes, and speak to us in appealing tones; they are clothed in a living human soul, with all its conflicts, its faith, and its love. Then their presence is a power, then they shake us like a passion, and we are drawn after them with gentle compulsion, as flame is drawn to flame." And yet it is *ideas* that the loud-voiced wisdom of the age would have us believe to be the salvation of the world! God is driven farther and farther into unknowable heavens, the Christ is made to figure only on a dim and blurred page of history, the Spirit is thrust out on some score of intellectual difficulty, all reduced to ideas and ghostly at that, and a selfish world is summoned to drop the principles that have made it what it is and that stand to it for the solidest realities, by a phantom-show of ideas for which it does not care, or but admires as some far-off unattainable glory! The Faith that is to redeem the world must have a surer method, it must have a vitalizing motive, and such a motive can proceed only from a person using the strongest force in a person — love. And thus the Christ comes before humanity, making God's love manifest in a human and personal way, so unfolding his divine beauty in word and deed that men kneel before Him, subdued into glad receptivity of his truth. Thus it was that the multitudes thronged about Him, that Zaccheus was won by his condescending pity, that this woman broke upon Him her fragrant tribute of honor, that Thomas said, "Let us also go, that we may die with Him," and Peter, with a devotion that outran his courage, "Even if I must die with thee, yet will I not deny thee," that John leaned upon his bosom, that the women of Jerusalem bewailed Him on the cross and lingered about his sepulchre, that Joseph claimed the privilege of his burial, that the disciples mourned while He lay in the tomb, that joy gave wings to their feet when they heard of his resurrection. And when He finally ascended, and the full scope of his love came to be realized, when his character and being began to stretch away into the infinite under the revelation of the Spirit, it stirred them to even deeper passion. His love, seen now to be divine, awoke in them all the divineness of love, and became the measure of their devotion. From that day to this, the faith of believers has clustered about the personal Christ, growing cold and effete as it has drawn off from Him towards philosophy, and waxing warm and effective as it has come near to his glorified person. I grant that this love varies in its external features. In these later days, it has the calm of thought, the sobriety of conviction, the breadth that springs from a realization of his work. The semi-erotic aspect it has sometimes been made to wear and that is still weakly cherished in some quarters, has largely passed. The love we now render is the fidelity of our whole nature, the verdict of our intelligence, the assent of our conscience, the allegiance of our will, the loyalty of sympathetic conviction, all permeated with tender gratitude; but it is still personal, loving Him who loved us and gave Himself for us.

There are reasons for the assertion just made, that it is only through such a love that we can be delivered from ourselves and our evil. It is no novelty even in the thought of the world. "George Eliot" says:[1] "It is one of the secrets in that change of mental poise which has been fitly named conversion, that to many among us neither heaven nor earth has any revelation till some personality touches theirs with a peculiar influence, subduing them into receptiveness." It only needs to make this assertion universal to have in it a definition of

[1] *Daniel Deronda*, ii. 36.

the process of Christian faith, and almost a vindication of it by its superb insight. How otherwise shall we begin to secure this process of conversion; how uproot the selfishness that makes it necessary? Authority fails; the commandments are in the Old Testament, also in other sacred books it is claimed, but they had not much honor in their fruits. But when they issued from the lips of the living Christ, they fell into men's hearts like fire, and wrought in them as a passion. Will not thought open a path between evil and good? Thought may resolve conduct and character into their elements, but it cannot separate them. Philosophy makes slow progress in saving men; it has eyes to see man's misery, but no hands to lift him out of it. If, upon such a basis, one begins to struggle towards the good, the result is a hard, painful life, sustained by mere will, without warmth or glow or freedom, often overshadowed by doubts and mazed by sophistries, for there are philosophies and philosophies, a life more deficient and less exalted than it seems to itself, because it is not constantly matching itself with a personal standard. The measure of rules and bare ideals has little working efficacy, it is unsubstantial, it does not recognize the complexity of life, for only life can measure life, it guides but imperfectly and lacks the strongest of motive-powers — inspiration. There is light enough but no warmth, matter enough but no attraction. Goodness that is enforced or devised has no propagating power. You cannot think, or plan, or legislate it into existence; it is not a product of syllogism, nor a deduction of knowledge, nor a fruit of experience, but is akin to life and must be begotten. And so character is placed under the lead of personal love. At the threshold of life we are met by affections that check and call us off from inborn selfishness, the love of parents and of brother and sister, and then that fiery passion that ushers in a love that makes of twain one, and then the diviner, downward-flowing love upon children; it is in such ways as these, all personal, that evil is kept or crowded out, and we become tender and generous and pure. But beyond lies the broader sphere of humanity, for which there is but small native passion, and hence but little inspiring force impelling us to its duties. Yet this is the field of our highest duties, for here are our widest relations. And it is here chiefly that Christ becomes an inspiration through the loyalty of love. Christ is humanity to us, He has hardly any other relation; He was not a father or husband, as son and brother his relation is obscured, his citizenship is not emphasized. In a certain sense, it is hardly necessary to have an inspiring and saving Christ in these relations, they enforce themselves, they are still full of their original, divine power. Not so, however, when we get outside of these domestic and neighborly instincts. Our relation to humanity at large is so blurred that it fails to enforce its duties. Hence Christ put himself solely and entirely into this relation, the Son of man, the Brother of all men, the Head of humanity, and there sets in play the divine forces of universal love and pity and sympathy. When our love meets his in the loyalty of faith, we find ourselves rightly related to humanity and to God. Faith in Christ has for one of its main ends the proper adjustment of the individual to society. The secret, essential relation of the Christ to humanity, and of humanity to God, flows to us along this channel of obedient, inspiring love, and so we come to love our neighbor as ourselves, and God supremely.

But the truth may be set in even a larger light. The love of Christ not only delivers us from evil and unites us to humanity, but it does the wider work of uniting us to God's eternal order both on earth and in heaven.

The one supreme truth is that *God is love*. This is the secret of the universe. Creation is the outcome of this fact; the whole order of all things is grounded in it; the harmony of the universe is its realization. There is therefore no possible relation for a human being to stand in to God and to his creation but that of love. Not to love God is to be in confusion, at odds with creation, aside from the order of the universe. The whole creation swims in a sea of eternal love. Every law and process and form, material and spiritual, angelic and human, individual and social; every relation, every method, is established in this love. This makes love the supreme and all-embracing duty; it is thus only that we come into accord with the world, and fall into the current that sweeps through eternity. Thus love, that seems the most voluntary thing, and the thing most to be kept at our own disposal, to be given or withheld as we see fit, becomes an imperative obligation, for it is the only possible bond by which we can hold our place in God's created order, the one highway between self and all other things and beings. Not to love is, at last, utter and absolute separation from all else — even from self; it is the outer darkness where existence itself becomes bewilderment. To get into this love, which is God, and respond to its mighty harmonies, and know its perfect peace, this is the great and final achievement. Consider this truth until you have mastered it, or, at least, got some glimpse of it, and then put beside it the revelation of this love in the Son of God, and you see at once why you are to love Him. It is simply putting yourself in accord with the ruling principle of the universe, it is falling into line with the eternal order; for the whole universe is wrought into Him; He is the only begotten Son of the Father; in Him the entire order of nature is set forth ; in Him the whole of God's will is perfectly obeyed; He is the perfect Righteousness. And in Him the full order and will of eternal Love is brought into humanity, where human love, your love and mine, may lay hold of it and play into it. Nor can there be conceived any other method by which human love can enter into the eternal Love; it must go by the eternally ordained path of personality, and the personality must be a manifestation of all the fullness of God. Hence there is no other name under heaven wherein we must be saved.

The great problem set before the Faith, — nay,

let us not generalize, — the imperative need of every man is to get over from the natural and evil side of life to the Christ side, to give up worldly ways of feeling and acting, and pass into the Christly way; to die unto self and let Christ be formed in him, the true son of God and of man taking the place of the Adamic self, — a very definite and imperative work lying before every human soul. It is the secret of life, it is the key of destiny. How to bring it about is the question. It is an achievement, for it is nothing less, wrought, so far as we are concerned, by love to Christ, and by the service of love. For the whole nature follows love. Whithersoever it goes all the faculties troop after it. It is the magnet of human nature; where the heart is there are all the treasures of mind and will and moral nature. Let this love be planted in Christ, — won and fixed by our ever deepening sense of truth and goodness and all moral beauty, — and we begin to go over to Him upon it as upon a bridge. Character itself cannot be imparted or exchanged, but everything that goes to make character may be imparted, or quickened into action. Using this love as if it were some broad stream, the truth, the strength, the humility, the sympathy, the spiritual insight, the obedience, the very righteousness of Christ float down into us and become our own, and so at last we are one with Him and one with God, for He and God are one.

Let us not strive to find any other path for individual or social regeneration; there is no other path. Here is the way, the truth, the life. We cannot save ourselves; we cannot think or will ourselves into the life of God; we cannot drift into it on the tide of time. We must go by the eternally ordained path of love to Him who is the revelation of eternal Love, — a Person, — and suffer his love to charm us into a kindred love; we must lay our hearts close beside his, that they may learn to beat with the same motion; our wills near his, that they may fall into its harmony.

THE CHRIST'S PITY.

"Nothing but the Infinite pity is sufficient for the infinite pathos of human life."

. . . .

"When you have lived longer in this world, and outlived the enthusiastic and pleasing illusions of youth, you will find your love and pity for the race increase tenfold, your admiration and attachment to any particular party or opinion fall away altogether." — *John Inglesant*, Vol. I., page 121.

"Thou wilt feel all, that Thou mayest pity all." — *Christian Year, Tuesday before Easter.*

"He came laying His hand upon our head in sickness, His fingers upon our eyes, sighing out His soul upon us, breathing His peace into us, touching, taking us by the hand as we sink, entering into our homes, lifting us up in fever, teaching, chiding, enfolding, upholding, enlarging, inviting, encouraging, drawing, calming, controlling, commanding." — REV. H. S. HOLLAND, *Logic and Life*, page 219.

THE CHRIST'S PITY.

"But when He saw the multitudes, He was moved with compassion for them, because they were distressed and scattered, as sheep not having a shepherd." — ST. MATTHEW ix. 36.

WE often speak of love as the ultimate passion, but there is a depth even beyond love. For love is largely its own reward, and so may possibly have an element of imperfection, but pity or compassion has not only all the glory and power of love, but it forgets itself and its own returning satisfactions, and goes wholly over into the sufferings of others, and there expends itself, not turning back or within to say to itself, as does love, "How good it is to love!" Hence Balzac, in "The Alchemist," in depicting an ideally perfect love, makes the object of it deformed, thus profoundly indicating that love is not at its height and perfection without the element of pity. It may be a factor in the solution of the problem of evil that it calls out the highest measure of the divine love; a race that does not suffer might not have a full revelation of God's heart. What! Create a race miserable in order to love it! Yes, if also thereby its members shall learn to love one another, and if thus only it may know the love of its Creator. In the same way it is man's consciousness of misery, or self-pity, that reveals to him his own greatness,—a thought that Pascal turns over and over.

Pity is love and something more: love at its utmost, love with its principle outside of itself and therefore moral, love refined to utter purity by absorption with suffering. A mother loves her child when it is well, but pities it when it is sick, and how much more is the pity than the love! How much nearer does it bring her, rendering the flesh that separates her from it a hated barrier because it prevents absolute oneness, dying out of her own consciousness, and going wholly over into that of the child whose pains she would thus, as it were, draw off into her own body! To die with and for one who is loved — as the poets are fond of showing — is according to the philosophy of human nature. Might not something like it be expected of God, who is absolute love? And how shall He love in this absolute way except by union with his suffering children? Such is the nature of pity; it is a vicarious thing, which bare love is not, because it creates identity with the sufferer.

The text is one of the peculiarly revealing passages of the Christ's life. Here we behold in Him the blending of the highest forms of both divine and human love: the incarnation of one, the perfection of the other, one in their expression, for love is the reflection of unity. We see Him moving through the villages telling the good news of the kingdom of God at hand, healing all sickness and suffering that came under his pitying eye, and moved with compassion for the multitudes He could not reach. The people throng about him, as they always will when a true teacher speaks. They open to Him their hungry hearts, their bewildered minds, their despairing hopes for this world and that to come. Or they stand before Him, dull and dead as the forms and doctrines under which they had been smothered, or they bring to Him their nearer sorrows of wearying, life-sapping disease. For this compassionating teacher takes in the whole range of suffering; He sees that man is one; that bodily sickness and spiritual ailment are not far apart; that both in physical disease and moral degradation the common need is *life*. And it is to restore life to humanity that He has come; not to save souls, not to save bodies, but to save soul and body; He has not come to build up "a faded paradise" in this world, nor to unlock the gates of a paradise beyond, but to establish an order here so strong and well founded that it shall endure forever.

But as He looks over these suffering multitudes and reflects how little He can do for them, how few He can reach, how slow are the processes by which they are delivered from their sufferings; as He reflects how soon they will lapse out of the inspirations He has stirred, and turn again to their blind teachers; as his thought goes out to the wide world of suffering of which this is only a faint sign, he is moved with compassion. How can He leave them when He can do so much for them; save them to bear their sicknesses alone, to wander about in this world that is so full of God's truth and love without any one to show it to them; to be harassed by fears of death and haunting thoughts of the future, and vague, fearful thoughts of God, and by the unrest of conscious evil and all the weariness of unexplained life! And so in a sort of despair — it is the only thing He can do — He turns to his disciples and says: "Pray ye the Lord of the harvest, that He send forth laborers into his harvest." It was not a vain request; the next we see is these disciples, themselves the answer of their own prayer, armed with saving and inspiring power, going out into this world of unredeemed suffering. They go on an errand of compassion; they are to declare the kingdom of heavenly love as at hand, to heal the sick, to cast out devils, to raise the dead, — all in that large-hearted measure which they had realized in themselves.

In speaking further, we will guide our thoughts by naming several points.

1. Christ's habitual look at men had regard to them as suffering. No other aspect of life seems to have struck Him with equal force or to have so claimed his thought, that He did not feel its sorrow. The foundation of his work is ethical, but the tone is drawn from his sensibilities rather than from his judicial sentiments; the ethical is but the instrument; to get rid of the sorrow is the end.

The painters, and especially that nearly greatest one, Da Vinci, have given us a man burdened with his own sorrows, but when the artist comes who apprehends the true Christ, he will figure a sympathizing Christ; the drawn lines of finest sensibility, a mouth tender and trembling with just uttered words of compassion, and eyes fathomless with unutterable pity. I do not suppose that Christ was unobservant of, or unresponsive to, the pleasures of men. He did not sit at feasts with sad words upon his lips, but still his thought struck through these gladder phases and saw the lack behind the pleasure, saw that the meat and the wine stood for no full satisfaction, that the laughter was not the echo of a real joy. Nor yet do I mean that Christ's thought did not strike deeper still and find back of all suffering the eternal joy that underlies existence; that He did not know and feel that the keynote of the universe is blessedness. He not only knew this, but He knew it as no other ever knew it. In the last days of his earthly life, when his eyes were lifted somewhat from their long gaze at the world and turned to the heavens, He spoke of little else. This eternal joy had become his own, its secret won by obedience and sacrifice, full and welling over in desire that it might be full in those about Him. But He did not habitually take this larger and deeper view; it was, in some sense, a reserved view. To have had it before Him in all its force would have bred a sort of ecstasy unfitting for his work. Instead He looked at men and life as they are in the present moment. It is a main point in studying the eternal Christ to separate Him from all time-conceptions. In nothing is his divinity more attested than in his sharing the divine conception of what we call time. Like God He inhabits eternity in all his thought and speech. We do not coördinate God with space and time, these are human and conditional; with God time is an eternal now. If Christ has any thought derived from God, it is this. He did not stand beside a man racked with pain and exult in his future health. He had a more present cheer for those who wept over their dead than the hope of a future resurrection. It is the significant feature of his thought and teaching that the forces and facts of eternity are drawn within the present; the kingdom of God is at hand here and now; the power of the resurrection is realized now in those who believe. It was the same with suffering; the divine perfection of his sympathy drew his thought away from its future and linked Him to its present.

2. The question arises: Is this a true or a false, a healthy or a morbid view of human life? When one reads Pascal, whose whole thought is based on the misery of men, one says, this is morbid, this cannot be the philosophy of life. But the airy sentimentality of the optimists satisfies us as poorly; we feel that Pascal has an acuter insight and the greater weight of facts. The question cannot be answered by determining whether there is more happiness or suffering. Of this it would seem there could be no doubt. It is a good world; God pronounces it such while He is making it. All good has not evaporated with moral evil; it was Pascal's intemperate theology that led him to the opposite conclusion. This great intellect did not draw his data from life nor from his own sufferings; he was a recluse and had small range of social facts, and his acuteness forbade him to reason from himself; he simply rea-

soned on the basis of a doctrine of original sin that emptied human nature of all its contents, — a miserable, not to say irredeemable, condition indeed! There is, no doubt, suffering vast and keen, but it is small and shallow to the happiness that enspheres life as the air enfolds the earth. In individual cases evil or mischance may turn the balance towards suffering, and sin dims the brightness of the inwrought joy of life for us all. But could we measure the satisfaction that comes from natural affection, from the exercise of bodily and mental functions, from our adaptations to the world and society, from the mysterious sweetness of life itself, we should find our miseries outweighed many-fold. The mere fact that we stay in the world is proof that we really make the unconscious estimate. If this were not so, not only would the race not endure existence, but it could not endure it. When it becomes as a whole miserable rather than happy, it will die by natural consequence as a man dies by disease. Suicide is not oftener an indication of insanity than that the scale has inclined to the wrong side in a personal estimate of happiness and misery. Pessimism has no need to urge its logical plea for a self-destruction of the race; it will destroy itself when it becomes conscious that the pessimist's creed is true.

But none the less is suffering real, and none the less will a sympathizing nature pause upon it rather than look through to the underlying joy, and especially a great pitying nature like Christ will pause upon it and see little else. It is not a matter of more or less, but of appealing anguish. The most imperative appeal made to love is that of suffering; joy takes care of itself. Jacob had eleven sons about him, but Joseph was not. The shepherd has ninety and nine safe-folded, but "one is away on the mountains cold." A group of happy children bless a fireside, but the parents watch them with a shaded joy, thinking of the wanderer, dead or living they know not, but lost to them and to goodness. Put yourself in a great city, walk its fine streets, visit its theaters and parks, watch the gay throngs; spend days thus, and then one hour where poverty and vice unite to create wretchedness, — for one hour only see the little children sick and starving, the sewing-women in garrets, the dying on their beds of rags; breathe the air, take in the squalor, the vice, the utter misery; get one glimpse of this life, and the gay multitudes are forgotten in the deeper impression made here. Or spend an evening in a pleasure-party, and then pass to the bedside of a sick child, hear its moans, watch its restless tossings and appealing look for impossible relief, — which of the two pictures stays longest in any feeling heart! It is not a matter of more or less suffering that gives the tone to one's thoughts, but sensitiveness to whatever suffering there may be. Hence Christ paused here in his look at mankind; nothing diverted his gaze from its suffering. In the weariness of the flesh, He sometimes withdrew from the aching vision into the secrecy of the mountains, and at moments He exulted as He saw the Satan of this misery falling like lightning from heaven, and the burden of sorrow rolling off from the heart of the world, but for the most his eye rested steadily upon the suffering before Him: a man of sorrows, but not his own sorrows; a man of griefs, but griefs that were his own only as He took them from others into his own heart!

It is not to be thought, however, that this Christly pity embraced only the conscious suffering of men. It is an undiscerning sympathy that reaches only to ills that are felt and confessed. We every day meet men with laughter on their lips, and unclouded brows, who are very nearly the greatest claimants of pity. Pity him who laughs but never thinks. Pity the men or women who fritter away the days in busy idleness, calling it society, when they might read a book. Pity those who, without evil intent, are making great mistakes, who live as though life had no purpose or end, who gratify a present desire unmindful of future pain. Pity parents who have not learned how to rear and train their children; pity the children so reared as they go forth into life with undermined health and weakened nerves, prematurely wearied of society, lawless in their dispositions, rude and inconsiderate in their manners, stamped with the impress of chance associations and unregulated pleasures. No! it is not pain that is to be pitied so much as mistake, not conscious suffering, but courses that breed future suffering. Who, then, calls for it more than those who have settled to so low and dull a view of life as not to feel the loss of its higher forms, content with squalor and ignorance and low achievement or mere sustenance? It is now quite common to say, at the suggestion of some very earnest philanthropists, that the poor and degraded do not suffer as they seem; that they get to be *en rapport* with their surroundings, and so unmindful of their apparent misery. This may be so, but even if the wind is thus tempered to these shorn lambs of adversity, it is no occasion for withholding pity. Nay, the pity should be all the deeper. The real misery here is, that these poor beings do not look upon their wretched condition with horror and disgust, that they are without that sense and standard of life which would lead them to cry, "This is intolerable; I must escape from it." Hence, the discerning Christ-like eye will look through all such low contentedness to the abject spirit behind it, and there expend its pity. Not those who suffer most, but oftener those who suffer least, are the most pitiable. The naked and starving, the widowed and orphaned, and even those about to die may have currents of life flowing quick through them, and life always contains the seeds of joy. Pity rather the man who is content with this world, and is governed by its small prudencies; pity him who is blind to God's inspiring presence; pity the man who is feeding himself with low pleasures and through beastly appetites. The deepest pity of all, "tear-dropping pity," will rest where it is impossible to awaken moral feeling or the sense of noble things. Then breaks out the divine cry: "If thou hadst known, even thou, at least in this thy day, the things which belong to thy peace!"

I speak at length on this point, because so fine a force as human pity ought to be wisely directed. It should be something more than an emotion springing out at the sight of suffering; it should be a matter of insight, of careful measurement, and just adaptation.

But, beyond the unrealized suffering, how much is there that is not so overlaid! It is not necessary to paint the picture that we see so often, so often indeed that we do not see it. Suffer? Who does not suffer! What body that is not at times racked with pain, what house long escapes sickness, what home that sooner or later is not overshadowed by death. Poverty, business troubles, domestic anxiety, mistake and its bitter fruit, regret for the past, darkened futures, the slow eclipse of bright hopes, the life that has missed its meaning, — let us not make little of these. They may not be the greater part of even any single life, but they are real. Get the verdict as you will; read it in the pages of the masters of human nature whose greatest works are tragedies, listen to it in the songs of the poets, or trace it in the faces of men, or find it in the sad pensiveness that grows with the years, and it will be the same. It is a suffering world, not wise enough to avoid disaster, not strong enough to wrestle with nature, not yet good enough to reap the rewards of virtue, not aspiring enough to attain the joy and peace of faith. It is a fallen world, fallen away from its ideals and inwrought methods, and hence it cannot be other than a suffering world. It is the mystery of humanity; beast and bird reach their appointed measure of bliss, but man fails of his. The fact itself bespeaks a remedy; the anomaly asserts a return of the law and reign of joy. Because infinite love pities, it will deliver!

3. It is not a long step from the Christ's pity to that it evokes in those who believe in Him.

There is something beyond a sense of justice and fair dealing, something beyond even good-will and love. The highest relation of man to man is that of compassion. Hardly separable from love in words, it may be in conception; it is love at its best, love quick, love in its highest gradation; it is the brooding, the yearning feeling, the love that protects while it enfolds. It is not laid upon us as a bare duty, but something to which we are born and trained, the evolution of the highest moral sentiment. Hence all suffer in common ways and in almost equal degree except when sin throws its leaden weight into the balance. Every throb of pain I feel is a divine call to pity your pain. When my child dies I am called to weep by the grave of yours. When poverty with its stings and constraints is your portion, God bids me enter into your condition with pitying heart and hand. Our sorrows are not our own, to be secretly wept over or soon dispelled. God forbid that any of us should pass through suffering and come out of it, not only unchastened, but with no tenderer feeling for the whole suffering humanity! It should be the first question with one who in any way suffers, as it is nearly always the first impulse: To what service of ministering pity am I called? For the ultimate purpose of God in humanity is to bring it together. No true thinker dissents when the process of history is defined as *reconciliation*. The main human instrument is that we are considering; it is the finest and most dominant force lodged in our common nature; it brings men up to the point from which they launch into the Universal Love.

The law and the method run very deep. One of the chief problems of the day is: how to reconcile the antagonisms of society. While there have been in previous ages a wider space between classes and far heavier oppression and wrong, never before have there been so intense a consciousness of oppression and wrong and so threatening restlessness under it. Communism and Nihilism and the universal organization of labor and capital into opposing forces, to-day at peace, to-morrow at war, are not happy prognostics. Nor do the thoughtful pass by the segregating tendency going on in all manufacturing regions, with its inevitable alienation, and only kept from revolt by steady prosperity; they know to what such alienation leads at last; the logic of history and of human nature points to one tragical conclusion. Argument will not close this chasm, force only widens it, prosperity but keeps it as it is for the hour. Other methods must be used to overcome these threatening evils. Social science is doing something, but knowledge does not lead the regenerating forces of society; it may marshal them and point the way, but the leader will be a diviner force, a subtler inspiration. The opposing classes must be brought closer to one another, first by the exercise of justice and then by the exercise of Christian sympathy. When the rich get near enough to the poor to feel the constraint and perplexity and bitterness of their poverty and so are moved to share its burdens, there will be peace in society; never before! Society itself will at last exact justice, but justice is but the portal of that fair temple in which a united humanity shall serve and love and worship.

Great care must be taken to keep this fine quality from sinking into a mere sentiment. There is indeed,

> "The sluggard Pity's vision-weaving tribe,
> Who sigh for wretchedness, yet shun the wretched,
> Nursing, in some delicious solitude,
> Their slothful loves and dainty sympathies."

It is not a gush of feeling, it is not made up of tears or sighs, nor is its exercise to be confined to actual pain, but is to be carried back into the region of *causes*, and here the wisest compassion will be busiest. A vast amount of pain and sorrow is due to injustice: the extortions of the strong and the rich, the unequal distribution of the burdens of society, the discrimination against woman in the laws and in payment for labor, the tyrannical oppression of poor women in cities, the greed of landlords, the horrors of tenement houses, the narrow margin between wages and living, the legal indorsement of dram-shops, the tragedies of the stock-market, the robberies of monopolies, the facility of divorce,— these are some of the fountains out of which flow steady streams of misery. Hence, a wise compassion will strive for just laws, and honest administration, and a better order of society. So of sickness: it mostly springs from lack of sanitary knowledge and regulations. It is beautiful, the pity that hovers by sick-beds and flies to pestilence-stricken cities, but it is a larger and wiser pity that strives to secure the conditions of health. So of intemperance, without doubt the greatest evil of the day; it is a true pity that lifts up the fallen, but that is finer and truer which goes back into the region of causes, — wise nurture, and restraint of the greed that lives on the evil. So a discerning pity will watch with jealous eye the great, deep wrongs of society, and when the conflicts that they beget come on, as come they must, it will know where to array itself; as Shakespeare, who never discourses more wisely than when he dilates on this theme in two of his dramas, says: —

"I show it most of all when I show justice;
For then I pity those I do not know."

There is indeed an orderly development of human society, not to be unduly hastened, but it is by struggle, and one of its factors is the human will and heart.

It was on the Judean counterparts of such sufferers that the pitying eye of the Christ steadily rested. The well-to-do, "the fat and greasy citizens," He passed by, giving his pity to the stricken deer of society; they that are whole have no need of a physician. Translate the phrase that describes the class He most sought, "publicans and sinners," and we have the vast *pariah* class, that outer fringe of society that has fallen away from its true order and is dragged along, a shame and a clog, hated and hating, redeemable by no forces it knows, and kept at the lowest level of misery and degradation by the contempt and neglect of the better classes; a mighty throng that renders needless any assertion of depravity or any argument for a redemption. Here was the special field of the Christly service. Life is complex and humanity is broad, and Christ covered it all, but because He was under the conditions of humanity He suffered Himself to divide his thought and pity where they were most needed. His example has all the weight of an express commandment:

> "— It most invectively pierceth through
> The body of the country, city, court,
> Yea, and of this our life."

The respectable, the rich, the ranks of orderly society, these have their claims upon us, but the payment of them belongs rather to the gospel of prudence and easy love. The true gospel of Christly pity points to these palsied and spirit-possessed children of sin and misfortune. A true recognition of it would well-nigh reverse the whole order of church procedure; it would put the grand church in the slums and the humble chapel in the avenue.

I have not been speaking of a sentiment but of a *law*, something that underlies not only Christianity but society, and underlying one because it underlies the other, for their spheres and methods must ultimately be the same.

It is the tenderness of eternal love that binds

God to his creatures. It is the tenderness of human love, wise, strong, and pitiful, that binds men together. And it is out of such sympathy only that peace is born for community or nation.

THE CHRIST AS A PREACHER.

"Goodness doth not move by being, but by being apparent."— HOOKER, *Book I.*, vii. 7.

"In Christianity nothing is of real concern except that which makes us wiser and better; everything which does make us wiser and better is the very thing which Christianity intends." — STANLEY, *Christian Institutions*, page 314.

"The New Jerusalem, metropolis of earth and heaven, is not a city built of stone nor of any material rubbish, since it has no need of sun or moon to enlighten it; but its foundations are laid in the eternal wants and passions of the human heart sympathetic with God's infinitude, and its walls are the laws of man's deathless intelligence subjecting all things to his allegiance. Neither is it a city into which shall ever enter anything that defileth, nor anything that is contrary to nature, nor yet anything that produceth a lie; for it is the city of God coming down to men out of stainless heavens, and therefore full of pure unmixed blessing to human life, and there shall be no more curse." — HENRY JAMES, *Society the Redeemed Form of Man*, page 473.

"We ought to receive with the utmost confidence those truths which pervade, like an atmosphere, the whole Bible."— REV. NEWMAN SMYTH, D. D., *Orthodox Theology*, page 139.

THE CHRIST AS A PREACHER.

"The Spirit of the Lord is upon me,
Because he anointed me to preach good tidings to the poor;
He hath sent me to proclaim release to the captives,
And recovering of sight to the blind,
To set at liberty them that are bruised,
To proclaim the acceptable year of the Lord."

ST. LUKE iv. 18, 19.

WHEN we have once measured these words, we shall be reminded of the tent of the Arab chief: when folded it could be carried in his hand, but when spread it was wide enough to shelter his whole tribe.

A study of the incident under which they were spoken in the synagogue of Nazareth is peculiarly rewarding, because it looks off in so many directions: into remote Jewish history, into present customs, to the nature of the gospel, to its manifold methods of working, to the heart of God, to the inspiration of Christ; and finally it discloses the weakness and evil of human nature when its prejudices and traditional thoughts are assaulted. It is so rich in material and association that a book could legitimately be made from it. It would be a book historical, ecclesiastical, political, theological, ethical, psychological, and the treatment would not be forced. Were a thoughtful student to sit down t the study of this passage, he would first be led to an investigation of the captivity of the Jewish nation in Babylon, and of the details of that captivity; the peculiar forms of suffering endured, and the effects in body and mind, and upon national beliefs and customs. He would then be led to study the literature of the book of Isaiah, and of the relation of the Hebrew prophet to the people, — almost a unique thing in history. He would then pass to a study of the political economy of the Jewish state, and especially to that peculiar feature of it by which every fifty years society was, to a certain extent, resolved into its elements and reconstructed; all alienated lands restored, all bondmen liberated, probably all debts canceled, — the most unique feature in human legislation, and one of the wisest and most gracious, affording, as it did, a barrier against the aggressions of capital, checking the growth of oppression, taking off the burdens from the poor and unfortunate, and giving them another chance by restoring them to freedom in their circumstances, an inwrought, constitutional defense of the people against their natural oppressors, a system instinct with liberty and grace and every divine quality. It was an arrangement full of wisdom, in that it was constantly restoring the nation to the great social principles on which it was founded, principles of righteousness and mercy and freedom, — an order linked in with its religion and with sacrifice for sins that were also burdens and bondage, — a vast, stupendous system, overwhelming in its significance, sweeping all about the life of every man, covering him with its grace, from the misery of outward misfortune and mistake to the guilt of secret crimes!

If it is asked where Jesus refers to this system, the answer is in the phrase, "the acceptable year of the Lord." We might read these words many times, and not suspect that Christ referred to this political feature of the Jewish commonwealth, unless we had learned that the year of jubilee was commonly known as "the acceptable year." The phrase is thus taken out of the hands of a narrow theology that uses it as a time-word, — a certain day beyond which there may not be another in which God is gracious, and instead is made to stand for the ushering in of an order and an age of the freedom and mercy and justice presaged by the year of jubilee, an age of spiritual and also political freedom, an eternal reign of righteousness and love.

Our student will then be led to study that pathetic story of the captivity, when the daughters of Jerusalem wept by the rivers of Babylon and hung their harps upon the willows, and the prophets sank into lamentations or rose into ecstatic visions of deliverance and return; thence to the special forms of that oppression, how it broke the hearts and bruised and weakened the bodies, especially inducing blindness, and thence into a study of the return and upbuilding. He will then pass to a study of the synagogue, find out when the people began to assemble in these edifices built, like our churches, throughout the country, in which the people met every Sabbath to hear the law read and discussed. He will, with awakened curiosity, be led to see in the synagogue the germ or framework of the Christian Church, and to suspect the reason why Christ said nothing about an external church, because here was one already existing in external form sufficient for all practical purposes,—a very simple, rational, and convenient institution, fit to shelter and house believers every one of whom has become a king and priest to God. He will see that the synagogue, and not the temple, furnished Christianity with its Church. And he will be apt to close his study with very slight regard for the vast hierarchical systems that envelop and weigh down the faith, and to conclude that the Church is a very simple thing; at most but a body of believers come together to repeat the words of their common faith, without any priest at all, but only a minister for simple convenience.

Our student will come to know much about the customs of the people, and of the procedure in the synagogue, notably that children were required to attend its service and hear the Law, and join in its simple worship. He will learn that certain parts of the sacred books were appointed to be read on certain days, and much also of ancient manuscripts, their shape, texture, how kept and read, and of Oriental ways of teaching. As he thus studies, he will be forced to the imperative conclusion that he is reading a history of the most trustworthy character, and not a tissue of myths and late remembrances; and if he has the gift of logic and insight, he will be drawn away from any thin, semi-learned theories that may have clouded his faith in the record.

He will then pass to a study of the matter of Christ's preaching. He finds that Christ read the appointed lesson for the day, which happened to be the day of Atonement, but not the whole of it; that He pauses in the middle of a sentence because the rest was not to his purpose, and he is flooded with revealing light shed by the omission, for the Christ has not come to proclaim " the day of the vengeance of our God." That conception was not to enter into the order He had come to declare. It was an undue presence of that conception that made Judaism imperfect, and John the Baptist less than the least in the kingdom of heaven. It was the absence of that conception of God that furnished the positive elements of the revelation of God which Christ was making.

Our student, as he scrutinizes this preaching, finds in it a twofold meaning, though but one spirit. This Gospel is primarily a deliverance shadowed by the year of jubilee ; it embraces the physical and social ills of men and their spiritual ills. The inextricableness with which they are united in the words of Christ suggests to him the profound mystery of body and spirit, mind and matter, environment and spiritual history. He will find in it a denial of all Manichean and Stoic notions that the soul is independent of the body, and is to be treated in another fashion, but rather will he find the broader philosophy, that man is to be regarded as a unit, body and soul making up one life, and that what truly blesses one blesses the other. He will discover a certain temper in these words that furnishes a keynote to the Christian system, and a prophecy of its work. He finds in them a theology and a life, a doctrine and a practice, and that the two are inseparable.

Our student, as he goes on in the history, gets as deep an insight into the human heart as into the divine. He reads again the oft-recurring story, a great spirit rejected by friends and neighbors; it is only the carpenter's Son, the boy who grew up in the midst of us, and now, forsooth! claiming to be a prophet! And they drive him out of their city. He finds in this no strange history, but only an illustration of a daily fact. Men never see the great in what is about them. We ride without eyes under Greylock, and go to the White Mountains for sublimity. The moon in Venice, and the sky in Naples, have more charm than here at home. The weeds of other climates become our flowers, and our flowers seem to us but weeds. There is little heroism, little devotion and nobility on our square mile; there are no epics or lyrics of human deed and feeling sung in our streets; the great, the beautiful, the excellent, is at a distance. Why we think thus it may be hard to tell, unless it is from instinctive reverence on the one hand, and on the other, because the realization of greatness makes us aware of our own littleness, and so provokes us to envy and anger.

Quite a broad field our student has traversed in

studying this short paragraph of St. Luke's Gospel, — from the political constitution of Judea down to the subtilties of our common nature!

We pass now to this preaching of Christ, and will speak of its substance, its philosophy, and its power.

1. Its substance. Without doubt we have here the keynote to his entire teaching. This was his gospel from first to last, whatever He may have said of an apparently different tenor on special occasions. It is a derogation and an absurdity to suppose, as is sometimes asserted, that Christ, finding this kind of preaching did not answer, changed his tone to a "woe." It may be reasonably supposed that Christ did not feel his way along, but that He understood himself and his work from the first, and struck at once to the heart of his business. This appears still more plainly as we realize that, here at the outset, He brings out the whole divine meaning of the Jewish economy. It is understood that great numbers of persons are still reading that purblind mass of crudities known as the "Mistakes of Moses." Does the author of that book know what the Jewish system means when you get down to the soul of it? Does he tell you that its keynote is mercy, and that its method and aim is simply that of deliverance and freedom from the actual ills of life? Does he tell you that it is a system shot through and through with great redeeming and liberating forces? Does he tell you that it takes a nation of slaves, ignorant, barbaric, besotted in mind and degenerate in body, and by a

shrewdly adapted system of laws lifts it steadily and persistently, and bears it on to ever bettering conditions and always towards freedom? Does he tell you that from first to last, from centre to circumference, it was a system of deliverance from bondage, from disease, from ignorance, from anarchy, from superstition, from degrading customs, from despotism, from barbarism, from Oriental vices and philosophies, from injustice and oppression, from individual and national sin and fault? Does he tell you that thus the nation was organized in the interest of freedom, planned to secure it by a gradually unfolding system of laws, educational in their spirit, and capable of wide expansion in right directions? Nothing of this he sees, but only some incongruities in numbers and a cosmogony apparently not scientific.

It is the peculiarity of Christ's preaching that He pierces at once to the centre of this great delivering system, and plants his ministry upon it. He takes its heart, its inmost meaning and intent, and makes them universal. He draws them to the front, leaving behind the outworn framework of laws and ordinances, and lays them directly before the eyes of the people. "This is the meaning of your law, this is the secret of your nation, namely, deliverance, freedom."

We cannot conceive a better Gospel nor a profounder social order than this. It accords with the largest view of humanity, whether it be scientific, historical, or religious. Science and history and religion tell a like story of deliverance, emergence from the lower into the higher, struggle towards the better, deliverance from evils, and so a passing on into righteousness and peace. Christ supplements and crowns this order of nature and providence by his Gospel. "I am come to save you in full, body and spirit, to make you free indeed by a spiritual freedom; I am come to declare that this deliverance, which is the secret of your national history, is to become universal, the law of all nations and the privilege of all men." Here is a gospel indeed!

The peculiar feature of this quotation from Isaiah, which Christ makes his own, is its doubleness. "The poor,"—but men are poor in condition and in spirit. "The captives,"—but men may be in bondage under masters or circumstances, and also under their own sin. "The blind,"—but men may be blind of eye and also in spiritual vision. "The bruised,"—but men are bruised in the struggles of this rough world, and also by the havoc of their own evil passions. Which did Christ mean? Both, but chiefly the moral, for He always struck through the external forms of evil to the moral root, from which it springs, and of whose condition it is the general exponent. And He always passed on to the spiritual end to which external betterment points. He was no reformer, playing about the outward forms of evil,—hunger, poverty, disease, oppression,—giving ease and relief for the moment. He does indeed deal with these, but He puts under his work a moral foundation, and crowns it with a spiritual consummation. Dealing with these, He was all the while inserting the spiritual principle which He calls *faith*. Unless He can do this, He is nearly indifferent whether He works or not. If you cannot heal a man's spirit, it is a small thing to heal his body. If you cannot make a man rich in his heart and thought, it is a slight matter to relieve his poverty. At the same time, Christ will not separate the two, for they are the two sides of one evil thing. Poverty and disease and misery mostly spring out of moral evil. They are not the limitations of the finite nature, but are the fangs of the serpent of sin. To refer evil, physical or moral, to development, betrays clumsy observation. The *imperfection* of *development* is a phrase the parts of which do not go together. In a true and orderly development, every part and point are perfect. A half-grown animal is never blind because it is half-grown, or paralyzed because it is young, or sick because it is immature. In the natural order, evils come in when the development has been reached, and its energies have ceased to act in full force. But those who contend that physical and moral evils are the necessary attendants of what they call imperfect development, reverse the very process from which they argue, placing them at the outset where they are never found in any other order. Plainly, we cannot reason from one to the other; plainly, there is a disturbing element in human development, for which no analogy can be found in the physical and animal processes. Human ills are not the sole products of ignorance, nor the chance features of human progress, but the fruit of selfishness,— not an order but a perversion. And so Christ sets himself as the deliverer from each, the origin and the result, the sin at the root, and the misery which is its fruitage. Therefore let no man think that there is any gospel of deliverance or helpfulness for him, except as it is grounded in a cure of whatever evil there may be in him,— evil habits, or selfish aims, or a worldly spirit.

2. The philosophy of this preaching, for I know not how else to name a certain feature of it.

Suppose some questioner had arisen in that synagogue of Nazareth and asked Jesus, not as to the substance of his preaching, for that was plain enough, but what was the ground of it. "You declare a gospel of deliverance; on what ultimate fact or reason do you rest your declaration?" A reasonable question, had there been any to ask it; there are many asking it to-day. I think the answer would have been of this sort: "I am making in this gospel a revelation of God, showing you his very heart, putting Him before you as He is, without any paraphernalia of symbol or ritual, translating Him into life. This is what God feels for you, this is how He loves and pities you, this is what God proposes to do for you; to cheer you with good news, and open your blind eyes, and free your bruised souls and bodies from the captivity of evil." And it is God who is to do this, not any human one, no trend of society or course of nature, no self-struggles or self-wrought wisdom, but God uncovered, revealed, brought abreast human life, and face to face with every man; this puts reason into the good words.

When shall we learn it, we of to-day? Troubles enough we all have; cheerless hearts all around us; blind eyes that see no glory in heaven and no path on earth; captives of lust and appetite and avarice and hard-heartedness and sordidness, conscious of the bitter captivity. They are all about us; they are here; perchance we are such; perchance I am! Do we know how to be healed? Do we know how to get free from these blinding, enslaving, tormenting sins? There is but one way, and that is by somehow getting sight of God, such sight of Him that we shall believe in, that is, trust and obey Him? Those words in the Nazareth synagogue were but the idlest breath except as they brought the delivering God before men. But when God is seen and known, the whole nature of man leaps into joyful and harmonious activity. Of all words used by those about to die, the commonest are these: "He is such a God as I want;" profoundest words of faith and philosophy! The only words in death, the best in life! It is God that we want! It is such a God and so revealed that we need! Under this revelation of Him our troubles shrink, our broken hearts are healed, our darkened minds are illuminated, our sins pass away in tears of shame and repentance, and our whole being springs up to meet Him who made us and made us for Himself; the secret of existence is revealed, the end of destiny is achieved!

3. The remaining point is the *power* of this

THE CHRIST AS A PREACHER.

preaching. In one sense its power lay in its substance, and in another sense, in the philosophy or ground of it, but there was more than came from these; there was the power that resided in Him who spoke these truths.

There is almost no power in words however comfortable in sound, or explicit in meaning; there is almost as little in bare truth. These are not the lacks of the world. Words! have not men spoken good words from the beginning? Truth! There has been no dearth of truth from the first. It is written in the heart of man. It cries perpetually in the street. It is graven on the heavens and the earth; philosophy has always taught it; literature is crammed with it. There has never been a civilization nor an age that was not overarched by a knowledge of the fundamental truths of character and duty, never an age without some nearly adequate conception of God. But how powerless! How slowly has the world responded to what it knows! How feebly does any man answer to his perceptions of right and truth! The reason is that truth has little power until it is transmuted into conviction in the mind of some person who utters it as conviction. In no other way has truth any force than by this alchemy of personal belief. There must first be a sight of it, and then a belief in it. There is, however, a wide difference or rather gap, between the two. The philosophers and religionists of old saw truth, but they saw it in detached forms and not as a system; they also failed to connect it with a personal, divine source, and hence had no ground of inspiration and no sufficient motive to duty. In other phrase, they were without the doctrine of the Holy Spirit. Compare, for example, Abraham and Zeno; the latter had an immeasurably wider culture and range of thought, but he could not elaborate a vital system. Abraham, on the contrary, with his one idea of a spiritual, personal God, and his one principle of obedient trust, inaugurated an order that instantly became vital and endures still as eternal truth. He did not look as widely, perhaps not as directly at life, as the Stoic, but he looked in truer directions. One truth, unless it happens to be an all-embracing truth, and no number of truths however clearly seen, have any inspiring or redeeming power until they are grounded in an eternal Person. Mozley, in one of his sermons, asks: "Have we not, in our moral nature, a great deal to do with fragments?" Yes, and it is the weakness of human nature when it undertakes to teach moral truth that it has only fragments to deal with. It is because Christ did not see truth in a fragmentary way, and because there was in Himself nothing fragmentary, that He teaches with power. There is no capability in man of resisting perfect truth; when it is seen, it conquers. The main thing therefore is to *see*, but men love darkness, and even when they begin to see, it is in a half-blind way.

We read that they wondered at his gracious words, and that later, at Capernaum, they were astonished at his teaching, for his word was with authority or power. Why astonished at his teaching? It was nothing new; it was mainly a quotation, but He spake it with power, or in a way that commanded assent. But in what lay the commanding power? Not in any impressiveness of manner, or felicity of presentation. It was something more even than sincerity and earnestness of conviction. None of these elements reach up to power. The impressive and felicitous manner is often weak. One may be very sincere and earnest and yet produce no great effect. Elements of power, they do not constitute power. The world is full of sincere and earnest men, advocating measures, pleading for causes, preaching sermons, who make little impression and gain no ends. The main reason is that they lack scope, their vision is small, they do not see their subject in its large relations and bearings. They have no measure or comprehension of it, but take some feature or incident of it and mistake it for the whole. The listeners feel consciously or unconsciously the lack or the error, and refuse to believe, or to be moved. There can be no estimate of the mischief often wrought by very good and earnest men, who by some fine qualities of zeal and honest purpose and fluency, get the attention of the multitude and preach a gospel shot through with narrowness and ignorance, tagging to its fundamental and unmistakable features some de-spiritualizing and cramping notion of a second personal coming of the Lord, or the like, and so dragging the whole system down to the level of a dead Judaism, opening breaches through which the whole faith of the people who first hear them gladly, at last flows out;

truth swept along with error because they have been taught to regard them as identical. There are many dangerous teachers in the world, but none equals the good man whose ignorance outweighs his goodness, the goodness floating the ignorance while it does its fatal work.

The main element of power in one who speaks is, an entire, or the largest possible comprehension of the subject. One may earnestly declare a truth, but if he does not *see* it, he will not impress it. But whenever one sees a truth in all its proportions and relations and bearings, sees it with clear, intense, absolute vision, he will have power over men however he speaks. Here we have the key to the power with which Christ preached. We read that the Spirit of the Lord was upon Him, He was filled with the Spirit, inspired, breathed upon through and through by the divine breath. But it was not the Spirit that spoke through the Christ, nor was the power that of the Spirit. The power was in the Christ whose being was set in motion by the Spirit. He was not an instrument played upon, a divine harp responding to heavenly winds, but an actor, a mind that saw, a heart that felt, a will that decided, all moving together. He was passive only in the freedom with which He gave Himself up to be possessed by the Spirit. It was a force behind and in his faculties, illuminating and arousing them to their fullest action. It is not the light that sees, but the eye illuminated by light. Inspiration is a mystery and it is not a mystery. It is not a mystery, in the respect that we know it to be a fact;

it is a mystery in the respect that we cannot understand it. We hear the sound thereof but cannot tell whence it cometh or whither it goeth. It is the witness put into humanity that it is kindred with God. We know not what it is, but when we feel its breath we know that it is the breath of God. But the Spirit is not the power of Christ; it is rather that which sets in action Christ's own power which lay in his absolute comprehension of what He said, and in a perfect comprehension of his position. He saw the meaning of the Jewish system. He knew what the acceptable year of the Lord meant. He pierced the old symbolism to the centre and drew out its significance. He saw that God was a deliverer from first to last, and measured the significance of the fact. He knew that God was the Father, and the full force and mighty sweep of that name. The whole heart and mind of God were open to Him. And because He knew God, He knew how God felt and what He would do, and have Him do. And so He takes his place as the One who is to declare and manifest to the world the absolute character and nature of God. This was the power of Christ's preaching; He saw God; He understood God; He comprehended God; He knew what God had done, and would do; the whole purpose and plan of deliverance and redemption lay before Him as an open page.

We cannot measure this knowledge of the Christ; we can but faintly conceive of it. But the measure of our conception of it, is the measure of our spiritual power over others. We speak, we teach, we live with power just in the degree in which we have got sight of God in the revealing Christ and through Him of the purpose and plan that underlie these mysteries that we call life and time.

LAND TENURE.

"The people forming the nation exists in its physical unity and circumstance, in a necessary relation to the land."

"The possession of the land by the people is the condition of its historical life."

"The right to the land is in the people, and the land is given to the people in the fulfillment of a moral order on the earth." — MULFORD, *The Nation*, Chap. V.

"The land is the essential condition of the normal and moral development of the state, and therefore it is absolutely holy and inalienable. It is here that the real moral spirit of the love of the father-land rests; originally it is a love of one's native land, and always retains this natural element, but in its completeness it is wholly interpenetrated with this consciousness of a moral relation." — ROTHE, quoted in *The Nation*, page 71.

"The generous feeling pure and warm,
Which owns the right of *all* divine,
The pitying heart, the helping arm,
The prompt self-sacrifice are thine.
Beneath thy broad, impartial eye,
How fade the lines of caste and birth!
How equal in their misery lie
The groaning multitudes of earth." — WHITTIER.

LAND TENURE.

"And ye shall hallow the fiftieth year, and proclaim liberty throughout all the land unto all the inhabitants thereof; it shall be a jubilee unto you; and ye shall return every man unto his possession, and ye shall return every man unto his family." — LEVITICUS xxv. 10-13.

ALL men ultimately get their living out of the soil. There seems to be a recognition of this in that inexhaustible storehouse of fundamental truths, — the first chapters of Genesis. Man is placed in a garden to till it and to eat its fruits. He has no other way of living, and will never have any other. There never will be a process by which the original elements that enter into food will be manufactured into food. We may fly in the air, or travel around the earth with the sun, but we shall never take the unorganized substances that form grass and grain and the flesh of animals, and directly convert them into food; they must first be organized into vital forms. There seems to be in this process a hint of the eternal truth that life proceeds only from life.

Hence, questions pertaining to land are the most imperative that come before men, because the first and most constant question with every man is, How shall I live, how get my daily bread? All other questions pertaining to life or condition come after this one. He may be free or enslaved, he may live in a city or on the sea, he may be educated or left ignorant, but first of all he must have food, and food, first or last, comes out of the ground. Every human being must have some real relation to a certain extent of soil. The relation may be an indirect one; he may never see his estate, he may live in a city and not know the grain that yields his loaf, but somewhere there is a certain stretch of land that stands for that man's life. Fifteen square feet, it is said, will furnish a Hawaiian enough to support existence; the Indian requires miles of hunting ground; the Belgian farmer lives well on two or three acres; here in New England we require many. But the main point is the imperativeness of the relation. Commerce, manufactures, schools, churches, government even, all these represent no such necessity as an open relation to the soil. You may burn all the ships, factories, churches, school-houses, annihilate government, and man still lives, but cut him off from the soil, and in a week he is dead.

I say this to explain the force of land questions, their interest to thinking minds, their place in history, and in political and divine economy, which, however, are one thing. To get man rightly related to the soil, in such a way that he shall most easily get his food from it, this is the underlying question of all history, its keynote and largest achievement. The chief struggles in all ages and nations have turned upon this relation. For a hundred years Roman history was colored by struggles over the agrarian laws, the patricians claiming the lands of Italy for their own, the people and the great conquerors claiming them for themselves and the disbanded armies; these struggles were the basis of Cæsar's fortunes. It was the apportionment of the lands of England by William the Conqueror to his followers, that laid the foundation of those conflicts between the nobility or land-owners and the people, that have never ceased, and that are to-day at white heat; questions in which there is technical justice on one side and eternal righteousness on the other. Why should not the Duke of Buccleugh own land over which he can ride thirty miles in a straight line, with a title good for nigh a thousand years? Why, again, should one man hold land from which thousands of people, on or near it, who are well-nigh starving, could get their bread? I do not attempt to answer these questions, because they are complicated and do not admit of brief answer, but the recent land-act of Mr. Gladstone shows how a great, philosophical statesman regards them, "marshaling the way they are going." The Code of Napoleon, which took the great estates of France, and even all landed possessions, and made them subject to division on inheritance, showed the same broad sense of human justice, with perhaps some lack of forecast.

There are two forces at work in the matter, both proceeding out of what seems almost an instinct for ownership of the soil. The earth is our mother, and she woos us perpetually to herself. To own some spot of land, and be able to say, "this is mine," is one of the sweetest of personal feelings; it declares our kinship with this natural world that nurses our life and upholds our feet. There is a sort of pathos always felt when one speaks of owning a burial lot, — a slight, tender satisfaction, as if it were fit that one should himself own the spot of earth where his earth-fed body is to be resolved into the elements. And thus it was that Abraham, though he was to have no country here, but only a heavenly one, still was suffered to call his own the cave where he buried his dead; so dear and natural a satisfaction was not to be withheld.

These two forces that draw men to the soil are, first, a natural, almost instinctive sense of keeping close to the source of life, as a wise general does not allow himself to be separated from his supplies. This is broad, every-day, common-sense. When a people are shut off from the soil, or denied ownership of it; when it is held by a few and farmed out even at low rents; when land is held in such a way that it no longer answers its end of feeding the people, but is kept for parks and forests and hunting grounds, there will be restiveness, complaint, and resistance, coupled with a defective life of the nation and of the family. Back of all claims of inheritance, above all laws, and deeper down than technical justice, is the ineradicable conviction that the soil is for the people simply because they live out of the soil; and it is a simple corollary that the living should be as easily got, and as generous as possible. The main reason why we have an annual immigration of over a quarter of a million from

Europe is that land can be owned here, while there it can only be rented. And this emigration is the reason why Europe is saved from agrarian revolutions, and the few are left in possession of the land. The injustice of ages lingers because there is an outlet for human indignation.

The other force is the pride and greed and love of power of the strong. Here is a triple-woven force out of which has sprung by far the greater part of the injustice and oppression that have afflicted the race. There is no pride so natural and persistent as pride in extensive ownership of land. It is figured in the temptation of the Christ, to whom was shown all the kingdoms of the earth. To climb a hill or tower, and say, "I own all I see," — this is merely the topmost reach of self-satisfaction. It is simply the broadest possible reflection to the man of his own importance. To own the earth, — that which feeds man and upholds him, that which endures while the generations flit across its surface, that whereon is wrought the perpetual mystery of growth, the arena of the unfailing goodness, the promise-covered and promise-keeping earth, — this is the most philosophic and well-nigh noblest form of human pride. It is innocent when it does not invade the just rights of others; when it does not forget that the earth is the common property of humanity, on the simple ground that it is necessary to its life.[1] But, in-

---

[1] I hardly need say that I do not here intimate any theory of Communism, or of arbitrary distribution of the soil, nor even in what the right consists by which any man holds a particular portion of land. I

stead, nearly the whole world is subject to the encroachments of this pride. And greed joins hands with pride. There is no form of wealth so permanent, because the earth endures forever; so unfluctuating, because based on the sure order of nature; so steady in its revenues, because drawn from the imperative demands of daily need. Hence the rich invest in lands. There is hardly a heavy capitalist in the country who is not a large landowner at the West; and these lands, lying unused in the track of advancing populations, become the cause of the high cost of farms bought by the poor. A Boston or New York capitalist early secures some thousands of acres; the poor emigrants push beyond, settle the country, and thereby advance the value of the tract many fold, — a shrewd and technically just operation, but essentially mean and eternally unjust.

And to pride and greed is added the love of power. The possession of the soil is the surest exponent and standing-ground of worldly force. Everything else may fail: the hearts of men, coined treasures, ships and houses, bonds and promises to pay, but so long as society keeps a man in the possession of land he is so far forth strong; he has a place to stand in, the fortifications built by nature, and the arms and defenses that spring perpetually out of the earth; he realizes the fable of Antæus.

am only speaking of a more general and primitive principle, namely, a close and direct relation of the people to the soil, — a stumbling-block in all history, — a relation yet to be realized in the larger part of the world.

It is through these impelling forces, the governing ones in human nature, that the land has commonly been held by a few rich and strong, while the great mass of mankind have lived upon it at second-hand, shut out from large portions, enslaved, serfs, payers of rents with no chance of purchase, suffered simply to draw from it their necessary bread, the profits of their toil passing to owners whose ancestors stole the land; — such, and worse, is the history of man's relation to the soil. In all ages, and in the immense majority of cases, the relation has been characterized by deep and cruel injustice. It is the chief field of that dark word and fact — oppression. The main oppression in the world has been a denial of man's natural rights in the soil.

There has been almost nothing of it in this country, except at the South, where the cycle of wrong and its retribution has been completed. Whenever it has taken form, — as in the State of New York, in the middle of the century, — it has met with summary repulse. In California, the evil of vast estates, not to be bought or cultivated, was becoming real, when recently the State enacted a new constitution, chiefly to secure a different system of taxation, under which these vast estates are crumbling into small farms, at purchasable prices. Happy nation, where every man who will, may sit under his own vine and fig tree! Not so is it with any other, and never before was it so in all the world, unless we except that little nation called Judea, the only nation that, at the outset, anticipated the inevitable evils of land-monopoly, and provided against them. All other nations have swept blindly into these evils, to emerge only after long ages of struggle and bloodshed.

The remarkable feature of the Jewish Commonwealth is its anticipatory legislation against probable, and otherwise certain abuses. The struggles of other nations, and the skill of statesmanship, have been to correct abuses; in the Jewish Commonwealth they were foreseen and provided against.

There are no words to express the wonder felt by the student of social science as he first measures the significance of that feature of the Jewish state known as the year of jubilee. It is little understood, hidden away in an uninteresting book, stated in ancient and blind phraseology, a thing of long past ages, nevertheless it remains the most exalted piece of statesmanship the world has known, — an example of social sagacity, and broad, far-reaching wisdom, such as we look for in vain in the annals of any other nation.

It is a singular fact that the enslaved of the colored race are the only class that seem ever to have measured the significance of the year of jubilee. It had a meaning and a hope for them that they drew out of these old Levitical scriptures, and wove into their songs and prayers and preaching and every-day speech; and at last their day of jubilee came! It was also understood by one of the other race: John Brown, — a Jewish prophet in the whole temper of his mind, a man who traversed a line of thought and action far above the level of technical justice and constitutional law, — found in this ancient law of Moses the inspiration that made him the defender of Kansas against the slave power and a willing martyr at Harper's Ferry. He had a favorite hymn, Charles Wesley's "Blow ye the trumpet, blow!" The poet saw in the year of jubilee a spiritual deliverance from sin, its ultimate and highest significance indeed, but this political iconoclast saw it in its direct and simple meaning as a deliverance from slavery, — the first and only man in the modern world who ever drew upon it for practical purposes.

A few words will give us the salient features of the institution, when we shall see the application of all that has been said.

The Jewish Theocracy had for one of its main features a system of Sabbaths curiously and profoundly arranged for the interpenetration of divine and political principles. The Sabbath was not as it is with us, a spiritual thing, but was both political and moral, yet so finely were the two features welded that they are inseparable. The Sabbath was thus made an assertion that life is of one piece, and that God is over and in all life. Every half-century, presumably the natural period of human life, formed a grand Sabbatical circle; first the seventh-day Sabbath, then the seventh Sabbatical month in each year, then the Sabbatical seventh year. When seven of these have been observed, there is ushered in a year of remarkable provisions, known as the year of jubilee. The weekly Sabbath was for the physical and spiritual rest of the individual; the seventh Sabbatical month is also for the individual, but it has a wider social significance, takes in the nation and winds up with the chief religious act of the nation, — the fast and sacrifice of atonement. The seventh Sabbatical year has an agricultural and political significance. The ignorance of later periods and the delayed wisdom of modern science are anticipated; the soil is to lie fallow one year in seven for recuperation. To-day the agricultural journal is urging upon farmers this bit of ancient wisdom. On this seventh year all debts were remitted, a custom retained even to the exact time by the laws of many States, notes outlawing at the end of seven years, and accounts at even a shorter period. The purpose was both prudential and merciful. It led to snugness in business, it avoided entanglements that outweigh memory and so render testimony difficult, it put a limit about the power of the presumably strong over the presumably weak and unfortunate, yet had no quality of injustice, as all transactions were based on a full understanding of it. It simply prevented a compounding of interest, a process fatal at last to both parties. But all this is moral as well as economic. It was a perpetual lesson in thrift, in carefulness, in forbearance and mercy; it was a continual rebuke to the hardness of avarice; it assured the poor and the unfortunate that by a *divine* law, his burden would be taken off. It constantly fed hope by giving every man a fresh start, not daily or yearly, which would be demoralizing, nor at the end of some remote and undefined period, which would be disheartening, but once in seven years, a period long enough to enforce the lesson of mistake but not long enough to crush the spirit.

A cycle of seven years also measured the limit of the bondage of any Hebrew slave, though not synchronizing with the seventh-year Sabbath. Humanly speaking, slavery could not be kept out of the Hebrew Commonwealth; it was too early in the history of the world. But it was hedged about by strenuous laws all merciful in character, and of such a nature in their operation that slave holding became unprofitable, and the system died out. Moses was wiser than this nineteenth-century nation of ours! He sapped the life-blood of the institution by wise statesmanship; we drowned it in a sea of blood and fire, — blood from a million hearts, fire that touched the hearts of forty millions.

But the fiftieth year, or year of jubilee, has a wider scope. It covers this prime question of land-tenure. It settled at the outset the problem that no other people ever solved except through ages of struggle and revolution.

The Hebrew nation existed under the consciousness of a covenant with Jehovah. It would be a petty criticism that pried into the origin of this belief, moved by contempt at the seeming presumption of this little nation of fugitive slaves, — petty and narrow indeed! It were wiser and more scientific to regard every nation as under covenant with God, if it but had the wisdom to know it. That this nation discerned the eternal fact, and wrought it into the foundations of their State, only shows its insight into the nature of the State, and its receptivity of inspired truth. Moses was no partialist, no conceited dreamer that Israel was a favorite of heaven.[1] This was but the poetic gloss put on the national career by the poet-prophets of a later age. He doubtless knew that every nation exists under covenant with God, exists in God and for God, and that this relation constitutes a covenant. In the same way, every man has a covenant with God; and this necessary relation, made up of promises and laws on one side and obligations on the other side, is the peculiar glory and hope of every life. But this covenant, whether with a nation or an individual, takes on special forms according to circumstances. It is in the covenant of God with this nation of ours to give us the continent, and to keep it forever, if it continues free and just. It is in the covenant of God with every man to grant him a certain, special success and reward if he keeps God's commandments. So when these Hebrews were on the way to Palestine there was elaborated for them, or inspired within them, a belief that God had given them this land. They drew on the traditions of their race and called it a promised land. They held the hope of possessing it from God, and so it was a covenant possession. This is not superstition nor conceit, but truth so large that we can hardly take it in. It were better to train ourselves

---

[1] I am not unmindful of the criticism as to the authorship and date of the Pentateuch now in progress; but will merely say that the point now under consideration bears internal and unanswerable proof of dating from the Conquest of Canaan; it could not, from its very nature, have originated at a later period.

towards a comprehension of it than look down upon it as a narrowness. But this promised land was for the nation, for all and each one; not for the heads of the tribes, not for the successful warriors, not for the strong, or rich, or high-born, if such there were. When the promised land was reached and secured there was allotted to every family a tract of land, a sort of universal homestead act. Recognizing the fact that man's ultimate dependence is upon the soil, the purpose is to keep the whole body of the people as near it as possible, and to prevent dispossession from it. They are not forbidden to sell it; such a requirement would have taken all freedom and elasticity out of practical affairs, it would have made men the creatures of formal rules instead of leaving them to the educating influence of commercial transactions. Inalienable estates make a man at the same time weak and too strong: weak because he has no call to preserve his own, and too strong because he has resources without corresponding character; he will be over-confident, willful and presumptuous.

But on the other hand, these Jewish estates could not be permanently alienated. Once in fifty years all land, that had been sold, reverted to the family to which it had been allotted: "every man returned to his possessions."

It does not lessen the wisdom of this legislation that it probably did not meet the exigencies of the later development of the nation, nor even that its details may have become a hindrance in the more complex state of society that followed the Captivity, when it probably ceased to be enforced. Its wisdom is to be found in its previsionary features, in its reversal of ordinary history, that is, it planted the nation on equal rights at the outset instead of leaving them to be achieved by struggle, and in its assertion of the general principle that it is wise to keep the body of the people as near the source of their subsistence as possible. It was not given up until it had educated and grounded the nation in those conceptions of practical righteousness that are found in the pages of the prophets, through whom they have become the inspiration of the world.

Its design and effect are evident. It was a bar to monopoly of the land. All greed and pride in this direction were limited. One might add field to field for a series of years, but after a time the process ceased and the lands went back to their original owners. The purpose was to make such a habit unprofitable, to keep the resources of society evenly distributed, to prevent the rich from becoming too rich and the poor hopelessly poor, to undo misfortune, to give those who had erred through sloth or improvidence an opportunity to improve the lessons of poverty, to prevent children from reaping the faults of their parents; one generation might squander its portion but the next was not forced to inherit the consequences. Thus once in fifty years society was rehabilitated. It was a perpetual lesson in hope and encouragement. It took off accumulated burdens. It put limits about the cruelty of man to man. It was a constant assertion of equality. It fostered patriotism, a virtue that thrives best on the soil. It kept alive in every man a sense of ownership of his country. It was, primarily perhaps, an inwrought education of the family, fostering a sense of its dignity, and guarding the sanctity of marriage and legitimacy of birth. All these influences and ends drew their efficacy, not from their formal perfection, but from the fact that they sprang out of a divine requirement, and were the expressions of a moral order that rested on God.

Such are some of the main features of this unique law. There are minor features that it is not necessary to speak of, details appropriate to its proper execution. For example, the fields lying fallow was necessarily incidental to a transfer of them. It also directed the attention of the restored owners to other forms of labor, such as the repair of houses and the like, that were needful. Thus we see how the seemingly trivial or superstitious features pass away under examination, and resolve into practical wisdom.

Though a political measure, it is informed with spiritual significance. It is throughout instinct with mercy. It taught humanity. It rebuked and repressed the great sins. It was in keeping with the underlying fact of the national history which was deliverance, and, as well, with the central idea of the world, which is redemption, — redemption from evil however caused and of whatever kind. It was an assertion of perpetual hope, — hope which, though long delayed, comes at last to all, and every man returns to the possessions his Creator gave him. It was in its profoundest meaning, a prophecy wrought into the practical economy of a nation. It shadows forth the recovery from evil, the undoing of all burdens that weigh down humanity, the eternal inheritance awaiting God's children when his cycle is complete. And so the Christ, when, on the day of atonement, he stood up in the synagogue of Nazareth to read, opened the book where it was written: —

> "The Spirit of the Lord is upon me,
> Because He anointed me to preach good tidings to the poor;
> He hath sent me to proclaim release to the captives,
> And recovering of sight to the blind,
> To set at liberty them that are bruised,
> To proclaim the acceptable year of the Lord."

And the eyes of all were fastened on Him as He said: "To-day hath this Scripture been fulfilled in your ears." The acceptable year of the Lord was this year of jubilee. Christ stood upon this great, sabbatical idea of the Jewish system, not upon the sacrificial and ceremonial idea, but upon this far loftier one of rest and deliverance, — rest in God, and deliverance by God from all the evil of the world.[1] He made universal what had been particular, general what had been restricted. He ushered in an age of jubilee, a restoration not to be undone, a deliverance never to lapse into captivity.

[1] The true relation of Christ to the Sabbath is to be found here, rather than in his chance allusions to it in his conflicts with the Pharisees, in which necessarily there was something of antagonism to it as a Pharisaic custom. Christ discerned the fact that the entire Jewish life, individual and national, was Sabbatical, — there was no time that was not a Sabbath; *i. e.*, the nation was grounded on and immersed in rest and deliverance. The question remaining for us to-day is, Shall we have a sign of these eternal facts and processes? Shall we have a Sabbath or not? I have never seen any elaboration of this view, namely, that Christ planted Himself upon the sabbatical, and not on the ceremonial idea.

This ancient piece of statesmanship is full of pointed lessons for these modern times. It cannot be reproduced in form, but it still teaches the ever necessary lesson, that nations and corporations and individuals are always forgetting that the world belongs to all men by the gift of God. It teaches the wisdom of showing mercy to the poor and unfortunate, and the unwisdom of permitting endless monopolies and limitless increase of wealth. It is the business of the State to see that these things are restricted, as both right and safe, as necessary for the rich as for the poor. The methods employed may sometimes seem to lack in technical justice, but there is a righteousness that lies back of formal justice. As the world goes, the forms of justice are apt to become the instruments of oppression in the hands of the avaricious, the proud, and the strong. These three always lie in wait to oppress the poor, the humble, and the weak; and their choicest instruments are those legal forms and institutions that are necessary to society. But they have their limits by a law which is above all such laws and formal institutions. When wealth oppresses the poor, or keeps them at the mere living point, when monopolies tax the people, whenever a few own the soil, however legal the form of possession, when there is any process going on by which the rich are growing richer and the poor poorer, there is a divine justice above all formal justice, that steps in and declares that such processes must stop.

Shakespeare saw this, as he saw so many things

that underlie social righteousness; Shylock was legally entitled to his pound of flesh, but there was a law of mercy that overruled technical justice, and Portia resorts to technical quibbles to save the unfortunate Antonio, only because the avaricious Jew would not heed this law of mercy. The dramatist thus sets forth the fact, that if the law of mercy is not fulfilled, *other means will be used to the same end.* Moses put these means into the constitution of the State. The Jewish theocracy was imbedded in mercy; its forms down to the minutest detail were instinct with the finest spirit of justice and equality, and tenderest regard for the poor and unfortunate. It reversed human history, beginning at the goal to which other nations are tending. Still, it is not exempt from the process of development, but the development pertains to the form; the spirit underlying the developing form is in keeping with the absolute perfection of God, and is the attestation of his presence in the forms.

There is a wisdom in laws that hedge about the courses of the avaricious and the strong, even at the expense of technical justice. For when the oppressions of the rich and the powerful and the fortunate reach a certain point, the oppressed multitudes turn like hunted beasts at bay, and destroy both their oppressors and the social fabric.

These dangers are never far off from any people. They have their seeds in human nature. We have once tasted their bitterest fruit, we may taste it again.

Three dangers confront us that we do not yet

much heed, but which are sure to take shape when the outlet now found in new land is closed, and the forces of society are shut up to themselves: the growth of monopolies, the antagonistic organization of capital and labor, and legislation in the interest of wealth. They can be met and averted only by a recognition of the fact that the nation is a moral order, and endures only through a realization of practical righteousness.

MORAL ENVIRONMENT.

"Though it is true that we cannot make ourselves feel at the time by an act of the will, acts of the will do eventually, not create feeling, indeed, for feeling is a divine gift, but elicit it and bring it into play by removing the obstructions to it. The formation of habits by acts of the will against inclination is indeed the working of the law by which the mind is prepared for a higher state, in which feeling, and inclination itself moves it to good." — MOZLEY, *University Sermons*, page 152.

"The problems to be solved in the study of human life and character are these: Given the character of a man and the conditions of life around him, what will be his career? Or, given his character and career, of what kind were his surroundings? The relation of these three factors to each other is severely logical. From them is deduced all genuine history. Character is the chief element; for it is both a result and a cause, — a result of influences and a cause of results."—PRESIDENT GARFIELD, *Memorial Address on Gen. Thomas.*

"He fixed thee mid this dance
Of plastic circumstance,
This Present, thou, forsooth, wouldst fain arrest;
Machinery just meant
To give thy soul its bent,
Try thee and turn thee forth, sufficiently impressed."

ROBERT BROWNING, *Rabbi Ben Ezra.*

MORAL ENVIRONMENT.

"Wherefore, my beloved brethren, be ye steadfast, unmovable, always abounding in the work of the Lord, forasmuch as ye know that your labor is not in vain in the Lord." — 1 CORINTHIANS xv. 58.

Is it for this that St. Paul has led us through his mighty argument, to confirm us in the homely duty of steadfastness? Is it for this only, mere everyday fidelity, that he has taken us along this grandest highway of thought, compassing the whole history of humanity, spanning the gulf of death, and tracing human destiny till it is lost in the ecstasy of final victory and eternal life? One would think that having lifted us to such heights, he would leave us there to bask in the eternal sunshine and drink the joy of the victory over death. It seems an anti-climax in thought and style, that after the mighty themes brought before us, — the sway of death from Adam to Christ, the resurrection from the dead set forth by analogies drawn from heaven and earth, the mystery of the spiritual nature and the deeper mystery of the image it shall bear, — it seems out of keeping that we should be called upon to fold the wings upon which we have followed him in his inspired flight, and drop back into the mere ploddings of every-day duties. Whether it seems an anti-climax or not, depends upon one's conception of what is high and low. A mere rhetorician would not have dared to add anything after the sublime assertion of the victory over death and the grave. A sentimentalist would have said: " there can be nothing higher or better than such a frame; here let us abide." But St. Paul, being no mere rhetorician and nothing whatever of a sentimentalist, saw that there was something higher than victory over death, something more essential than comfort in the revelation of destiny; and so he leads us on to what he conceives to be highest and best. It is an interesting disclosure of the underlying traits of his mind that is made by the purpose lying back of, and running through, this chapter. His aim is not to enlarge our knowledge of the future, not to reveal our destiny, not to comfort mourners, not to take away the fear of death; all these ends are gained, but they are not the primary ends before him. He sets this matter of resurrection from the dead right in the minds of the Corinthians because false views of it were injuring and perverting the *service* they were to render. So long as they believed that resurrection meant some spiritual transformation already past, they were incapable of true service; their hope was behind them, their inspiration was a spent force, there was no sufficient motive for thorough fidelity; for in morals the motive is always ahead. They had dropped a definite and inspiring hope and taken up in its stead some fantastic notion that resurrection from the dead meant simply an awakening of their spiritual nature, type of mistake made now as well as then, and followed by loss as great. Such are they who deny all validity of fact to gospel narrative, and shrink all the objective revelations of God into the interplay of their own emotions. Take definiteness and outward reality away from the Faith, and there will be no more strong, definite service, but instead endless and useless introspection upon the mysteries of our nature, the rehearsal of which comes to be regarded as the fulfillment of all righteousness, — a very tiresome thing, and so dropped, or exchanged for the startling assertions of atheism; for between a God revealed and atheism there is no resting-place. St. Paul is careful that they of his day shall fall into no such mistake; hence these words that sound like the trump of doom, awakening echoes in the under-world, and calling in the courses of the stars to aid him in his saving work. His single aim is to keep men from lapsing out of a true and rational service to God. Service! service that is steadfast, that flows out of unmovable convictions, that always abounds in work, that is kept to its standard by the most inspiring of hopes, that is confident of success, knowing it is not in vain in the Lord because he is the Lord of an actual resurrection. Such is the height to which he leads us, beyond which there was, in his mind, nothing higher, as there can be nothing higher in the mind of any one who rightly measures human life. For service unites in a practical form the two highest qualities or forces of our nature, — love and fidelity; one covering our emotional, the other our moral faculties; one fixing us in the eternal order of human sympathy and oneness, the other turning it to practical ends and holding it steady to its work.

Thus service becomes the height and sum of human duty. Servants exalted into friends; servants understanding the glory of their calling and also the secret of blessedness; servants in the one work of doing good in an "evil world;" such is the name and the vocation of all who are born into the world. Its finest characteristic is steadfastness, the holding on quality, persisting, not by mere force of will, but by sympathy with, and faith in, the end to be reached.

This steadfastness requires first of all, that one should be steadfast in his own moral condition; and of this point we will now speak.

As it is the finest feature of service, so it is the one we are most apt to fail of. Alternations of feeling that find their way into conduct, lapsing away from purposes, the fading out of clear perceptions of truth, the slothful neglect of plain duty; here is the fault of us all. But there are reasons for it that it is well to understand.

1. The high standard of requirement makes it hard of attainment. This is one of the features of Christian service that tends to throw it out of general acceptance; in one way or another men are always trying to escape claims that are otherwise so attractive. Ask anything of me, but do not ask me to be perfect; take much from me but do not require all; leave me some little space where I may be my own master and hold something as my own: so men have ever said, not discerning that a perfect

standard is both a necessity and a blessing. Thus only can God declare his perfect will; thus only is highest effort evoked; thus only do we learn the perfectibility of character, one of the unique features of the Faith; thus only is the divine element within us summoned to its fellowship with the Spirit. But while the high standard awakens enthusiasm, it also begets discouragement; we are like men climbing some tall peak, who draw strength from its very height, and start afresh as they see the glory of the light that plays about the distant summit, but are also wearied by the same conditions. The greatness that inspires also weakens; the perfection that stimulates our finer qualities presses heavily on our weaker ones. We hold our lives under this two-fold condition of perfect requirement and human weakness, and the result is an experience sharing in the qualities of each. But it is better that there should be fluctuation under high requirement than uniformity under low requirement. For the kingdom of Heaven aims only at the best; it does not concern itself with what is inferior; it is gauged throughout upon the scale of the perfect and the infinite.

The struggle of the ages, the inmost purpose of human development, is to bring men up to the point of enduring the highest motives. It is one of the unique features of the Christ,—a sinless man demanding sinlessness, ending the preparatory stage of inferior requirement, and of winking at the hardness of the human heart, and launching upon the world the utterly new conception and demand of perfection. Yet He makes it in no bare way, but with a corresponding disclosure of motives and with gracious provision in case of failure. In a moment, and for the first time, the world of eternity is thrown wide open, the absolute nature of God is revealed, the assertion of perfectibility and the demand for it laid upon men, destiny lifted out of time into the timeless ranges of eternity; and along with these overwhelming revelations, enough indeed, it would seem, to crush the human spirit, a redeeming revelation of grace and pity and patience and inspiring aid. Such is the miracle in the world of thought and history that Christ presents! Such is the absolutely new conception and method that He inserts into society for its adoption, a method that combines infinite stringency of requirement, with provisions that render them effective in every weakest child of humanity.

2. Steadfastness finds another hindrance in the stronger power of the world, stronger because nearer and always present. We have only to put out our hands and we feel it; our eyes always behold it; its voices fill our ears; it is built into the structure of our bodies; our flesh is wrought out of its dust; our nerves vibrate in unison with its electric pulsations; our blood is red and vital with the nourishment drawn from its bosom. It is but a short road between our bodily desires and their fulfillment; it is not a long road between worldly desire of any sort and its gratification. It is all before us, near at hand, unmistakable, very real and substantial. It is not strange, that when the

claims of this world conflict with those of the eternal world, the former should often win us. For the eternal world, though near, is not visible, nor has it a voice always to be heard amidst the clamor of this world. Its tones are low, its movements are fine and delicate like the touch of spirits, its rewards and satisfactions are parts of a wide-circling system, the full force and results of which we do not yet experience. Now, it is almost a law of our nature that the nearest motive governs us. That it is not wholly a law is the foundation of religion. That we can reject the nearer motive, and yield to the remoter or higher one, is the basis of spiritual life. The use of this possibility of our nature constitutes character in its higher ranges.

With such hindrances as these, it becomes a vital question how to fortify ourselves in a steadfast habit of spiritual life. For fluctuation is weakness and misery; the heart as well as the judgment protests against this serving two masters. There is no peace nor strength nor success save in steadiness and unity of purpose. How to gain it is the question.

It is evident that the first and main thing to do is to set the whole current and habit of life against these temptations. We must cherish the enthusiasm of the high standard; we must resist the nearer motive, and hold the two worlds of sense and spirit in their right relation; we must recognize the fact of human weakness, and treat it accordingly, bringing up fresh reserves of will to fill the place of drooping purposes, inducing higher moods that shall lift us out of the lower. All this is very evident, but is it not possible to come into some condition, some moral fortress, that shall be in itself fortified against this tormenting fluctuation? Mere acts of the will, the proddings of conscience, the enthusiasms of the spirit do not avail; the fault is in the will itself, in the conscience, and the flesh-encased spirit. Something is needed to steady the will, to supply the place of an intermitting conscience, to take up the irregularities of the emotions; something to keep the moral machinery in action, when will and conscience and emotion flag or cease to act.

We are driven to that old-fashioned thing called *habit*, which I shall now speak of under the modern phrase of *environment*.

It is a point greatly overlooked just at present, that faith needs an environment. Because faith is spiritual in its essence, we are too ready to conclude that it is spiritual in its substance; that because it is inward and invisible, it has no need of an external and visible form. So it is left unhoused, — a spirit without body, a tartarian ghost in this very concrete world.

It is a practical as well as curious question as to the relation of character to the external world. Is character the result of inward forces, — using the world simply as a field of action, a mere standing ground, — or does it actually draw upon external forces? Does all come from within, or is there an interplay of forces upon the moral nature from both worlds? Does environment contribute to character? It is a strange feature of an age that deems itself thoughtful, that it takes opposite sides of this question according to the department of life to which it is applied. If it is the spiritual department, the whole drift of the age is towards inwardness, with denial of, or indifference to, any force or value in environment. Faith and spiritual condition are deemed so wholly interior in their sources and arena of action, that they are hardly allowed a place even in conversation; much less do they require an environing form and habit. But if the question refers to education, to health, to social habits, to culture, there is a disposition to make much of environment. Strange inconsistency of an age that imagines itself logical! It has taught us the great word and truth of environment; we ask it to be consistent in its application of it.

This word *environment* has become a sort of keyword in modern thought. It would not have so fastened itself on common speech were there not a fresh and intense sense of some truth for which it stands. It is an old word, as old as the language, but the fact or force that it represents is far larger, or rather is far more plainly recognized, than heretofore. The ancient and also the eternal truth is that man grows from within out. It is from within, — thoughts, principles, beliefs, desires, affections, purposes, — that a man's life takes shape. This is eternal, unchangeable truth; the Christ declared it, the poets and philosophers repeat it, it underlies the great theories of education, it is the first principle of the Christian faith. But all truth is double. Man grows also from without. If the seed of growth is sown within him, the moisture and light and air that determine the growth are from without.

It has been recognized of late that the environment of men has affected them far more than has been supposed. The immense variety in all animal life is, how far we know not, but to an immense degree, the result of varying external conditions, or change of environment. The favorite scientific thought of the day holds to a certain unity of life at the outset, and that the variety is due to external causes. This probably is not a universal truth, but it is a truth of immense sweep. Physically, man is molded by climate, by food, by occupation. Mentally he is molded by institutions, by government, by inherited beliefs and tendencies. It is a truth of wide range and significance, and just now rather overshadows the other and greater truth, that man grows from within, and has his shape in a spiritual germ wrapped up in himself.

There is, however, a general inconsistency in its application. In the natural sciences, especially those pertaining to plants and animals, the environment is studied quite as much as the nature of the plant or animal. So the peculiarities of races and nations and communities are explained by their surroundings; there is less talk of blood and more of condition. The social science of the day plays about the external condition of the degraded masses, and wisely so, for the without must be reformed as well as the within. In short, in every department of thought except one, there is a deep sense of the value and power of environment.

The department from which it is excluded is religion; everywhere else proper external conditions are insisted on; the organization of society must aid and reflect its culture; a city must have public buildings and institutions that correspond to its growth; the value of art in shaping mind and character is thoroughly felt, the influence of good houses, pure air, sweet water, shapely architecture, fine proportion and color is everywhere recognized, and justly. But when we come to religion, we find that the favorite thought of the day has halted.

There is no graver accusation to be brought against the age than this inconsistency, and especially on the part of those who make the most of environment, emphasizing it everywhere until they come to this part of life, where they stop and say: "Religion is a spiritual matter; it is all within; it is something not to be spoken of; a spirit of reverence is all that is needed — the form may go; be humble, but you need not pray; fear God, but you need not trouble yourself about church or worship; keep children pure, but don't burden their minds with the forms of religion." We recognize in this a very general and popular habit of thought, especially in two classes, — the scientific class, and the vast bulk of the people who have caught its way of thinking. There are two classes yet exempt, — the humble, believing class, and the few who are too intelligent to be deceived by the transient fallacy.

I think those of us who still hold on to the value of the external forms of religion may well ask of those who do not, to be consistent. They have taught us the immense truth in that word environment; we ask them, by their own logic, to carry their idea into religion, instead of coming to a dead halt on its threshold. We ask them not to turn their backs on their philosophy by making the spiritual culture of a man an exception to his physical and mental culture. We ask the man who is particular that his children should live under the disciplining influence of fine art, and good society, and beautiful scenery, and healthful surroundings, to act on the same wise principle in training his children in eternal morality. As things are going, the latter is left out; the forms of religion are passing away from the family; there is no daily grace over meat, no household prayer and hymn, no systematic teaching of religious truth and duty; the church is void of children; young men, for the most part, do not attend church; the act of worship no longer is esteemed of value for the young; the great mass hold it to be of small importance for any. And so the entire matter of environment in religion is dropping away from society more and more. It is a fact of immense significance that young people no longer frequent the churches, — which means that a generation is coming on that is not trained in worship and religion. What will come of it cannot be accurately foreseen; but it will be a state properly named as atheistic.

The difficult point to contend with in this state of things is a certain conceit and assumption of superiority. It used to be said that the religious man assumed to be better and wiser than the outsider, but to-day it can be said that the assumption is on the other side. There is a suppressed sneer for those who still go to church, and worship God in any outward way. It is a common and not suppressed boast, especially on the part of young men, that they are "not much of a churchman," for such is the phrase for stating that they have thrown away the whole thing,— outgrown it, they claim. They rather pity you that you also have not outgrown it, and look down upon you from their agnostic heights as very deluded and quite behind the age. There is nothing so difficult to contend with as conceit, unless it be fashion, and, alas! this practical atheism is supported by these two buttresses. The man who still holds on to the forms and strict observances of religion meets a subtle current of mild, pitying contempt. The young man who goes to church puts himself outside the vast majority, whose jeers are not lacking.

The reason of this inconsistency is that, as yet, there is but little recognition of any environment except a physical one; there is failure to see that our twofold nature implies a twofold environment; that as a material world enfolds the body and plays into it with educating forces, so there is a world of moral and spiritual fact that is the theatre and condition of moral and spiritual culture. I am aware that the reality of this world is questioned. But let us consult the poets, who are the best philosophers. It is in the very essence of poetry that it recognizes this double environment;

without it, it would have no vocation, no field, no possibility of existence even. Pegasus loses his wings and becomes a plow-horse. All thought is reduced to a bare realization of material facts, — man a thinker, but with nothing to think of except matter! All poetry, all high art, is a protest against this degrading conclusion. By its own inspired instinct it assumes a moral and spiritual order that enfolds man and plays into him. Shakespeare, almost without fail, puts every great moral action into a framework of corresponding physical likeness. The tempest in Lear's heart is linked to the tempest of the elements by more than a fancy. The moonlight sleeping on the bank, and the distant music, have a logical relation to the lovers' hearts. When "fair is foul, and foul is fair," these moral confusions " hover through the *fog* and *filthy* air," and are uttered on " a *blasted* heath." When the noble king draws nigh to the castle in confiding love and gratitude, —

> " The air
> Nimbly and gently recommends itself
> Unto our gentle senses."

As the hour of Banquo's murder draws on, —

> " Good things of day begin to droop and drowse."

Macbeth appeals to night to aid him in his crime. Thus, throughout, this master of thought throws back into the physical world the reflections of the moral acts done within it, but on what ground, except that in and behind the physical there is a moral order on which they repose. He could not find in nature a reflection of moral acts, if nature itself were not an expression of moral realities. The physical itself is environed and contained by the spiritual. Indeed, the whole relation of man to nature runs up into morals for its explanation, nor can it be found elsewhere. Thus, the uniformity of natural law, when brought into contact with the free will of man, means a fixed moral habit. Thus, his recurring natural wants tend to fix him in wise and orderly ways that are more and higher than physical customs. And so the uniformity of nature's forces and operations have not only a moral significance, but become sources and educators of moral habits. Man is thus being trained as a moral being into a certain affinity with the courses of nature; the stars rise and set in him; the steadiness of gravitation is reduced to a moral equivalent in his obedient heart. This steadfast environment of natural law is simply a plan and method, so far as it goes, for getting man into a corresponding moral state, — uniform but free, and so tending to produce a fixed yet free character, — brought up, at last, to the nature of God whose perfect freedom finds expression in the uniformity of his laws.

It will not answer to shut out character from these external orders, and confine it to an interplay of emotions and convictions in our secret bosoms; it must have another world than its own to secure and draw out its development. And such a world is provided. The nation when viewed as a moral order and citizenship is made sacred, the family when regarded as divine and eternal, society when it is felt to be a relation of righteousness, the church when it is recognized as the necessary and natural condition of spiritual life, — these are the outer walls of the environment upon which high character depends, and by which it is shaped in its general features. But as within a walled city there are other walls environing household life, and within these still other walls enclosing the individual, and as the body itself is a sort of wall about the spirit, — all needed to secure a full, sound life, — so character must have successive rings or layers of environment about it in order that it may have fullness and strength.

I believe it to be one of the chief mistakes of the age, the fruit of an excessive individualism, that the value of such environment in shaping and fixing character is overlooked. There are more vital points on the other side, life is from within, but truth is double; it can reach no height but on the balancing pinions of the within and the without; clip either wing and it circles round and round and at last comes to the earth. The outward drill of religious observance and spiritual habit is as needful as the devout feeling, even though, like the river of life, it flows out of the throne of God. One logically implies the other, but it does not necessarily secure it. One may run the risk of formalism, but the other runs the risk of extinction. It is a matter of regret that to stand within or without the church is getting to be regarded with indifference. And if within, the recurring duties of the relation are regarded as hardly obligatory or even important. Now, this framework of Christian service is indispensable to Christian character, and the necessary condition of its permanence and steadiness. The outward habit tends to create an inward habit; the external method favors the internal disposition and becomes its measure, as in a plant the soil and light are the conditions and the measure of the growth of the vital principle within it.

Here lies the secret of public worship; we do not worship because we feel like it, but that we may feel. The feeling may have died out under the pressure of the world, but coming together from mere habit, and starting on the level of mere custom, we soon feel the stirring of the wings of devotion, and begin to rise heavenward on the pinions of song and prayer. This is well understood in England, and underlies the much criticized "Cathedral system." To one who goes for the first time from our simple American churches into an English cathedral, York or Westminster, and encounters its elaborate ritual, repeated twice every day, often to almost no congregation, a service composed largely of singing, the prayers intoned, the Scriptures read in a strange penetrating monotone, — it seems the vainest form, a relic of popery, a thing kept up to please the ear and eye, and to reap the fruits of the rich endowments. There is, indeed, much to criticize, much that might well be changed, much that might well be added; but the longer one thinks of this system and usage, the more one suspects there may be in it solid sense and far-reaching wisdom; he sees in it a nearly indestructible embodiment and assertion of worship.

The building itself is of stone, its history shades off into dimly recorded ages. In its crypt lie the ashes of the great for a thousand years; on its walls are the names and effigies of statesmen and soldiers and philosophers and saints; its pavements are worn with the tread of generations. It is vast, beautiful, solemn, enduring; it spreads wide and generous over the earth, resisting the encroachments of this world's eager hands, and rising high into the pure spaces of heaven. St. Paul's is not a beautiful structure, but it overlooks the Bank of England and the Exchange. And thus all over England, in towns nowhere two hours apart, are found these great churches, with their corps of clergy and choirs, with daily service heralded by softly chiming bells, uttered by divinest music, and invested with the solemn usage of long ages. There is no interruption of this service, no vacation, no holiday, no break from pestilence or war or political change. Here is a mighty fact tremendously asserted; it forces a sort of inevitable reverence, not the highest and purest indeed, but something worth having. It becomes the conservator of the faith, and in the only way in which it can be conserved, through the reverent sentiment and poetry of our nature. Hence, it has reduced the entire service to song and chant. The prayers and creeds are not said but sung. Translated thus into sentiment, etherealized into poetry, the hard and outworn part of them vanishes away, and their real spirit lays hold of the spirit, and is sent up into the spiritual heavens on the wings of song; for a creed is not made to be read as prose, but to be sung as poetry; and it is all the truer and more truly confessed because so rendered. The fresh critic says of much of this service, why not change it? Why not suit it to the times? And indeed one may justly press such questions, but the answer also has force: "We want an unchanging assertion of our faith in the worship of God: it ought not to change with the fickle tide of human thought; its real meaning is keyed to unchanging human need; it has met these needs in ages past, and it will meet them for years to come; if you require changes, make them for yourself as you go along — the church is broad and tolerant."

The practical question arises, Has this great system real power; does it keep alive reverence and speak back to the lives of the people? It would be idle to claim that it is the only or main channel of religious life in England. The dissenting churches reach more of the people and enforce a more direct and cogent influence; but neither will or ought to yield to the other; the wise men on either side do not antagonize one another; each has its field and method. The main value of the established church is its lofty and unshaken assertion of the worth of worship — keeping alive reverence, which is the mother of morality, and furnishing a public environment of the common faith.

This system of form and worship is kept up because the highest culture and intelligence in England believe in it. There is there as here a tide of shallow and conceited thought setting against external observance; it will not deny God but will build Him no altar; it will be reverent but it will not worship by voice or knee. The service, as it is observed in the cathedrals and in the parish churches all over England, and in the Presbyterian churches of Scotland, which are presided over by men equally intelligent and robust in intellect, is the protest of the best minds in Great Britain against the divorce of religion from the forms of religion. We have not, in our country, the aids and bulwarks against this disintegrating influence that are there so effective. The immemorial usage and the thorough organization of worship afford, at least, a covert while the fitful winds of unbelief sweep over the people. Here we have no antiquity that commands veneration, and our organization of worship is slight and shifting. But all the more we need, as individuals and churches, to hold right principles on this subject and cling to good customs. We cannot afford, in this day, to let anything in the way of religious observance pass away without the severest challenge. We can do nothing better for ourselves, for our families, for the faith, than secure for each a full, ministering environment of religious custom. A man should have for himself certain religious habits and usage, — something of an external nature that shall speak back to him in confirmation of his belief; it helps to make it definite, to keep it constant; it bridges over the weak and languid spots in one's experience; it is a body holding together the soul and playing into it from the external world. It is the belief of all churches that the sacraments are an outward sign of inward grace. It is a relation sanctioned by the highest thought of all ages; without religious observance there can be no full, strong, rewarding spiritual life, and hence no real life.

More imperatively is it needed in the household. A family without prayer, without a domestic ritual of worship, is an anomaly; it is as though the body were without an eye or a limb; it will be weak where strength is most needed; it will lack a certain fine flavor and sweetness, and will grow hard and dreary, and at last desolate because the avenues of light and lasting joy and peace have been kept closed. And for like reasons, the claims of the Church should be heeded. It is the altar before which every man should worship, because he is linked to an external world, and also to a world of fellow-men.

If you would have a faith, put under it a solid earth, and overarch it with an infinite heaven; stand firm on one, and look steadfastly into the other.

IMMORTALITY AND SCIENCE.

> "And hear at times a sentinel
> Who moves about from place to place,
> And whispers to the worlds of space,
> In the deep night that all is well.
>
> "And all is well, though faith and form
> Be sundered in the night of fear;
> Well roars the storm to those that hear
> A deeper voice across the storm."
>
> *In Memoriam*, cxxvi.

"The foundations of a faith in a future life lie outside of Revelation, and ought, therefore, to be disclosed independently of it. . . . It is immortality which gives promise of Revelation, not Revelation which lays in our own constitution and in the government of God the foundations of immortality." — PRES. BASCOM, *Philosophy of Religion*, page 185.

"There is in man the suspect that in the transient course of things there is yet an intimation of that which is not transient. The grass that fades has yet in the folded and falling leaves of its flower that perishes the intimation of a beauty that does not fade. The treasures that are frayed by the moth and worn by the rust are not as those in which love and faith and hope abide. There is a will that in its purpose does not yield to mortal wrong. There is a joy that is not of emulation. There is a freedom that is other than the mere struggle for existence in physical relations, and is not determined in its source or end by these finite conditions." — MULFORD, *Republic of God*, page 243.

IMMORTALITY AND SCIENCE.

"Seeing that these things are thus all to be dissolved, what manner of persons ought ye to be in all holy living and godliness, looking for and earnestly desiring the coming of the day of God, by reason of which the heavens being on fire shall be dissolved, and the elements shall melt with fervent heat? But, according to his promise, we look for new heavens and a new earth, wherein dwelleth righteousness." — 2 PETER iii. 11-13.

It is a singular fact that these words have far more probability of truth than they had a generation ago. Then, the stability of the physical universe was held to be a settled fact of science; it is not so regarded now. The science of to-day is inclined to the opinion that the physical universe will undergo great catastrophes and probably be extinguished. But while science thus adds its weight to Scripture, it throws difficulties in the way of belief in future existence by destroying the only known theatre of life. If this world and the universe of worlds are to undergo at times such catastrophes as science and Scripture indicate, even to possible destruction, where shall immortal man abide? Where is he when the heavens are on fire and the elements melt with heat? The Scriptures do not heed the question, but modern thought stumbles over it into unbelief.

The question most eagerly urged to-day is that of

human immortality. It is doubted and assailed on all sides, consciously and unconsciously. It is discussed and denied under definite form; it mingles with the current thought of the hour; it haunts the most thoughtful minds; it disturbs the faith of the most devout. It is doubted not only by science but by theology. There is springing up a school of religious thinkers, learned and devout, that denies the inherent immortality of man, regarding it as an achievement, or result of faith and virtue. The religious form of this opinion is immortality conditioned upon holiness; its scientific form is the survival of the fittest. They are the two sides of one theory and tend to support each other, though the advocates of each work their vein of inquiry independently of the other. It is not impossible that the scientific theory, the survival of the fittest, so far as it relates to the past of existence and up even to the very verge of the working of the Christian system, will prevail, and win common acceptance; but it is a question if Christianity is not the exact reversal of this principle, and the introduction of another phase of God's eternal laws. Christianity teaches not that the strongest only survive but also the weak. Indeed Christianity is not itself except it teaches this. Its inmost principle, its entire significance, is the salvation of the weak. Its contrast with nature is that it saves and does not destroy. It abdicates its place and function when it admits that any part of humanity perishes at death.

But the common, every-day skepticism of immortality springs from a somewhat general though not very thorough knowledge of the scientific theories as to life and origin now at the front. It is the influence, rather than the knowledge, of these theories that lies behind the doubts.

Physical science chiefly touches human destiny at two points of what is technically known as the principle of Continuity; namely, the resolution of thought and feeling into molecular changes; and the development of man from preceding lower orders of life. The principle is thought to militate against immortality, as it implies that all the potency of life is within matter, and that all mental and moral activities are but the operation of organized matter. Under this hypothesis thought and feeling are resolved into the whirl of molecules and the formation and destruction of tissue, a wholly material process, necessary in its character and admitting of no permanent personality. To find anything outside of this all-comprehending law of which immortality can be predicated, anything that survives when the bond breaks that holds the whirling atoms together, is an impossibility under this conception. On the contrary, its analogies seem to point to an opposite result. Personality under this theory is but a momentary lifting up of certain particles and forces from the ocean of being into which it soon falls back, like a wreath of spray snatched by the wind from the crest of a wave, drawing its energy from it, never ceasing to play into it, and finally mingling with it. The main thing is not personality but the all; the chief object is not to erect lasting personalities but to keep the great ocean of activity in full working order; the real value of existence lies not in yielding an order of enduring persons, but in the undiminished energy of itself, throwing up, for a moment, such phenomena as trees and beasts and men, as if for its own secret delight. So long as science held only this view of the world it was not wholly devoid of nobility of sentiment. It could speak of immortality if not of enduring personality; the forces entering into and passing out of human life do not cease but live and act forever; men perish, but man survives; the generations pass away, but the race endures. Here, indeed, is a certain kind of immortality, capable even of sustaining a lofty, if not real theory of altruistic morality.

But of late, these fine sentiments have been losing their force. There are indications that leading physicists are getting somewhat concerned at their own conclusions, and are surmising if there may not be some world or order outside the reach of their tests; or if in that *something* that lies back of whirling atoms, — that something which it is forced to recognize though it cannot lay hold of it, — there may not be a universe spreading out in regions as vast as those revealed by the microscope and telescope; if this universe of suns and planets, of earth and air, of revolving atoms and continuous force, is not, after all, a hemisphere against which lies another universe as real as this, a universe of causes and beginnings, and therefore perhaps of ultimate destinies. For science is now asserting that the material universe is limited in its duration. It is simply a vortex-ring, like a puff of smoke, having its origin in friction, and at last to be brought to an end by friction. It is matter diffused by heat, losing its heat and uniting again as cold cinder. The sun once was all, and all once more will become the sun, and the reunited sun will lose its heat in space, and when heat is gone, all motion will cease, and eternal silence and death will reign throughout space. Not a cheerful gospel certainly, this that science last reveals to us. It is not strange that the dreariness of such conclusions repels the mind towards some better hope, and that physicists are working other veins of truth, if for no other end than to escape the horror of desolation their own triumphs have compelled them to face. Mr. Fiske says: "There is little that is even intellectually satisfying in the awful picture which science shows us of giant worlds concentrating out of nebulous vapor, developing with prodigious waste of energy into theatres of all that is grand and sacred in spiritual endeavor, clashing and exploding again into dead vapor balls, only to renew the same toilful process without end — a senseless bubble-play of Titan forces, with life, love, and aspiration brought forth only to be extinguished." Such sentiments characterize the ablest physicists of the age.

It is a great achievement to have traced this physical universe down to its end, and taken an intellectual measure of it. One of three possible destinies is now held to be certain: it will either cease to exist, or it will exist as a frigid mass of dead matter; or it will forever repeat a process of alternate vaporization and condensation. Whichever it be, the question rises with infinite emphasis: What is the end of creation? The study of the material universe takes us farther and farther from life and meaning and use. We reach, at last, either nothingness, or a cinder, or a ceaseless clash and repulsion of vapor-balls called worlds, with possible moments of life amidst vast cycles of lifeless ages. We reach the end of a road but find nothing to tell us why it exists. The question forces itself upon us, if by looking in other directions we cannot reverse this process and find some worthy end of creation, *something* instead of nothing, the play of mind instead of the whirl of molecules, life instead of death. The recent verdict of science as to the fate of the material universe, drives us with irresistible force to belief in an unseen, spiritual world, — not the belief of religious faith, but of cold, hard reason. The profoundest depth of absurdity into which the mind can sink is the denial of *purpose*. Meaning, worth, use, there must be somewhere. If we cannot find it in the seen, we must search for it in the unseen. If the path into the visible leads away from it, we must open one into the invisible to see if it cannot be found there. There is no theory that lays hold of the universe with so comprehensive a grasp as the principle of continuity, but like all other materialistic theories, it leaves a *somewhat* unexplained and outside its grasp, a somewhat that embraces its beginning, consciousness, moral freedom, and the main-spring of its activity; but it may be considered as favorable to immortality by reaction from its own triumphs. It remands us with terrible emphasis, to some other order for light which it has demonstrated to itself that it cannot find, finding only darkness.

The other main point at which physical science touches human destiny, is in connection with that part of the doctrine of physical evolution which holds that all forms of life are developed from preceding forms under the impulse of some unknown force,—a theory not yet exactly defined and far from being fully proved. So far as it is accepted in its extreme form, it seems to violate the hope of immortality by bringing all life into one category, and under one law, with the apparent inference of one destiny. If personal identity can be predicated of one set of beings, why not of all, if all are one? The very vastness of the hope seems its own destruction. Bishop Butler, encountering the same objection from another line of argument, boldly accepts this logic, and does not withhold immortality from the brutes. Aside from logical considerations, it may be a harmless belief, but while the verdict of human thought has always been in favor of the immortality of man, it has rejected that of the brute; and the permanent impressions of the race are not to be disregarded. It does not follow that because all lives may be developed from a preceding order, one destiny awaits them. It is a process of involving as well as evolving, and the former may introduce new conditions, if not new forces, that affect the final issue. It may even be granted that all the potentiality of life is drawn from preceding orders, without being forced to the conclusion that their destiny is the same. This potentiality has an accretive quality, in so far at least as to form new combinations. It may thus unite energies that shall enable it "to shoot the gulf we call death." Take the extremest form of evolution, — matter having all the potency of life within itself, — it does not necessarily exclude future existence. The space between an ascidian and a thinking brain is as wide as that between temporary existence and unlimited existence. If an ascidian can evolve mind, the brief life of an ascidian may evolve endless life. Somewhere along the process it may pick up the quality of continuance as somewhere, according to the theory, it picks up the sense of moral freedom; for there is nothing in this assumed potentiality of matter adverse to continuance. On the contrary, as the theory presupposes the eternity of matter, and the continuity of force, the probability would be that the vital potentiality of matter embraced a principle of eternal duration that would at last come out in some of the higher forms of life. If matter can attain to mind that longs for immortality, may not its potentiality be able to achieve it? If it can develop the conception, may it not be able to develop the fact? A matter that can work itself up into such forms as a Shakespeare or a Newton, might be expected to reach corresponding achievements in regard to time.

If the question still recurs, at what point in the

process of evolution, granting its truth for the moment, the principle of immortality is inserted, or gets possession?—a question of great pungency under the principle of continuity, we answer it by instancing an analogy. At what point of its growth does a plant acquire the power of self-perpetuation? As a shoot it utterly perishes if cut down; the lusty after-growth of stem and branches also withers into nothingness; the flower is not "a self-reviving thing of power;" but the flower, gathering light and dew into its glowing bosom, intermingles with them its own life-essence and so bears a seed around which it folds its faded petals as a shroud, and falls into the dust, no longer to perish but to live again. This is more than illustration, it is an argument. A living thing under the law of development comes to have a power of self-perpetuation that it did not have at first; why should it not be so with the life that has culminated in man? He is the flower of life, and in his heart alone may there be found the seed of eternal existence.

But this phase of the subject is unsatisfactory; it is not necessary to consider it under these suppositions, and we turn to another. We want not mere continuance but some solid ground for belief in *personality* after death. An immortality of force, of vital energy, of impersonal life, is a matter of small concern to us. If this be our destiny, all personal hopes, plans, and motives must be confined to this side of the grave. Our little life is indeed rounded with a sleep, a brief journey from nothingness to nothingness. But reason and human nature itself forbid us to accept any theory of existence that can only be named with a sigh, as this must be. The keynote of the universe is joy, and every theory of destiny must harmonize with it. Evolution cannot impair the fact of personality here or hereafter, simply because man transcends nature, which is the field of evolution. It is true that we are very thoroughly mixed with the nature about us, and physically may be one with it. We give our bodies over to the evolutionist to predicate what he will of them, but we draw a line that science is forced to respect, between our physical and moral nature, and claim for the latter a diverse set of laws and a diverse destiny. Man may comprise all that has gone before him in nature, but he is not summed up by it. As the grand proof of this, we adduce the fact of the moral nature with its prime characteristic of freedom. This takes man out of the category of the material world, and exempts him from its destiny. He covers, but he also transcends nature and is a *supra*-natural being. It is absurd to suppose that the order of law that reigns universal in the realm of nature should yield such a thing as free-will. Mr. Darwin himself admits that "free-will is a mystery insoluble to the naturalist." Necessity, which is the equivalent of law, never could evolve freedom. But choice, or freedom, is the constituting characteristic of man, upon which is built the whole fabric of his life and moral nature. It makes him a person; it is the basis of his history. It puts him above the order and on-going of nature. Make the chain of evolution as strong as you will, bind man down to nature by every muscle and nerve and bioplastic cell of his body, here is something unaccounted for, and by far the greater part of him. As a moral being, he is utterly inexplicable on any theory of evolution that attempts wholly to account for him. As moral, he is attended by a vast array of faculties, experiences, and phenomena, that evolution cannot explain, such as consciousness of identity, abstract conceptions, moral obligations, the sense of God, the consciousness of a will. If natural science refuses to accept these as legitimate phenomena, or treats them as mere enlargements of physical instincts, so much the worse for natural science; it thereby abdicates its function of explaining phenomena. The greater physicists perceive this. Professor Tyndall says that the chasm between brain-action and consciousness is impassable, that "here is a rock upon which materialism must split whenever it pretends to be a complete philosophy of the human mind." The admission is valuable, not merely because of its origin, but for its impregnable truth. With such a chasm between the two parts of man's nature, — molecular processes and perpetual flux on one side, and conscious identity, moral sense, and freedom on the other side, — we need not feel troubled at anything physical evolution may assert of man: it simply cannot touch him. We may now build our argument as to his destiny, unhindered by any clamor that may reach us from the other side of this chasm, — a chasm that science itself recognizes in our composite nature.

Thus far we have simply outlined some of the reasons why such theories as that of the continuity of force, and physical evolution throw no barrier in the way of possible immortality. The former fails to account for man, and is intolerable to the human mind. The latter does not account for the beginnings of life, for the plan of any life, for the source of 'the potency that works in life, or for the reason that guides its workings; it does not account for the difference between the instincts of the brutes and the mental and moral faculties of man, nor for the sense of personal identity; nor can any theory account for it that is limited by matter with its universal law of constant flux and atomic change. Personal identity is impossible under any theory whatever of materialism. A consciously enduring being cannot be got out of a perpetual flux. It can proceed only from a non-atomic, and therefore non-fluctuating substance, — from something therefore wholly opposite to matter. Matter cannot uphold the consciousness of identity. When this is apprehended, we shall have little difficulty in believing that we are far outside its limits, — of another substance and destiny.

But other difficulties may arise, such as the thought that this sense of personal identity may be temporary, that as it slowly grew within us, so it may slowly die out; that as our life was drawn out into separateness from the great ocean of being, so, having some cycle within itself, it will sink back into it, as a star rises and sets. Age and infancy are very like, especially when each is normal; sleep and unconsciousness mark both. As there is no identity before infancy, is there any after age? The fact that, notwithstanding the extreme plausibility of this familiar analogy, the human mind has never accepted the suggestion, has great significance; it has instinctively felt that this resemblance does not indicate a reality. Descartes argued: "I think, therefore I am." Had he continued, I am, therefore I shall continue to be, he would have uttered as cogent logic. Granted the consciousness of personality, and it is impossible to conceive of non-existence. If *self* is a unit and not a conglomerate of atoms, how is it to be got out of existence? We cannot conceive of the annihilation of an ultimate atom. We can conceive of an organism being resolved into ultimate atoms, but not of their destruction; science and reason agree in this. But man is conscious of himself as an entity, — a moral unit, — a non-fluctuating, unresolvable, and hence indestructible thing. This is the logical expression of the common belief in immortality, and is the basis of the remark of Goethe, that "it is to a thinking being quite impossible to think himself non-existent."

The thought that we may sink back into the life-flood of the universe from which we came, as a drop of water lifted by the wind falls into the ocean, is checked by the same sense of the impossibility of the loss of personal identity. Whatever may be our relations to the source of life, the I, the self, must remain. Anything else is, as Goethe says, unthinkable. Tennyson asserts the same: —

> "That each, who seems a separate whole,
> Should move his rounds, and fusing all
> The skirts of self again, should fall
> Remerging in the general soul,

> "Is faith as vague as all unsweet;
> Eternal form shall still divide
> The eternal soul from all beside."

But it may be said, if there is another life, there must be another world. Where is it? Of what composed? If it is within the limits, or under the laws of matter, it can have no endurance. The soul must have a sphere like itself,—permanent, unfluctuating. And because it must have it, its existence may be asserted on common and well accepted grounds of reasoning. Whatever is needed to account for and explain any well attested truth or phenomenon, may be accepted as real. Thus, when the undulatory theory of light was established, it was necessary to assume the existence of the luminiferous ether, and there is still almost no other proof of its existence than that the nature of light demands it. Science has thus created by simple deduction a universe of matter. Surely if philosophy may create a universe in which to float the worlds, and convey those quiverings of burning suns that we call heat and light, it will not withhold a fit sphere for the soul when it breaks away from the bonds of matter. We base our proof, however, not on mere analogy, but on the simple ground that the nature of the soul demands a proper and answering sphere, as wings demand air, and fins water. Otherwise, creation is without order and coherence. It is nothing against the existence of such a world that we do not see it, or get any report of it. The sense of this came over me with great power as I once stood upon a spur of the Contra Costa Range at New Almaden, and looked down upon the valley of Santa Clara that stretched away from its base, a floor of emerald, twenty miles to the Bay, and twenty miles between the enclosing mountains. A thin, blue haze — the miracle of beauty in that land — spread gauze-like over the landscape, deepening to purple in the hollows of the hills, obscuring all traces of human habitations, and leaving visible only the vast stretch of fields without motion or sound or other indications of life, — *a visible* world. But, I mused, how much more real is the world hidden under its distance and shroud of azure, the unseen world of human life, the play of passion, the strife of ambition, the ache of sorrow, the joy of hope, — a world *unseen*, but so real and intense as to blot the other into insignificance.

Were we to search for this sphere of the soul, we would not look for it in any refinement of matter, nor in any orb beyond the "flaming walls of the world," but rather in an order over against this visible order, as mind stands over against the body. If, however, it be said that the mind must always have a body, or something like it, to hold it up, a *sub-sto*, — a something like quicksilver upon a mirror, to take up and turn back its operations, something to sustain reaction and perhaps necessary to yield consciousness, — we may follow a hint dropped by science in its latest suggestions. Physicists of the highest rank hold to the existence of a pure or non-atomic fluid filling all space, in which the worlds swim, a sort of first thing to which atomic matter is a second thing. But while science thus acknowledges a non-atomic fluid filling the interstellar spaces as a basis upon which the universe is a cosmos, or a united whole, it cannot impugn the analogy of a non-atomic soul fluid, or ether, as the basis or body upholding the mind, if we care to claim it. As we can imagine all the worlds from "Blue-eyed Lyra's topmost star" to the smallest asteroid, swept together into some far-off corner of space — a not improbable result — and leave it clear of atomic matter yet filled with ether ready to float and unite another universe, so the material atomic body may be swept away and gathered to its original dust, leaving the immaterial body intact, a basis for the mind and its action as it had been before. Science and Revelation here draw very near to each other: science demanding a non-atomic substance as the only possible basis of conscious identity, and Revelation asserting "there is a spiritual body;" and "God giveth it a body even as it pleased Him."

The subject leads us into a region of mystery, where indeed all truth conducts us, shading off in quicker or slower degree, according to the nature of the truth. What can you say of human life? Where will you get your terms for describing life? Where will you stand as you draw off and look at life — being? Make being objective, and where are you when you contemplate it? What upholds your feet; what is the light of your eyes as you look at this fact of existence? You cannot tell; you are in a region of mystery. Outside of all our thinking lies this unknowable region, a land of mystery. Every true thinker reaches it quickly. It is ignorance to overlook this field, into which run paths from every department of study. A crystal of salt is as mysterious as conscience. Question it with What? Whence? For what? and you are at once in the realm of darkness. As the mystery of space invests the physical creation, so do our thoughts lose themselves in mystery whenever certain crucial questions like these are connected with ourselves. But mystery implies faith; they are correlatives. I do not mean faith in any specific sense, but rather that as all thought runs at once into mystery, all knowledge has in it an element of faith. And by faith, I mean a fixed hope that there is truth that cannot be attested except as it bears witness to itself. And no man is a thinker who shuts this faith-element out of his speculations. For no man can be called a thinker who does not follow the paths opened by the study of any fact or thing. The secret of thought lies in tracing the connections and bearings of truth. I go farther: no man is in any high sense a thinker upon whom these questions, Whence? Why? For what? are not pressing down for answer. The secret, the soul of thought, is not disclosed till, in the shrouded chambers of stillest meditation, these questions are raised in respect to whatever the hands touch and the eyes see and the ears hear. And whenever these questions, Whence? Why? For what? are asked, the questioner finds himself in depths of mystery. If it be life that he questions, it is dumb before him. If it be a crystal, its gleam dies out; it cannot tell whence it came, or whither it goes, or why it is. Into this region we are driven when once we begin to think, a region where we have no light but such as comes from our hopes, no assurance but such as is generated by the assertions of our own souls. Finding myself here, I question no longer the dumb unanswering world about me, but I question *myself*. I ask, as I have a right to ask, What do I want? What do I need? What is the meaning of these voices that never cease utterance, like the echoes of tides within sea-caverns, voices that speak of God and self and destiny. I question these, and though it be still a world of mystery about me, I get answers that are plainer, and that reach deeper down, and higher up, than when I look into the face of gleaming planets, or drop dredging plummets into the depths of the sea. I get, at least, affirmations that yield me repose, and take something of the vanity and jangle out of life. And if here I raise the question of destiny, I find myself at liberty to believe in what I want. I need life, and I take it, and no philosophy of matter or origin can pluck it out of my hand.

IMMORTALITY AND NATURE.

"Who forged that other influence,
That heat of inward evidence,
By which he doubts against the sense?

"He owns the fatal gift of eyes,
That read his spirit blindly wise,
Not simply as a thing that dies.

"Here sits he shaping wings to fly:
His heart forebodes a mystery:
He names the name Eternity."
>> TENNYSON, *The Two Voices.*

"For love, and beauty, and delight,
There is no death nor change; their might
Exceeds our organs', which endure
No light, being themselves obscure."
>> SHELLEY, *The Sensitive Plant.*

"Life loveth life and good: then trust
What most the spirit would, it must;
Deep wishes, in the heart that be,
Are blossoms of necessity."
>> DAVID A. WASSON, *Seen and Unseen.*

"I cannot believe and cannot be brought to believe, that the purpose of our creation is fulfilled by our short existence here. To me the existence of another world is a necessary supplement of this to adjust its inequalities and imbue it with moral significance."
>> THURLOW WEED.

IMMORTALITY AND NATURE.

"If a man die, shall he live again?" — JOB xiv. 14.

It is a strange fact that the human mind has always held to the immortality of the soul, and yet has always doubted it; always believing but always haunted by doubt. Yet this throws no discredit upon the truth; rather otherwise. A belief that remains persistently rooted in the mind of the race, generation after generation, yet ever beset by an adverse influence, must have a vitality drawn from truth itself; were the belief not true, the doubt would long since have vanquished it, for nothing but truth can endure constant questioning. The fact, though strange at first sight, is not inexplicable. It is a truth that takes up, and sets forth the antagonism found in man's own nature as a moral being put under material conditions, a mind shut up in a body. The consciousness of mind and moral nature is always asserting immortality; the sense of our bodily conditions is always suggesting its impossibility. It is the same thing that has always showed itself in philosophy; idealism denying the existence of matter, and materialism denying the reality of spirit. But the true philosophy of the human mind is both idealistic and materialistic; *I am, the world is*, — this is the general verdict; it holds both to mind and matter; but they tend to war against each other, mind consciously preëminent over matter, and matter forever doubting the reality of mind, claiming it to be a part of itself. Hence, when the practical question of immortality is raised, the mind asserts the continuance of itself after death, subject, however, to the doubts raised by our close subjection to matter. It is under such conditions that we hold all high truths — spiritual, ethical, mental. We do not reach unquestioned ground till we come to truths of mathematics, the unshared domain of matter.

In keeping with this, we find that nearly all doubt or denial of immortality comes from the prevalence of a materialistic philosophy; nearly always from some undue sense or pressure of the external world. The skeptics are those who study the physical world exclusively, or those who are peculiarly sympathetic with the order of the material universe, or those who fall in with a prevailing habit of materialistic thought. Great sinners very seldom question immortality. Sin is an irritant of the moral nature, keeping it quick, and so long as the moral nature has voice, it asserts a future life.

Just now the doubt is haunting us with unusual persistence and power of penetration. Certain phases of science stand face to face with immortality in apparent opposition. The doctrine of continuity or evolution in its extreme form, by including everything in the one category of matter, seems to render future existence highly improbable.

But more than this, there is an atmosphere, engendered by a common habit of thought, adverse to belief; for in morals, everything goes by atmospheres. There is a power of the air that sways us, without reason or choice. But, as usual, public opinion lags behind its origin. While there are schools of science that hold immortality to be impossible, still if the verdict of the broadest and highest science could be reached it would be found in sympathy with the doctrine of a future personal existence. For science is rapidly changing its spirit and attitude. It is revealing more and more the infinite possibilities of nature. Its own triumphs have made it humble and believing; it does not now say: it is improbable; but rather, nothing is improbable. The trend of tendency is outward, taking in more and more. Its lines of perspective do not converge but spread outward, taking in more of spirit as they take in more of matter. It is also getting over that stultifying principle of positivism that nothing is to be believed that cannot be verified by result, the most shriveling doctrine that ever found place in philosophy. True science admits that some things may be true that it cannot verify by result, or by any test that it can use. The most thoughtful believers in the doctrine of evolution understand very well that it does not account for the beginning of life, for the plan of any life, for the potency that works in matter, for the facts of consciousness, for moral freedom and consequent personality. Here are facts and phenomena that it sees must be accounted for; and it also sees that they intimate and perhaps demand a future life. In short, science is broadening into philosophy, and is getting philosophic insight and outlook.

In considering immortality, it is quite safe to put science aside with all its theories of the continuity of force, and the evolution of physical life and inwrought potentiality, and the like. There is nothing here to hinder faith in whatever may be asserted of immortality from other sources. It matters not what the evolutionist says of our past, or through what gradations of being he may trace our physical history; it matters not how we came to be what we are. We are what we are, moral beings, with personality, freedom, conscience, moral sense; and because we are what we are, there is reason to hope for immortal life. Whatever may be the origin of our moral nature, it cannot affect its destiny; our past does not determine our future. So much for science; if it cannot say anything for immortality, it cannot say anything against it.

In any attempt to prove immortality, aside from the Scriptures, we must rely almost wholly upon reasons that render it probable. Our consciousness of personality and moral freedom declare it possible, but other considerations render it also probable and morally certain. Indeed, our faith in immortality, aside from revelation, rests upon indications that point to it, omens that presage it, inwrought prophecies that demand it for their fulfillment. But let us allow no sense of weakness to invest the word *probability*. Many of our soundest convictions are based on aggregated probabilities. In-

IMMORTALITY AND NATURE. 241

deed, all matters pertaining to the future, even the sunrise, are matters of probability.

We propose to name some of the grounds for believing that the soul of man is immortal. I speak chiefly to those whose faith in the Scriptures is not absolute, and to those who are troubled with flashes or seasons of doubt that blind them to their better hope; to those also, who, by some state or habit of their minds, demand other testimony than that of revelation.

1. The main current of human opinion sets strongly and steadily towards belief in immortality. Whenever the question has been raised, it has been decided in the affirmative. It is a permanent conviction of the race, varied only by solitary voices of denial, and by periods of doubt, like the present, through the over-pressure of hypothetical and seemingly antagonistic truth.

2. The master-minds have been strongest in their affirmations of it. We do not refer to those who receive it as a part of their religion. In weighing the value of the natural or instinctive belief, Augustine's faith does not count for so much as Cicero's, and Plato's outweighs Bacon's; Plutarch is a better witness than Chrysostom; Montesquieu than Wesley; Franklin than Edwards; Emerson than Channing; Greg's hope is more significant than Bushnell's faith. All the great minds, often in spite of apparently counter philosophies, draw near to the doctrine, and are eager to bear testimony to it. Even John Stuart Mill, whose religious nature was nearly extirpated by an atheistic education, does

not say *nay* when the roll of the great intellects is called. Blanco White, another wanderer from the fold of faith, wrought into the form of a sonnet so perfect that we instinctively call it immortal, an argument, the force of which men will feel so long as " Hesperus leads the starry host : " —

> " If light can thus deceive,
> Wherefore not life ? "

Wordsworth touched the high-water mark of the literature of the century in his ode on immortality, and Tennyson's greatest poem is throughout exultant in the hope that " Life shall live forever more."

3. The longing of the soul for life, and its horror at the thought of extinction. Emerson profoundly says : " When the master of the universe has points to carry in his government, he impresses his will in the structure of minds." That this inwrought desire should only guard the mortal life would be an unworthy use of so deep a passion, even if it did not come nigh to deception. The universe is adequate to meet the wants of all its children. It does not use infinite thoughts for finite ends. There must be correlation between desire and fulfillment.

4. The action of the mind in *thought* begets a sense of a continuous life. One who has learned to think finds an endless task before him. He comes to the end of nothing, solves nothing, reaches no full truth, only a few hints and stepping-stones "that slope through darkness up to God." The brute probably has a clear understanding of all subjects upon which it thinks ; that is, the bounds of perception and thought are identical ; but man

reaches the bounds of nothing. The atom may hide a universe, and the seen heaven of stars may be but an atom to the whole. We speak of cause and effect, but we grasp only a little section of an infinite series. We trace *cause* till eye and thought can go no farther, when we reverently say God, spanning, in our ignorance, worlds of unattainable truth. We trace *effect* only to lose it as the drop is lost in the ocean. Thus, with a sense of truth, we cannot absolutely measure any truth. All things are linked together, and the chain stretches either way into infinity. It is a necessity of thought to follow it, and the necessity indicates the fact. There can be no fit and logical end to thought till it has compassed all truth. It is unreasonable to suppose that we are admitted to this infinite feast only to be thrust away before we have well tasted it.

5. A parallel argument is found in the nature of love. It cannot tolerate the thought of its own end. "It announces itself as an eternal thing." The spontaneous forms it assumes in language put it outside all limitations of time. It takes us over into the field of absolute existence, and says: Here is native ground; I cannot die; if I perish I am no longer love, but misery. Love has but one symbol in language — forever; its logic is, there is no death.

> "What vaster dream can hit the mood
> Of love on earth?"

6. There are in man latent powers, and others half revealed, for which human life offers no adequate explanation. Worship demands for its justi-

fication a broader field than this life. Time might possibly explain obedience, but not rapture; reverence or dread, but not the longing of the soul after God. There is within us a strange sense of expectancy. As Fichte says: "My mind can take no hold of the present world, nor rest in it for a moment, but my whole nature rushes on with irresistible force towards a future and better state of being." A divine discontent is wrought into us, — divine, because it attends our highest faculties. It is true that one who has reached the higher grades of life has learned not to fret against time, but it is equally true that he is not content with time. The repose of the greater spirits is not acquiescence in the allotments of time, but the conscious possession of eternal life. Time and mind are not truly correlated. Hence the delight we take in all symbols of vastness and power. The child claps its hands as it looks upon the sea and hears its "wild uproar," — feeling a secret kinship with it. The peace brought by the mountains is but the content of the mind in having found a somewhat truer measure of its own vastness. The repose of the soul when night reveals the immensity of the universe, springs from its contact with a truer symbol of itself than the day affords. Hence, in the night, all the passions of the soul have greater sweep; it is then we pray, that inspirations breathe through us, that imagination opens widest her doors; the upper deeps of space call to the deeps within. I would not weaken what I believe to be sound argument by any admixture of mere sentiment. I refer therefore, in the soberest and severest way, to those blind emotions that fill the mind whenever we listen to the music of the masters, or look upon true art, or in any way come in contact with what is highest and best. So far as they are translatable into thought, they assert a perfection and a life of which this is but a foretaste. So also the wind blowing through reeds upon the margin of a lake or the branches of mountain pines, or perchance over grasses that cover the graves of the dead, has a Memnonian tone that foretells the dawn of an eternal day. The perfect of whatever sort, whether the purity of a flower, or the harmony of sounds, or the perfection of character, awakens a kindred sense within us that is the denial of all limitations.

7. The imagination carries with it a plain intimation of a larger sphere than the present. It is difficult to conceive why this power of broadening our actual realm is given to us, if it has not some warrant in fact. If this world is all, an intense perception of it would seem to be of more value than any imagining of what is not and cannot be. But our minds are not set more to a realization of world-facts than to dreams of what is possible. How blind were the earlier civilizations to the material world while they sang their great poems and built their still enduring philosophies. The most natural thing the mind does, is to break through its visible barrier and fall to enlarging its domains. It finds itself in a cell, it builds a palace; roofed over and walled in, but will own no limits save the infinite spaces of heaven. The imagination is plainly the

open door of the mind by which it escapes its limitations, but into what does it open, illusion or reality?

8. The same course of thought applies to the moral nature. It has been claimed by some that they could have made a better universe. An audacious critic has asserted that he could have done this very thing, made a better world, as La Place said he could have constructed a better planetary system. When asked how he would alter the present order, he replied, "I should make health catching instead of disease;" a very bright answer, but its wit is not so great as its apparent wisdom. Any mind at once says, Why not? The critic is not far wrong, if this world is the only theatre of human life. It is true that if the element of disease were taken out of life, there would go out with it that strength that comes through struggle with adverse conditions; if we had not disease to contend with, we should have instead mental weakness. And if health were contagious, instead of being the result of virtue and wisdom, we should have so much less wisdom and virtue. A South Sea Islander does not trouble himself to make bread when he can pluck it from the trees; and a man would not question his mind or conscience in regard to health if he could secure it by contagion; hence mind and conscience would be feeble so far as they depended upon the discipline of health-seeking. But, after all, this critic of eternal Providence is not far wrong, if all this struggle with disease, and other great evils, have their only reward in this life.

Time is not long enough to compensate man for so mighty conflicts. It is not presumptuous, however, to say that *man* could have been better made, if he is not to live after death; this one life of earth would be better if his moral nature were emptied of the greater part of its contents, and their place filled by instincts. A round of utilitarian duties, of low prudencies and calculations covering the brief span of existence, would be the highest wisdom. If this life is all, we are over-freighted in our moral nature, like a ship with the greater part of its cargo in the bows, ever drenched with the bitter waters of the sea, instead of floating freely and evenly upon them. If this life is all, there is no place for such a faculty as conscience with its lash of remorse in one hand, and its peace like a river, in the other. It is out of proportion to its relations. It is like setting a great engine to propel a pleasure-boat, or like building a great ship to sail across a little lake. A strong, well grounded instinct, that led us to seek the good and avoid the bad, as animals avoid noxious food, would be a better endowment than conscience, unless it has some more enduring field than this from which to reap. The step from instinct to freedom and conscience, is a step from time to eternity. Conscience is not truly correlated to human life. The ethical implies the eternal.

Let us now turn from human nature to the divine nature, where we shall find a like, but immeasurably clearer, group of intimations. Assuming, what no intelligent skepticism now denies, the theistic conception of God as infinite and perfect in character, this conception is thrown into confusion if there is no immortality for man.

1. There is failure in the higher purposes of God respecting the race; good ends are indicated but not reached. Man was made for happiness, but the race is not happy. Man was made for intelligence, but the race is ignorant. Man was made for social order, but war is his habit. He was made for virtue, but the race is vicious. Only now and then does one fulfill the evident ends for which he was made. As a whole, there is the direst failure, and unless there is another field where these hideous wrongs and lacks may be set right, we must conclude that a wise and good God organized society upon the plan of failure, with the result of immeasurable, hopeless misery. The possibility of ultimate earthly success does not lessen the weight of this fearful conclusion. What is the perfection of some far off generation to us and to our generation?

2. The fact that justice is not done upon the earth involves us in the same confusion. That justice will sometime be done gives us peace; that justice should never be done throws the soul into a chaos of endless cursing and bitterness. The slighting of love can be endured, but that *right* should go forever undone is that against which the soul, by its constitution, must forever protest. The remonstrance — it was not a question but a remonstrance — of Abram with God: "Shall not the judge of all the earth do right?" is the privilege of every soul, not an expectation but a demand.

The sentiment of righteousness underlies all else in man and in God, for we cannot conceive of God without attributing it to Him. But justice is not done upon the earth, and is never done, if there be no hereafter. Multitudes suffer what they do not deserve, incurring the penalties of vices and crimes not their own. It is the nature of certain vices to yield their bitterest results in posterity, the offender himself escaping with but little suffering. Here justice is blind indeed, failing both to inflict and to spare. A babe that suffers from an inherited vice, and dies in moral purity, might pass to nothingness, but the injustice could never perish. It would endure, a blot on the white robe of divine righteousness; it would forever prevent the universe from being a moral order. Were there no God, the wrong would pass into the elements to work eternal discord; it would haunt the ages; for if there is no immortality for the soul, there is immortality for wrong till it is set right. The martyr dying in the arena, while the tyrant jests above him, is an eternal injustice if there be no future. If all the unjustly treated of the earth were to pass before us, — the oppressed, the persecuted, the victims of unjust wars, of priestcraft, of enforced ignorance, of false opinion, of bad laws, of social vices, — the sad procession would number well-nigh the whole. Shelley calls this "a wrong world;" St. Paul, "a present evil world." They saw it alike, but the Apostle put into the word *present* a hope that the wrong and evil world will at last yield to a right world.

3. Man is less perfect than the rest of creation,

and relatively to himself, is less perfect in his higher than in his lower faculties. So marked are these facts as to suggest a failure of power or wisdom on the part of God to carry out the best part of his plan; which is actually the position taken by John Stuart Mill. And Mr. Mill is right unless a broader sphere than this world is allowed for the development of man. In the animal races, there is but little falling short of typical perfection, but the perfect type of humanity transcends experience, and can be known only by an ideal projection of hints and fragments drawn from the worthiest and greatest. How perfect also is the material universe, and with what harmony it "still quires to the young-eyed Cherubim;" what exact obedience, and hence what order, in all realms save our own, which is the highest. What conclusion can we draw but that the Creator succeeded in his lower works but failed in his higher, — a conclusion so monstrous as to render plausible any theory of human destiny that avoids it; for a Creator is responsible for his creation; and every act of creation must be justified by its wisdom. There can be no justification of a creation that is characterized by failure.

4. As love is the strongest proof of immortality on the man-ward side of the argument, so is it on the God-ward side. Divine love and human love are alike, and act alike. Love demands sympathy; it is enduring by its own nature. Absolute and infinite love must love forever. Love also, by its nature, suffers from anything that hinders its expression, or brings it to an end. It is so with man;

it must be so with God in a more absolute sense. But God has set us in relations of love to Himself, his love for us being the basis and reason of our love for Him. Life has no higher end than to come into a conscious love of God. Grant now, for a moment, that this life is the end of all, — what sorrow does God inflict upon Himself by allowing the objects of his love to perish! Nay, what more than sorrow, what folly to train men to love, to lead them through years up to the point of mutual recognition and sympathy only to snuff them out of existence! What then are we but bubbles floating on the summer air of existence, reflecting for a few fleeting moments the image of our Creator, and bursting to destroy both ourselves and the image we reflect! Why should love allow the end of what it loves? If it cannot prevent the end why does it create? It is as though a father should rear children till their love for him had bloomed into full sweetness, and then dig graves into which he thrusts them while their hearts are springing to his, and his name is trembling upon lips that he smothers with eternal dust. It is related of an Arab chief, whose laws forbade the rearing of his female offspring, that the only tears he ever shed, were when his daughter brushed the dust from his beard as he buried her in a living grave. But where are the tears of God as he thrusts back into eternal stillness the hands that are stretched out to Him in dying faith? If death ends life, what is this world but an ever-yawning grave in which the loving God buries his children with hopeless sorrow, mocking at once their love and hope, and every attribute of his own nature. Again we say, the logic of love upon the divine as upon the human side, is, there is no death. Divine as well as human love has but one symbol in language — *forever*.

The probabilities might be greatly multiplied. If stated in full, they would exhaust the whole nature of God and man. Immortality has been named "the great prophecy of reason," — a phrase that is in itself an argument. We cannot look into ourselves without finding it. The belief is a part of the contents of human nature: take it away, and its most unifying bond is broken; it has no longer an order or a relation; the higher faculties are without function: eyes, but nothing to see; hands, but nothing to lay hold of; feet, but no path to tread; wings, but no air to uphold them, and no heaven to fly into. To doubt immortality is to reverse instinct; to reject the loftiest verdict of reason; to withhold from humanity its inspiration; to blast the only hope of mankind. It is a lapse, a regression; it crowds man back into his animal nature, and makes him a thing to eat and drink and perish. It cuts every strand that binds man to God, and destroys all conceptions of God. In place of the moral and spiritual truths that underlie and feed the life of society, it puts a creed of negation and despair: —

> "The pillared firmament but rottenness,
> And earth's base built on stubble."

Let us take heed then how we allow ourselves to think on this subject except with the utmost solemnity and carefulness. Let no presumptions against it stand till they have been tested and weighed by absolute knowledge. And let not the reasons for it be given up till we have some other theory of man and his destiny that shall clothe him with equal glory, and secure for him an equal blessedness; and if we cannot solve immortality as a problem, let us cherish it as a hope, holding that such a hope is better than the wisest perplexity.

IMMORTALITY AS TAUGHT BY THE CHRIST.

"The faith of immortality depends on a sense of it begotten, not on an argument for it concluded." — DR. BUSHNELL, *Moral Uses*, page 16.

"It would seem that the highest and holiest soul carries with it like an atmosphere a perfect serenity, a sense of present eternity, a presage of immortality." — GEORGE S. MERRIAM, *The Way of Life*, page 156.

> "But souls that of his own good life partake,
> He loves as his own self; dear as his eye
> They are to Him; He'll never them forsake;
> When they shall die, then God Himself shall die;
> They live, they live in blest eternity."
>
> HENRY MORE.

IMMORTALITY AS TAUGHT BY THE CHRIST.

"Because I live, ye shall live also." — St. John, xiv. 19.

SCIENCE may throw no barrier in the way of belief in immortality; nature and the heart of man may suggest clear intimations of a future life; human society may demand another life to complete the suggestions and fill up the lacks of this life; but, for some reason, all such proof fails to satisfy us. It holds the mind, but does not minister to the heart. It is sufficient to extinguish the horror of great darkness that falls upon us at the thought of death, but it does not kindle the sense of life into a flame of joy. It is a matter of experience that the faith in immortality that is based upon the logic of our own nature and conditions, is not a restful faith. It is forever going over the proofs to see if there be no flaw in them; it is startled by the new discoveries of science; it grows weak before the pressure of the physical world and its laws; it is ever haunted by questions: after all, may not the mind be as the body and perish with it? — is not this law of waste and destruction that wars continually against life and everywhere conquers it, stronger than life? — stronger in the visible world, may it not be stronger in the invisible world? And so this faith stands with a question upon its lips, tremulous at times, peering into the future with a troubled gaze, hoping rather than believing, and passing into the future with the peace of resignation rather than the joy of assurance.

It is noticeable also that the faith of natural evidence awakens no joyful enthusiasm in *masses* of mankind. Plato and Cicero discourse of immortality with a certain degree of warmth, but their countrymen get little comfort from it. Their joys and hopes still play about the present life; death is still terrible; mere continuance of existence yields no inspiring joy. The reason is evident when we refer to our own experience. The mere fact that I shall live to-morrow, does not sensibly move me; it awakes no raptures; it does not even awaken reflection. Something must be joined with existence before it gets power. Or, to come at once to the point, immortality must be united with character in order to solace and inspire men. Or, striking to the very heart of the matter, immortality must be connected with the living God, in order to be a living and moving fact.

We will now consider the way in which Christ treated the subject; and so I trust we shall come to see how it is that a Christian faith in immortality differs in power from any otherwise suggested.

When Christ entered on his ministry of teaching, he found certain doctrines existing in Jewish theology; they were either imperfect or germinal truths. He found a doctrine of God, partial in conception;

He perfected it by revealing the divine fatherhood. He found a doctrine of sin and righteousness turning upon external conduct; He transferred it to the heart and spirit. He found a doctrine of judgment as a single future event; He made it present and on-going. He found a doctrine of reward and punishment, the main feature of which was a place in the under and upper worlds where pleasure was imparted and pain inflicted; He transferred it to the soul, and made the pleasure and pain to proceed from within the man, and to depend upon his character. He found a doctrine of immortality, held as mere future existence; He transformed the doctrine, even if He did not supplant it, by calling it *life*, and connecting it with character. His treatment of this doctrine was not so much corrective, as accretive. He accepts immortality, but He adds to it character. He puts in abeyance the element of time, continuance, and substitutes quality or character as its main feature. Hence He never uses any word corresponding to immortality (which is a mere negation — unmortal), but always speaks of *life*. The continuance of existence is merely an incident, in his mind, to the fact of life. It follows inevitably, but is not the main feature of the truth.

For a moment, we will speak of the subject without regard to this distinction. We find Christ holding to immortality; He does not assert but assumes it, and not only assumes it, but at once begins to build upon the assumption. He never makes a straight assertion of future existence except once, when the Sadducees, pressing him with a quibbling argument against the resurrection, are led away from their point to the matter of future life itself, and are confounded by the simple remark, that when they speak of the God of the patriarchs, they confess that the patriarchs are alive because God is the God of the living and not of the dead, that is, the non-existent. Elsewhere, He simply assumes a future life. But an assumption is often the strongest kind of argument. It implies such conviction in the mind of the speaker that there is no need of proof. Christ calmly takes it for granted that there is a proper field for the play of his truth. He will not stop to prove that such duties as self-denial, love, faith in God, obedience, prayer, are based upon a future existence. They presuppose it, and of themselves are a sufficient argument for it. Without it, how inconclusive all his teachings become, how meagre, how untrue! Why put men under a law of self-denial that may even involve death, as it did in his own case, if death ends all? Why reveal to men the powers of eternity, if they are the creatures of time? Why mock them with revelations of the upper world, if they are never to enter it? And if Christ perished at death, what a jangle of inconsistency his own life becomes? His dying words, "Father, into thy hands I commend my spirit," become mere dying breath wasted in empty space.

In Christ's own mind, the intense and absolute consciousness of God carries with it immortality, as it does the whole body of his truth. Hence, if I were to construct one all-embracing argument for immortality, and were I to put it into one word, it would be — *God*. The last word of science in regard to the physical universe is that it is probably limited; there is an outer edge beyond which is empty space; within this limited universe, at its centre, is a world around which all others revolve, the sun of suns, the centre of all systems, whose potency reaches to the outermost verge, holding them steady to their courses, a world invisible perhaps to us but felt in the harmony with which our planet fulfills its appointed journeys. It is not otherwise in morals. Given the fact of God, and all other truth takes its place without question. The worlds of fact and duty, the meteoric flights of genius, the nebulous clouds of speculation, the burning suns of devotion, the cold, unlighted realms of physics — all fall into true place and function when they centre about God. A belief in God clarifies all subjects at once. There is no longer such a thing as mystery when God is known. Hence, when there is an overpowering, all-possessing sense of God as there was in Christ, truth takes on absolute forms; hence it was that He spoke with authority. His vision of God made his perception of truth absolutely perfect; hence his teachings are beyond criticism. It is the marvel of the world that it has never been able to lay its finger convincingly upon a weak spot in all the various utterances of the Christ, nor even show that He did not speak with utter and absolute knowledge of every theme he touched. He saw the whole of every truth, and saw it in the clear light of absolute vision. It is not necessary to refer this to his essential divinity; it is due rather to his utter and perfect sense of God; for God is light and in Him is no darkness at all. When we come into that light, all darkness of doubt and mystery flies away, and we know all truth even as we are known. It was Christ's realization of the living God that rendered his own conviction of eternal life so absolute.

We can but notice how grandly Christ reposed upon this fact of immortal life. He feels no need of examining the evidences, or balancing proofs; no doubts overcloud his faith; death offers no hindrance; it is but a sleep. He regards nothing from the stand-point of time or this life, except worldly work. He stands steadily upon *life*, life endless by its own nature. He cast himself upon this eternal fact of life and immortality without hesitation or reserve, and died with Paradise open to his sight. Death was no leap in the dark to Him; it was not even a land of shadows: it was simply a door leading into another mansion of God's great house.

It is a proper question to ask here, "Is it probable that Christ was mistaken? Is it possible that his faith in immortality was but an intense form of a prevailing superstition?" If we could find any weakness elsewhere in his teachings, there would be ground for such questions. But as a moral teacher He stands at the head, unimpeachable in the minutest particular. His wisdom was the finest, his judgment the truest, his analysis of life the deepest, his assertion of duty the most authoritative that human ears have ever heard. Is it probable that, true in all else, He was at fault in this one respect? Is it probable that this faultless structure of harmonious and self-witnessing truth is built upon a phantasm, cosmos resting upon chaos; that a body of truth all interwoven and suffused with life is based upon an illusion of life? Here is where personally I rest. I see nature devouring life, a law of death reigning everywhere; I see the star of life rise and set; I see life yielding to silence, and all that held it going to mix with the elements; I look into the unseen world, but I get no report or vision of it; I gaze into the infinite heavens and am shriveled to nothingness; I look into the infinity of animal life with its law of destruction and death and I say, Is it not so with man? But I turn from the doubts thus suggested to Christ and they vanish like morning mists. Dr. Arnold defined faith as "reason leaning on God." So here, we do not abdicate reason before mere words, but suffer it to lean on one to whom the Father has showed all things. If one tells me ninety-nine truths, I will trust him in the hundredth, especially if it is involved in those before. Build me a column perfect in base and body, and I shall know if the capital is true. When the clearest eyes that ever looked on this world and into the heavens, and the keenest judgment that ever weighed human life, and the purest heart that ever throbbed with human sympathy, tells me, especially if He tells it by assumption, that man is immortal, I repose on his teaching in perfect trust. This is the highest possible exercise of reason, for that is not reason that isolates itself from the wisest and best, and says, I will solve my problems alone. It is reason to see with the wise, and to feel with the good. Still another distinction must be made; we do not accept immortality because Jesus, the wise, young Jew, wove it into his precepts, but because the Christ, the Son of God and of man, — Humanity revealing Deity, — makes it a part of that order of human history best named as the Reconciliation of the world to God. Immortality is not an aspiration of the devout, nor a guess of the wise, nor a conclusion of the logicians, but is the centre and soul of God's order in the world; and the achievement of a faith in it is wrought out by an understanding of this order, and by obedience to its eternal laws.

We may now return to our main point and consider *how* Christ taught immortality. As I have said, He makes no straight assertion of it, but assumes it. He speaks rather of life, and life implies immortality. He does not think of it as a future, but as a present fact. The element of time does not seem to have entered much into his thoughts. He was too wholly at one with God to think of past and future. As time, in the divine mind, is an eternal now, so it seems to have been with Christ. We do not find Him peering into the ages upon ages of futurity, and drawing comfort from the thought that He is to live on and on throughout them all. Neither an infinite nor a perfect being regards time as we do. If the cup of life is full, there is little sense of past or future; the present is enough. To dwell on the future is an impeachment of the present. Hence, a little child whose angel still beholds the face of the Father, does not repine over the past, or sigh for the future. The very law of innocence and perfection, whether in child or angel or God or perfect man, tends to exclude the sense of time. Continuance becomes a mere incident; the main and absorbing thought is quality of life. When Christ speaks of eternal life, He does not mean future endless existence; this may be involved, but it is an inference or secondary thought; He means instead fullness or perfection of life. That it will go on forever, is a matter of course, but it is not the important feature of the truth.

And thus we are brought to the fundamental fact that Christ connected life or immortality with character. Life, as mere continuance of being, is not worth thinking about. He does not withhold future existence from the wicked and unbelieving, but plainly regards it of little account. Of what value is the mere adding of days to days if they are full of sin? Practically such life is death, and so He names it. Life is not the living on of a wicked soul through endless ages. Forever to hold a conscious being together as an organism, is not a real immortality. We may go even farther in this direction; there can be no real and abiding faith in immortality until it becomes wedded to the spiritual nature. So long as we hold it as a mere persuasion of the mind, or as an idea, it is subject to the chances of an idea; it meets the challenge of science; it ebbs and flows with the alternations of our mental clearness; it is overclouded by exhalations that rise out of the physical order to which we are linked. Hence I would not attempt to convince one skeptical of immortality through his reason alone. But when the spiritual nature is brought into exercise, it generates not only a faith in eternal life, but reasons for it. When life begins to be true, it announces itself as an eternal thing to the mind; as a caged bird when let loose into the sky might say: Now I know that my wings are made to beat the air in flight; and no logic could ever persuade the bird that it was not designed to fly; but when caged, it might have doubted, at times, as it beat the bars of its prison with unavailing stroke, if its wings were made for flight. So it is not until a man begins to use his soul aright that he knows for what it is made. When he puts his life into harmony with God's laws; when he begins to pray; when he clothes himself with the graces of Christian faith and conduct — love, humility, self-denial, service; when he begins to live out of, and unto, his spiritual nature, he begins to realize what life is, — a reality that death and time cannot touch. But when his life is made up of the world, it is not strange that it should seem to himself as liable to perish with the world. Hence we are not to regard the prevailing general belief in future existence as a genuine faith in immortality; this is the product alone of spiritual life. Christ made no recognition of immortality, except in connection with faith, and by faith He meant the *result* of faith, righteous character. Those who *believe* have everlasting life.

Others may exist, but existence is not life. Others may continue to exist, but continuance is not immortality. Here we find the significance, and the self-witnessing reality of the miracles in which Christ raised the dead. They are specimens of his universal work, a dramatic setting forth of the process of life He is bringing to light, an overflow of the fullness of life behind the veil, dawn-streaks of a sun not yet risen. But these pre-resurrections, these interruptions of the course and order of death, are wrought only in an atmosphere of faith; and thus He asserts that life has no value, except as it is linked with goodness. Of what avail to restore one to life, unless it be to life indeed! To have brought forward these images of the resurrection upon a background of sin and unbelief, would have been a discord; the drama of eternal righteousness that He is enacting in living ways would thus have no unity. Not even in hint, or symbol, not even to do a work of apparent mercy, will He deal with life, except in connection with morality. He will have nothing to do with bare existence, — that stands forever fixed in the sure order of creation; when it is under sin, He will not recognize it as life. To lift men out of existence into life, was his mission.

Christ not only gave us the true law of immortality, but was Himself a perfect illustration of it, and even named Himself by it — the Life. It is a great thing for us that this truth of immortality has been put into actual fact. Human nature is crowded with hints and omens of it, but prophecy does not convince till it is fulfilled. And from the divine side also we get assurances of endless life; but in so hard a matter we are like Thomas, who needed the sight and touch to assure him. And in Christ we have both, — the human omen and the divine promise turned into fact. In some of the cathedrals of Europe, on Christmas-eve, two small lights, typifying the divine and human nature, are gradually made to approach one another until they meet and blend, forming a bright flame. Thus, in Christ, we have the light of two worlds thrown upon human destiny. Death, as the extinction of being, cannot be associated with Him; He is life, — its fullness and perfection, and perfect life must be stronger than death. The whole bearing of Christ towards death, and his treatment of it, was as one superior to it, and as having no lot nor part in it. He will indeed bow his head and cease to breathe in obedience to the physical laws of the humanity He shares, but already He enters the gates of Paradise, not alone but leading a penitent child of humanity by the hand. And in order that we may know He simply changed worlds, He comes back and shows Himself alive; for He is not here in the world simply to assert truth, but to enact it. And still further to show us how phantasmal death is, He finally departs in all the fullness of life, simply drawing about Himself the thin drapery of a cloud.

I cannot close without directing your attention to a lesson implied in all that has been said, namely, a true and satisfying sense of immortality must be achieved. It cannot be taken second-hand. We cannot read it in the pages of a book, whether of nature or inspiration. We cannot even look upon the man Jesus issuing from the tomb, and draw from thence a faith that yields peace. There must be fellowship with the Christ of the resurrection before we can feel its power; in other words, we must get over upon the divine side of life before we can be assured of eternal life. A full predication of immortality can only be made through the moral and spiritual faculties. It is because we are, in part, under the dominion of the world, and worldly sense, and worldly maxims, that we doubt, or see dimly; we are like Milton's "tawny lion" in creation, fully formed in head, and "pawing to get free his hinder parts," which are still one with the dust of the earth; or like the Sphinx, of human head and the body of an animal, —

"Gazing right onward with calm, *eternal* eyes;"

intelligent of eternity, yet linked to perishable nature. And so there are two voices within us: the voice of our earthly nature and the voice of the spirit, and they utter conflicting words. It is our business in life to silence one, and give full ear to the other. By humility, by self-denial, by unworldliness, by spiritual thought, by devout aspiration, by silent communion with God, we grow into an abiding sense of eternal life. "Join thyself," says Augustine, "to the eternal God, and thou wilt be eternal." Just in the degree in which we attain height of spiritual nature are we able to predicate immortality of ourselves. It is not a thing announced by any "Lo here" or "Lo there," but is within us, the fruit of faith, the achievement of spiritual endeavor. It will be strong or weak, steady or fluctuating, just in the degree in which our life is rooted in the eternal verities of God's kingdom. Yet it will ever be a matter of degree so long as faith is weighted with present conditions; a matter of degree, yet doubt ever lessening to the vanishing point of nothingness, and faith growing towards the fullness of utter knowledge; as one climbing a mountain sees an ever-widening horizon, till, upon the summit, he beholds the circle of visible things melt into the infinity of space.

THE CHRIST'S TREATMENT OF DEATH.

"'T is life, whereof our nerves are scant,
Oh, life, not death, for which we pant;
More life, and fuller, that I want."

TENNYSON, *The Two Voices.*

"It can hardly be gain for us to die, till it is Christ for us to live."
PRES. BASCOM, *Philosophy of Religion*, page 187.

"Sleep is a death; O make me try,
By sleeping, what it is to die:
And as gently lay my head
On my grave as now my bed.
Howe'er I rest, great God, let me
Awake again at last with Thee.
And thus assured, behold I lie
Securely, or to wake or die."

SIR THOMAS BROWNE, *Evening Hymn.*

"O living will that shalt endure
When all that seems shall suffer shock,
Rise in the spiritual rock,
Flow through our deeds and make them pure,

"That we may lift from out the dust
A voice as unto him that hears,
A cry above the conquer'd years
To one that with us works, and trust,

"With faith that comes of self-control,
The truths that never can be proved
Until we close with all we loved,
And all we flow from, soul in soul."

In Memoriam, cxxxi.

THE CHRIST'S TREATMENT OF DEATH.

"Jesus said unto her: I am the resurrection and the life; he that believeth on me, though he die, yet shall he live; and whosoever liveth and believeth on me shall never die." — St. John, xi. 25, 26.

It is only from great inspired natures that we hear so contradictory words as these. It is not until we rise somewhat above the level of ordinary thought, that we perceive the doubleness, or twofoldness, that invests life, the assertion of which yields apparent opposition in language. In one breath, Christ says that if a man dies and believes in Him, he shall live; and in the next breath He says, that whosoever liveth and believeth on Him shall never die. Language could not be made more violently contradictory; believers shall never die; dead believers shall live; yet every docile reader of the Bible, coming on such a passage, feels that it contains a truth too subtle to be grasped with words. Language attempts it, but is turned hither and thither in vain attempts to embody the meaning, and the result is wild and contradictory statements. But the very ambiguity of the language is an indication of the value of the truth hidden underneath it. When the strata of the rocks are twisted and upturned, the miner looks for gold, deeming that in the convulsions that so disposed them, a vein of the precious metal may have been thrown up from the lower deep.

And not only is there a certain blindness in the treatment of the subject, but the subject itself is a mystery. We see but one side, or, as it were, the gate-way; beyond, all is uncertainty and darkness. But this blindness and apparent contradiction has its ground in us, in our feeble capacity to understand and to believe. To the Christ it was clear and radiant truth. He was dealing with the actual fact of death. Women were weeping for their dead brother before him. It was no time for fine, mystical talk, for ambiguous words of comfort, and it was this very desire to administer a higher comfort, that made his words seem strange and doubtful. In order to get at their meaning, we must keep in mind that Christ was drawing comfort for these afflicted friends, not from the old sources, but from Himself. Martha has expressed her faith in the common doctrine of the resurrection at the last day. Christ does not deny nor assent to it, but passes over it, as though it had little power to assuage the actual suffering of death. If it be true, it is a far-off event, ages hence, at the last day; it hardly touches the present fact of death. It has nothing definite, immediate, or specially consolatory in its character, being simply an affirmation of future existence. So little power had it, that Martha did not think of it, till led to it by Christ's question. She doubtless shared the vague belief of the Jews, that "her brother would ascend some time or other on angels' wings into a place somewhere above the stars;" but how could that comfort *her?* She could not bridge the gulf of time and space between herself and that event. She could get from it no assurance that her brother would ever be known by her; that the ties sundered by death would ever be joined again. There her brother lay in the tomb, dead, fast passing to corruption, soon to become as the dust of the earth, and there he would lie for ages, *dead;* herself soon to die and lie beside him, and sleep the long sleep of utter forgetfulness. What comfort is there here for yearning human love that longs for nearness and response? God's love may wait patient through ages, because ages are nothing to Him, but human love is impatient, because it is human and under finite conditions. We cannot endure that the object of our love should be beyond our knowledge and reach, and the bitterness of death springs from this fact of utter separation and apparent loss. A future, general resurrection, is only a slight mitigation of this suffering, because its operation is so distant and vague. Our little ones die — children that we scarcely endure to have out of our sight; the winter day seems long if they are absent, and the journey wears tediously away that separates us from their caresses; when these die, it is small comfort to know that ages upon ages hence, when great gulfs of change and place are passed, they and we shall live again. Instead of dwelling on that, we cling to the form and mementos spared by death; we visit their graves and keep alive the past instead of making alive the present. Christ, there by the tomb of Lazarus, strove to give these mourners a more substantial comfort than these far-away fancies of the common tradition.

He did this by a word and an act, — the one to show how true was the other; but we will speak only of the word.

1. His first purpose was to get their minds away from death; He will not let them think of it, but gives them instead *life*, and crowds it upon them in all ways possible.

There is but one natural fact to which Christ showed antipathy. We have no indication that climate, or storm, or heat, the weariness of deserts, or the roughness of mountains, moved Him to any word or thought of dissatisfaction. There was no impatience with youth; no sadness over age. He did not sigh over the brevity of life, or human frailty, or the variety of allotments. So far as we can gather, He was in profound sympathy with the natural order of the world, and of human life, save only in respect of its end. Death itself is a natural and fit event, and must have been regarded by Christ with no more aversion than the night or the tempest. But the fact had been so sunk in its associations, and identified with fears so horrible and conceptions so false; it stood for so much that was antagonistic to Himself, that He regarded it with aversion, and shrank from all mention or recognition of it. He set the whole weight of his thought and speech against what was known as death. There is a fine, illuminating significance in the fact of his indisposition to use the word. We observe in ourselves a reluctance to utter certain words because their associations are so bad or painful. The word is an open gate through which all the evil and bitterness it represents pours in upon us, and we seek for ambiguous and milder phrases when forced to utterance. And the finer the nature, the keener is the sensitiveness to such association of speech and fact. Death, as it was commonly regarded, was a hateful thing to Christ, and He would not name it. And so He said that the daughter of Jairus was not dead, but asleep. The mortal change had come, but that which the people meant had not come. They thought that some dark and dreadful change had come upon her spirit; that she had entered upon a long and gloomy sleep in the grave; that a cessation of life in its fullness has taken place till the last great day. But Christ will not countenance such views, and says that no such change had come: she is rather *asleep;* her life itself, in all its grand and beautiful functions, is still going on aside from the closed eyes and the pulseless form. He showed the same reluctance to apply the word when Lazarus died, and spoke of him as *sleeping*, till the dullness of his companions forced him to use the ordinary word. He evidently intends to teach another use of words as to the close of life, to inaugurate another phrase in place of "death." The conception He desires to establish is so different, that He clothes it in a new word, instead of striving to put a new meaning into an old word.

Why have we not learned the blessed lesson, or rather why have we forgotten it? for the early believers, fully taught by the resurrection of Christ, caught at once the remembered hints, and always spoke of physical death as sleep. St. Luke writes of Stephen, though his life was "dashed out by cruel stones," that he "fell asleep." And St. Paul writes many times over of those who have "fallen asleep," and St. Peter of the fathers who "fell asleep." They cherished the new word with fondness, wrote it upon their tombs, and devised emblems to set it forth. Even now in the catacombs of Rome, may be read such words as these: "Sleeping in Jesus;" "He sleeps in peace." Sleep is peace; to sleep in peace, then, how restful! How fresh and strong must be the awaking after such sleep!

If Christ had done nothing more for humanity than give to it this word *sleep* in place of death, he would have been the greatest of benefactors. To that which seems to us the worst thing He has given the best name, and the name is true. It is a great thing that we are permitted to take that almost dearest word in our tongue — *sleep* — and give it to death; sleep that ends our cares and relieves us from toil, that links day to day and shuts out the horror of darkness, that checks with pleasant suggestion the current of evil, that soothes and ends the fever of daily life, that begins in weariness and ends in strength, that keeps soul and body quiet while God fills again the exhausted lamp of life, that lets the mind into the liberty of dreams and perhaps suffers it to bathe in the original fountain of life; it is no small or unmeaning thing that

Christ taught us to apply this word to that seeming loss and horror hitherto called death. This is not sentiment nor poetry, except as sentiment and poetry stand for what is most real and substantial. Christ did not utter pleasant deceptions by the grave of his friend Lazarus; He taught new truth about death, that it is not what it seems, — a loss and horror, a matter of entombment and corruption, of ghostly waiting in the under-world, of disembodied and half-suppressed existence till the last great day at the end of the world. He puts all this aside, and invests it in a new atmosphere and surrounds it with different suggestions. It is to life what sleep is to the day. Sleep rests and restores the body to a fuller and fresher life. Christ would not have called death *sleep* merely because of its external likeness; his thought struck deeper than that. He meant that death does for us what sleep does for the body: repairs, invigorates, and repeats for us the morning of life.

Amongst the profoundest words of Shakespeare are those in which he speaks of sleep as "great Nature's second course." In a profounder sense still, the sleep of death ushers in the "second course" of nature, even the life that shall never know death nor sleep.

2. His next purpose is to get them to identify Himself with the resurrection; or, rather, to supplant it and the far-off life it indicates, with Himself and his life. Martha had spoken of a general resurrection in the last day — not necessarily a spiritual fact nor having a spiritual bearing, — a mere

matter of destiny, like birth and death, a distant mysterious event. Christ draws it near, takes it out of time, vitalizes it, puts it into the category of faith, and connects it with Himself. He says: Do not think of the resurrection in that way, as a final, world-end event, and thus suffer all the natural gloom and bitterness of death; instead, transfer your thoughts on the matter to me; consider me as the resurrection, and that whoever believes in me is absolutely beyond the reach of death, as it has been hitherto regarded.

But how is it that believing in Christ thus puts us beyond the reach and power of death? — a fit question and capable of answer, for this process has a philosophy and traceable order. Some may prefer to believe that this assurance is of the nature of a promise, and that those who believe in Christ are greatly strengthened and upheld by Him in the hour of death. This is undoubtedly true, but it is the small part of a much larger truth. Christ had in mind something of greater scope than momentary ministration to the dying. This is comparatively a small matter; for how many die instantly; how many sicken and die in utter unconsciousness; the vast majority with benumbed perceptions and sensibilities. It was doubtless intended we should go out of the world as unconsciously as we came into it. It cannot therefore be to meet so rare and brief an experience as conscious agony of death that Christ makes this statement. The entire truth that Christ had in mind was this: that faith in Himself, by its own law, works away from death towards life. For, Christ is life; to believe in a person is to become like that person, or one with him. Hence, to believe in Christ the Life is to become a sharer with Him in whatever He is, therefore in his life. We are told that Christ could not be holden of death; faith in Him works toward the same freedom.

The assimilating power of faith, that is, the power of faith to make those who believe like that in which they believe, is a recognized principle. The whole nature follows the faith, and gravitates towards its object. A moulding process goes on; faith is the workman and the object of faith is the pattern. Starting within, down amongst the desires and affections, it works outward, till the external man becomes in form, feature, and expression like the absorbing object. We meet men every day in whose faces we see avarice, lust, or conceit, as plainly as if it were imprinted on their foreheads. They have so long thought and felt under the power of these qualities that they are made over into their image. A man who worships money comes to wear the likeness of a money-worshiper down to the tips of his fingers; his eyes and nose and the very posture of his figure, bear witness to the transforming power of his faith. The Hindu who worships Brahma sleeping on the stars in immovable calm, gets to wear a fixed expression. The mediæval saints who spent days and nights in contemplation of the crucifix, came to show the very lineaments of the man of sorrows, as art had depicted them, and sometimes, it is said, the very marks of his torture in their own bodies. It is a principle wonderful in its method and power. We are all passing into the likeness of that in which we believe. There is no need that men should be labeled, or that they should make confession with their lips. Very early the faith hangs out a label, and soon the whole man becomes a confession of its truth. You have but to look, and you will see here a voluptuary, there a sluggard; here a miser, there a scholar; here a bigot, there a skeptic; here a thinker, there a fool; here a cruel, unjust man, there one kind, generous, true; here one base throughout, there one radiant with purity. It is wonderful, this power of faith first moulding, then revealing. It is the power of love directed by will, which together makes up faith; and as it works out so it works within, shaping all things there in like manner. It is by this principle that Christ unites men to Himself. It is at this point that He inserts Himself as a saving power into the world. He brings men to believe in Him in order that they may become like Him, and if like Him, then one with Him, sharers of his nature and his destiny. And if one with Him, then his life is their life; whatever pertains to Him pertains to them. The fellowship and oneness engendered by faith is an abiding fact and endures through life and the change called death. Christ is the Life: He stands in humanity for that eternal reality, and He came that men might know and realize it. If they believe in Him, they shall have life, and shall never die. By faith, we get over upon Christ's side in this terrible matter of death. Taught and inspired by Him, we are able to predicate life of ourselves, even as He predicated it of Himself.

But the question rises, Did not Christ die, and do we not die, even if we believe in Him? In the old-world, and still common, sense of the word, the sense in which Martha used it, Christ did not die, He did not go down into the grave and lie there, soul and body, in unconsciousness, nor did He pass into some nether place to wait till summoned again to life; there was no loss, no forlorn stay in a disembodied state, as the heathen pictured the under-world. In this common, and still existing sense of death Christ did not die. He refused to countenance such an idea of death. And those who believe in Him get deliverance from these false and terrible views of it, and come to share in Christ's view. Thus those who believe in Him never die.

In another sense Christ did die. He suffered this housing of the soul to be torn away, the tabernacle to be taken down, but He will not call it death. It does not touch the life: that flows on, an unbroken current, and rises into greater fullness. And so Christ says that those who believe in Him, and die in this sense, do not really die: though dead, they live.

And yet the fact and process of death remain. Its thick darkness may be taken away, but a heavy shadow still overhangs it. Why, having come into a consciousness of life, must I still undergo death? — A curious and pertinent question. It is not a sufficient answer to refer it to the course of nature.

I can conceive no answer but this: Man needs for his supreme development to undergo the supreme experience, which is death. He can have no full test of himself, except by the death of himself. When he can say: "Life is my all, but I can lay down my life," he utters his highest word; nothing more eductive can be experienced or conceived. There is thus reflected back to him the assertion and proof of his manhood and highest attainment. So, to die fearfully, or dumbly, or in passive submission to the inevitable, is below man. But to die bravely and calmly, or for a cause, is the prime achievement. Hence man alone is made conscious of death; he alone can freely and willingly die. In doing this he puts on himself the seal of a perfect personality; no test short of this would reveal him to himself; none less would measure him. It would be a vain thing, however, if it were a conscious ending of existence. I can die, but I must die to some purpose; I can lay down my life, but I must hope to take it up again.

We might pursue the subject into a most attractive field of thought, and show how a life of faith in Christ is, in itself, a wholesome, life-giving, life-nurturing process. It is always turned towards life. It fosters growth and increase; it strengthens and enlarges. It always keeps in view a fuller, broader, and deeper life, and thus repudiates the idea of death; it does not look in that direction. One who believes in Christ, and is therefore pure and true and just and kind, has in each of these qualities a cable binding him to eternity; for purity and truth and justice and love are eternal things.

It is a fact of unspeakable moment that the whole matter of Christian believing and living is summed up as *life*. And by *life* I mean *existence in the perfect fulfillment and enjoyment of all relations*. Unfold this short definition into its full meaning, and we have life as Christ used the word. This is the final, comprehensive, definitive term that stands for the Christian idea. We misname it salvation, but salvation is subservient to life. We talk about going to heaven or hell, but Christ speaks of eternal life; of saving the soul, but Christ bids us save the *life;* forfeit the world, if need be, but keep that full and unharmed. We transport the matter into some future world; Christ puts it into the hour that now is. It is the devastating mistake of ages of imperfect faith that the emphasis and crisis of life is carried forward into the next world, robbing this of its dignity, disrobing it of its loftiest motives, cheapening by withholding from it its proper fruitions. There is no juster word used amongst men than *probation*, and none more perverted. Life is indeed probation, but the judgment that decides is in perpetual session; not for one moment is it adjourned; every hour it renders the awards that angels fulfill; daily and forever does the Christ of humanity judge according to the deeds done in this present life of humanity, and send to right or left hand destinies. There is no day of eternity auguster than that which now is. There is nothing in the way of consequence to be awaited that is not now enacting, no sweetness that may not now be tasted, no bitterness that is not now felt. What comes after will be but the increment of what now is, for even now we are in the eternal world. The kingdom of heaven has come and is ever coming; its powers and processes, its rewards and punishments are to-day in full activity, mounting into ever higher expression, but never more real in one moment of time than in another. Thus seen, life begins to get meaning and dignity, and this world becomes a full theatre of God's action, — for here and now is his throne of judgment set in the heart of every man and in every nation. And so *life* is the single theme of the Christ, — life and its fullness. God gives his children one perfect, all-comprehending gift — *life*. It is his own image, his very substance shared with his creatures. Life carries everything with it; if true, it may be trusted to the uttermost; all things belong to it. By its own law it is endless; why should life ever cease to be life? It has but one enemy, — sin. So long as life is true to its own laws and relations, it knows no diminution of its forces. If there had been no sin, no law-breaking, there would have been nothing that we now call death. Change there might have been, successive phases of life, as the bud yields the flower, and the flower the seed, but nothing like that we call death. Even the body would not really die. Had its powers not been impaired by sin it would have filled its round of years without evil defect, and sunk into sleep, ending life as it began, with slowly fading consciousness, not dying, but changing bodies as the butterfly emerges from the chrysalis. Heredity almost teaches this in certain exceptional lives. Nor would we ever have known this lethargy of mental faculties, this dullness of spiritual vision, this apathy of moral feeling, this that we truly call deadness of spirit, if in all generations the laws of our whole nature had been observed. But when sin came, death also came. And so the entire system began to work towards death, in body and spirit, in men and nations. Christ introduces a reversing power, and turns the stream of tendency toward life. It is no mystery or miracle, unless it is strange that one being should change another into his likeness, or bring him under his power. We can conceive one so recipient of Christ's truth, so in sympathy with Him, so obedient to Him, as to have little sense of yesterday or to-morrow, to care little for one world above another, to heed death as little as sleep, because he is so filled with the life of God. It is towards this high state that Christ conducts us, sowing in our hearts day by day the seed of eternal life, — truth and love and purity. For if order is restored to our souls, the mind and body will follow after, and spiritual life will assert its preëminence over physical death.

The subject leaves us with two leading impressions : —

1. Comfort in view of the change called death. That was Christ's aim, to comfort Martha as she wept by the grave of her brother. He does not strive to annihilate her grief, but to infuse it with another spirit. As Jesus Himself wept, so we would not have love shed one tear less over its dead ; but there are tears that are too bitter for the human

eyes to shed, — tears of despair; and there are tears that reflect heaven's light and promise as they fall, — tears of hope. Death in certain respects can never be other than it is, but there is a despair, a horrible sickening fear to which Christ will not consent. He takes death as the world has conceived it, and, because He so changes the thing, He gives to it a new name; He takes away its sting by taking away the sin of which it is the shadow. If a strict separation between sin and death can be effected, there is no evil in the latter except something of physical suffering, and of pain in parting from friends; but this is taken up and submerged in that vast flood of hope that flows out of the gospel. Aside from this we may approach death as we approach sleep, as a grateful ordinance of nature, not longing for it, not dreading it, but accepting it as God's good way: a step in life, and not a going out of life. Here is where the comfort of Christ's revelation centres; it does not leave death a horrible uncertainty, a plunge into darkness, an entrance into some ghostly realm of torpid, waiting existence. It is instead, from first to last, a matter of *life*, life enlarged and lifted up, fuller and freer: " I came that they may have life, and may have it abundantly."

2. The subject leads us up to a new sense of the value of faith in Christ.

It is no small thing to be delivered from false views of death. Consider with what a hopeless gaze the heathen regard it, what dreary visions of an under-world, peopled with shivering, bodiless shades, working out the penalties of earthly sins, or revisiting the earth in degraded forms. The Jews even got no farther than some vague notion of a resurrection at the last day. There is no certainty till we come to Christ, and no deliverance from fear except through faith in Him. And by what rule shall we measure the value of this certainty and deliverance? We who have looked the last upon faces dear to us, and seen the life spark vanish from sight, can feel, though we cannot measure, the value of the faith which assures us that death is but the shadow of a coming greater life. It is a matter of unspeakable comfort, a blessing not to be compassed by thought, that Christ has inverted all the meanings that nature and habit have put upon death. The question is often put, What has Christianity done for the world? It has, at least, done this: When a mother lays her babe in the grave, life of her life, and loved more than life, she can believe that it is not dead but alive; that elsewhere its sweet life is going on with full function and personality. It is no small matter that human love is thus kept alive in hope, rather than crushed under the nether millstone of despair. What has Christ done for the world? He has delivered human love from the bondage of despair, and brought it under the inspiration of hope. And this is nothing more nor less than keeping love alive and strong; for nothing is surer than that the constant blighting of love by hopeless death wears away its fineness and weakens its power as an element of civilization. Few heathen wives are like Phocion's, of whom

Plutarch tells, who, when her husband was unjustly put to death by the Athenians, herself lighted his funeral pyre and gathered up his bones in her lap and brought them to her house and buried them under her hearthstone, saying, "Blessed hearth! to your custody I commit the remains of a good and brave man." What love, and yet what despair! Under the strain of such unrelieved suffering, love shrinks and hardens: —

"Death with its mace petrific, smites it into stone."

Love must have hope to feed on or it shrivels into mere animal instinct; but when soothed and drawn up to heaven by its hope, and spiritualized by a sense of eternal life, it asserts its infinite energies, and works in its own mighty way for the regeneration of the world. It is in such ways that Christ ministers to civilization. He invented no machine, neither engine, nor loom, nor compass; He taught no science; He laid down no theory of public education, no system of government; He organized no school of social science. It is a superficial view that regards civilization as depending upon these things. Christ went deeper: He took off the pressure from the human heart so that it could beat freely, and send full pulses of healthy blood to the brain and hands and feet of society. The human heart lies back of and underneath all else; out of it are all issues of life, for society as well as for individuals. Unless love, parental and social, is kept strong and vital, there will be no civilization worth the name. But love cannot be constantly smitten by death and its despair, and preserve its high and ministrative functions. What has Christ done for civilization? He secured free action for the mainspring of civilization. Get down to its heart and there you will find the brooding, creative spirit of Christ, filling it with hope and strength.

By what mighty arguments are we thus led up to Christ? Come, then, all ye who are in bondage to the fear of death; and ye who have laid away beloved ones in the sleep called death, and ye who are cherishing seeds of sin that make death real, come all to Christ, sit at his feet, believe on Him; be one with Him; and as He lives, ye shall live also, and shall never die.

THE
RESURRECTION FROM THE DEAD.

> "Then long eternity shall greet our bliss
> With an individual kiss." MILTON, *On Time.*

> "Then, soul, live thou upon thy servant's loss,
> And let that pine to aggravate thy store;
> Buy terms divine in selling hours of dross;
> Within be fed, without be rich no more;
> So shalt thou feed on Death, that feeds on men,
> And, Death once dead, there's no more dying then."
> SHAKESPEARE, *Sonnet* cxlvi.

"This wonderfully woven life of ours shall not be broken by death in a single strand of it; it shall run on and on, an unbroken life, upheld by the will of the Eternal. Death cannot break it, but it shall change it. It shall draw from it all perishable dross. While the life remains the same, some elements of which its strands are woven shall be changed; instead of the silver cord shall be the thread of gold; for the corruptible shall be the incorruptible; and there shall be no more entanglement and imperfection, no more strain upon any strand of it; the flesh shall not chafe against the spirit, nor the spirit against the flesh, but there shall be at last the one perfectly accorded, incorruptible, and beautiful life."
— REV. NEWMAN SMYTH, *Old Faiths in New Lights,* page 366.

THE RESURRECTION FROM THE DEAD.

"He is not here; for He is risen, even as He said." — ST. MATTHEW xxviii. 6.

"If there is a natural body, there is also a spiritual body." — 1 COR. xv. 44.

THE doctrine of immortality and the doctrine of resurrection from the dead stand somewhat in the same relation as a block of marble to a finished statue. The Christian doctrine of resurrection is the natural fact of immortality wrought into shape. We may know there is a statue in the marble, but how beautiful it may be, in what grace of posture it may stand, what emblems may hang upon its neck or crown its head, what spirit may breathe from its features, we do not know till the inspired sculptor has uncovered his ideal and brought it to light. The analogy may go farther. As an artist works a mass of marble into a statue, putting mental conceptions and meanings into it that are no part of the marble, so Christ has given a divine shape to immortality and filled it with beautiful suggestions and gracious meaning. We see in the statue the mind of the sculptor as well as the marble; so in the doctrine of the resurrection we see the mind and purpose of Christ as well as the bare fact of future existence.

The doctrine has fared ill in previous ages, as have all the great doctrines. But the perversion of truth is due not so much to ignorance as to an overmastering desire to guard against corresponding errors. Over against nearly all the false and gross forms that Christian truth has taken on from age to age, may be discerned the shadows of errors that have faded from our view, but were very real to the men whom they first confronted. It has been the way of the world thus far to meet error by exaggerating the truth. The human mind loves the truth and is ever seeking it, but it has not yet reached the point of resting calmly and steadily upon it; its action is like the swing of a pendulum rather than like the poise of the needle, — vibrating across the centre of truth instead of pointing straight towards it. We must not allow ourselves to be either shocked or disgusted by the forms given to the doctrine of the resurrection in the early Christian centuries. Let us rather remember that the generations after us may hold our views of truth, on many points, as cheap as we hold those of the ancients on the subject before us. Not that there is no attainable standard of truth; we have a compass pointing to the exact truth as well as a pendulum vibrating about it, — a divine revelation whose source is in the heavens, as well as a human reason swayed by the forces of earth. We find in the Scriptures the doctrine of the resurrection set down in forms that not only agree with reason, but stimulate it to higher exercise. Neither in Christ nor in St. Paul do we discover the pressure of worldly influence in their treatment of it. Christ was Himself the resurrection; He did not so much teach it as act it; and therefore we find in Him the absolute truth of the subject. St. Paul's discussion of it grows more and more luminous as it is subjected to the advancing thought of the ages. It cannot be denied, however, that very early it took on a crude and gross aspect. The Fathers taught not only the resurrection of the flesh, but drew it out into the most absurd particulars; the hair, the teeth, the nails, and every specified organ of the human frame would be raised up; some claiming that the bodies would be raised as they were at death; others as in their highest perfection; others that the hair and nails cut would not be lost, neither would they be raised "in such enormous quantities as to deform their original places, but shall return into the body, into that substance from which they grew." Such views strike us as ludicrous, but there is an explanation of them.

Two great enemies threatened the early life of the Church: Pantheism and Gnosticism. There are but two philosophies — the Christian and the Pantheistic: one asserting the personality of God and man; the other denying all personality. The doctrine of the one ever-living God kept the Jewish nation free from the latter; for the personality of God carries with it the personality of man. Christianity reasserted it, and gave it intensity by exalting man, and investing him with supreme duties, and assigning to him a personal destiny. It is this single fact that underlies modern civilization, an intense sense of the personality of man. It is the mainspring of the energy, the humanity and the faith of Western civilization as contrasted with the Oriental and the Ancient. If the question be raised again that is now so often raised as a taunt— "What has Christianity done for the world?"— we answer: it established a philosophy of man that has inspired whatever is great and good in modern civilization, and it supplanted a philosophy that unnerved man's spirit, stripped him of all dignity, and made him not only an easy victim of tyrants but of little worth in his own sight.

Wherever the Christian theory does not prevail, the Pantheistic does; it is the only alternative of the human mind; it haunts the world continually; all lapses of Christian faith are in its direction. It was the philosophy of the world when Christ entered it; it will be the philosophy of the world if Christianity is ever driven out of it. Its effect is to blast human energy by destroying human personality. The Fathers felt its encroachments upon the Church, and well understood its influence. By assailing personality, it denied an *enduring identity*, which is the total significance of the resurrection. In order to meet the Pantheistic spirit and influence, they went to an extreme and claimed that the resurrection covered the whole man, flesh and bones as well as mind and spirit. In the main they were right; in the details they were wrong. It is common to flout the memory of these great names by holding up the unseemly details of their teaching, but they did not act under the inspiration of ignorance; they were guarding the most sacred truth ever committed to human keeping against the most insidious foe that ever assailed it. Their philosophy was not yet fine enough to teach them that personal identity consists not in flesh and blood, and so, in their noble zeal for this vital truth, they asserted the resurrection of the flesh.

Another enemy that threatened the Church, more definite and specific than Pantheism, was Gnosticism with its Oriental doctrine of contempt of the body, holding that there is an antagonism between the flesh and the spirit, and that the flesh itself is evil, — a dangerous doctrine, as it makes sin external, transfers it from the heart to the body, and so turns all the forces of religion into mere discipline of the flesh. The Fathers perceived its danger, and not only denied that the flesh was evil, but emphasized their denial by asserting its literal resurrection. Again, they were right in the main but wrong in detail. This doctrine of contempt for the body was not only injurious to religion but to civilization. Its tendency was to paralyze society by reducing the wants of the body to the lowest point. Had the Fathers allowed this doctrine to prevail, not only would the Church have been subverted, but civilization itself would have been checked. Thus we see that the assertion of the resurrection of the flesh, with all its gross absurdity, was an assertion in favor of breadth of thought and of toleration; it was a protest against narrowness and bigotry. We are accustomed to think of the ancient creeds as putting limitations about thought and belief, but they were rather assertions of liberty, — veritable bills of human rights, prescribing not so much that men shall think in right ways, as that they shall not think in narrow and shriveling ways. It is very easy, it costs but little mental effort, to throw contempt upon the doctrines of the early church, but no broad thinker, no wise, charitable mind, will indulge in such a habit. The forms given to the early doctrines may be criticised, but they are not to be despised.

It was this sturdy defense of great imperiled interests that secured for the doctrine of the resurrection the place it has so long held in the Church. The occasion for the form first given to it has passed away, but the form itself remains. We still assert in words a literal resurrection of the body, but none of us believe it. Our hymns, our prayers, our epitaphs, and too often our sermons, imply that the dust of our bodies shall be reanimated in some far-off future and joined to the waiting soul. At the same time, we know that science declares it to be impossible; our reason revolts from it; it is sustained by no analogy; it is an outworn and nearly discarded opinion. There is, however, a general feeling of perplexity in regard to it. The present state of the question rather breeds skepticism than ministers to faith. Teach a thinking man chemistry and he must be skeptical; mathematics even is against the traditional view. It is an unhappy thing when one revelation of God is set in apparent opposition to another. When such is the case, the higher revelation commonly yields before the lower one; we side with the lower because it is nearer. The wiser way is to harmonize them; for God cannot be inconsistent with Himself.

The view now offered is substantially this: that the resurrection is from the *dead*, and not from the *grave;* that it takes place at death; that it is general in the sense of universal; that the spiritual body, or the *basis* of the spiritual body, already exists, and that this is the body that is raised up, — God giving it such outward form as pleaseth Him, and thus preserving that dualistic state essential to consciousness, if not to existence itself. I hold these views as both scriptural and rational, as according with the essence of the doctrine and with the analogies of nature.

Let us notice some considerations that render these points probable.

The analogy of nature. The continuance of life in the succession of plants and animals does not depend upon the transmission of matter, but of an *immaterial principle* or *entity* folded within the least possible amount of matter. The matter does not seem to be essential to the future life except as holding it during a very brief crisis. When an oak is about to become another oak, its life is committed to an acorn, — a slight wrapping of matter, and thus left for a few days till the oak can begin again its general method of existence by air and light and moisture, when it lets go the enfolding matter which decays and becomes to the new oak no more than any other matter. It may foster its life by its decay, but it does this incidentally, as any other matter might. The acorn simply covers a crisis in the life of the oak; the continuance of the oak does not depend upon the continuance of the acorn, but rather upon getting rid of it. The principle is universal. The law of succession does not consist in one bodily form entering into another, but in something quite different. As applied to the resurrection, this analogy indicates that future life does not depend upon the *preservation* of the physical body, but rather upon its loss.

We find a similar analogy in the animal world. The butterfly emerges from the chrysalis — a perfect creature — not by working up the substance of the worm into itself, but by a growth within it. At a certain stage, the chrysalis may be opened, and the members of the winged insect may be seen, two bodies in one: one fed through the agency of the other, but not identical with it. The butterfly gains its perfect form, not by assimilating the worm, but by getting rid of it. It is the most beautiful analogy in nature, its very gospel upon the resurrection, — at first a creeping thing, dull and earth-bound, a slight period of dormancy, and then a winged creature floating upon the air and feeding upon flowers; one life, yet possessing from the first the potency of two forms. The Greeks early saw it, and adopted it into their philosophy and literature, using it, however, better than we do. For, misled by false notions of a carnal resurrection, we have argued back upon the analogy and treated it as though the substance of the caterpillar were transmitted into the substance of the butterfly, which is not scientific truth. But the Greeks regarded it as both a body and a soul, not a soul made out of a body.

The entire significance and value of the doctrine of the resurrection from the dead, centre in the fact that it sets forth human identity. There are two general types of thought in regard to the nature of man. One asserts that he is a person; the other that he is an essential part of nature. All special theorizing ranges itself under one of these types. Pantheism asserts that man is merely phenomenal, and at death sinks back into the general whole. Christianity asserts that man is an immortal person. It is the antagonism of these two systems that led St. Paul and the Fathers to lay such emphasis upon the resurrection. The latter, hard pressed by Pantheism in defending identity, did not carefully or correctly define in what identity consists, and so pushed on to the extreme of asserting a resurrection of the flesh. It remains for modern thinking to clear away the slight rubbish left by them about the foundations of the great truth, and make it consonant with revelation and science. Pantheism says that man is a part of nature; Christianity says that man is made in God's image, — a person and forever to be a person, or that he has an enduring identity. The resurrection is mainly the assertion that this identity continues after death in opposition to Pantheism, which claims that man is resolved into the elements. Any theory that preserves full identity is sufficient to meet the demands of faith, for this is the main point that the doctrine is designed to teach.

The question now rises: In what does identity consist?

Identity does not lie in matter, nor is it dependent upon matter. If it does, then matter and the will are the same; then mind is as phenomenal as matter and is under the same laws. Hence fatalism; hence pantheism; evil is good and good is evil. By a fiction of language, however, we apply identity to material things. It is on the assumption that this is a true use of the word, that the puzzles of the metaphysicians are constructed as to the sameness of a thing with changing elements; as a knife whose parts are lost and replaced successively, till no single part of the original remains. Is it the same knife? If the lost parts are found and reunited, is that the same knife? Did the original knife lose its identity; and if so, when? These insolvable puzzles show the logical impropriety of applying the word *identity* to matter. Matter has no real identity. Matter is one; it is in perpetual flux. The mist rising from the river is a visible illustration of an invisible, universal process. The lichens upon our granite hills are transforming rock into gas and soil as really as the sun is changing the river into mist. Neither rock, nor lichens, nor the gas and dust into which they change have identity. The only identity we can apply to matter is that of appearance. We say the river is the same, but it is the sameness of appearance only, it changes every moment. A ray of light, a column of smoke, a flame of fire, — these are the same only in the sense that they offer the same appearance. The hunter leaves his cabin in the morning, and before he enters the forest, turns and sees the blue column of smoke ascending from his hearth. He returns at evening and sees the same column of smoke, but in reality it is another column in the same place. I go back at times to the spot where years ago I used to watch the coming and going of the ships, and I say to the dear friend who watches them still from that place of matchless beauty, "There are the same white sails we used to see twenty years ago." But they are not even the same ships; there is simply the same appearance and impression.

Now what is the identity of the human body? Have we anything different when we come to the "human form divine?" There is one ever-acting enemy of material identity — oxygen — unceasing combustion. No material thing remains the same for the millionth part of a second. We see this transformation in flame; we do not see it in flesh, but the flesh is burning as really as the wood. If it burns too fast there is fever and death; if it burns too slowly there is also death. The chemists tell us that we are ablaze to the tips of our fingers. Food is the fuel, and the fire runs along the veins as flues, burning up certain particles that are replaced by others. This process makes up physical life. Stop it, that is, establish positive identity, and death speedily follows. Thus material identity, instead of being a factor of life is a factor of death. It is on the wrong side of the question for those who would connect it with the living fact of the resurrection.

Such facts as these show us the difficulty of connecting identity with the material body, and of supposing that it enters, in any way, into the fact of the resurrection.[1]

The ancients, having no science to instruct them, regarded the body as always the same and imperishable. Hence the Egyptians embalmed their dead and hid them within mountains of stone; hence the Jews buried within caves and rock-hewn sepulchres, sealing the entrance with stones, looking for a physical resurrection. But the knowledge of oxygen puts another face upon the matter, and we must not forget that God made oxygen and ordained its function. We do not set science against the Bible, but we may use science as an aid in interpreting it.

We now answer our question positively. Its negative side shows us that personal identity cannot lie in matter; then it must lie outside of matter.

What is the living creature *man?* He is not the matter that makes up the perpetual flux known as

---

[1] If there is any organized matter of which identity can be predicated, it must be a form that is beyond the known laws of matter, — some refinement of it too delicate and ethereal to admit of disorganization. This is indeed supposable, and seems to some to be called for in order to explain the connection between mind and matter, but we have not, as yet, any grounds for accepting it; nor even thus could the gulf between the external world and consciousness be bridged. It offers, however, an interesting field for the united studies of the metaphysician, the physiologist, and the chemist. The acceptance of an interstellar ether as a simple logical inference from the nature of light, affords a hint that there may be discoveries of even another kind of matter.

the human frame; he is nothing that the chemist can put test to. He must be something, not material, that endures, upon which the shifting phenomena of animal life play themselves off. We may not be able to say what it is, or to get a clear conception of it; but we know there is *something* that sustains the fleshly existence. Call it an organization, a dynamic essence, a substance, that which *stands under* the phenomena of life; call it, as does St. Paul, a spiritual body; any name answers so long as we recognize the thing. It may be well to regard the Scriptural distinction of *body*, *soul*, and *spirit* as organic and not rhetorical, and to think of man as a threefold being: a physical body, a human soul, and a living spirit. It is at least a convenient distinction, and so using it, we claim that identity resides in the two last as making up human nature, and in no sense in the first. Thus we do not come to the man, the unchanging person, till we get outside of matter. There, beyond the reach of the chemist and his tests, in the immaterial soul and spirit, in the underlying organization, in the living type, it matters not what we call it, lies the proper identity of man. No addition or withdrawal of matter can increase or lessen this identity. He is as perfectly *man* without as with flesh. And for aught we know, his mental and spiritual operations might go on without the physical system, though not without some sort of a body. If separated, the soul would quickly have another body suitable to its place and needs, for the soul is the builder of man; as Spenser says: —

"For of the soul the body form doth take,
For soul is form, and doth the body make."

Now as identity is the central *idea* of the resurrection, what is the *fact* of the resurrection? Taught by so many ages of traditional belief, it is not easy to rid ourselves of the thought that it is in some way connected with the physical body, that something goes into the grave that is to come out. It is interesting to recall how clear a conception Socrates had on this matter. "In what way would you have us bury you?" said Crito to him. "In any way that you like; only you must get hold of me, and take care that I do not walk away from you." Then turning to those about him, with a smile, he continued: "I cannot make Crito believe that I am the same Socrates who have been talking and conducting the argument; he fancies that I am the other Socrates whom he will soon see a dead body, and asks, How shall he bury me? And though I have spoken many words in the endeavor to show that when I have drunk the poison I shall leave you to go to the joys of the blessed, these words of mine with which I comforted you and myself, have had, as I perceive, no effect upon Crito. I would not have him say at the burial — Thus we lay out Socrates, or, thus we follow him to the grave; for false words are not only evil in themselves, but they infect the soul with evil. Be of good cheer then, my dear Crito, and say that you are burying my body only, and do with that as you think best."

Our thinking on this point will correct itself if

we keep in mind that the body is not the man, and that it is the man who is raised up. He goes into the other world simply unclothed of flesh, there to take on an environing body suited to his new conditions. As here we have a body adapted to gravitation and time and space, coördinated to physical law, a body with cycles of time — day and night, months and years, wrought into it, — a body that feeds upon organized matter, that responds to heat and cold, and is simply a pathway of nerves between the mind and the external world, so doubtless it will be hereafter; the spirit will build about itself a body such as its new conditions demand.

This change necessarily takes place at death. A disembodied state, or a state of torpid existence between death and some far-off day of resurrection, an under-world where the soul waits for the reanimation of its body; these are old-world notions that survive only through chance contact with the Christian system. Christ did not teach them; his ascension was an illustrative denial of them. He found such beliefs existing as a part of the religion of the day, and did not contradict them in set terms, but taught higher truth in regard to the subject, and left them to fall by their own weight. This higher truth was the announcement of Himself as the Resurrection and the Life. This simple phrase, *when thoroughly understood*, is the repudiation of all these ghostly theories that overhung the ancient world, and have floated down into the Christian ages. It takes the element of far futurity out of the resurrection, and dissipates the shadows of the under-world, by putting life in place of death.

We will glance at some of the texts bearing on the subject. The Sadducees propose a question that implies the resurrection of the flesh at the last day, a doctrine of their rivals, the Pharisees, and fairly stated. Christ's answer is directed mainly to the dogma, not to either sect. Its central idea is that because the Patriarchs are alive, they have been raised up. "But that the dead are raised, even Moses showed; He is not the God of the dead, but of the living; for all live unto Him." Their resurrection is the pivot upon which their present life turns. If Christ's words do not mean this, we must despair of language as a vehicle of thought.

His words at the tomb of Lazarus are equally plain, and are of the same tenor. Martha states the doctrine of a resurrection at the last day; Christ sets it aside as a cold, comfortless superstition, and announced faith in Himself as covering the whole matter. The plainest feature of this narrative is the *contrast* Christ makes between Martha's words and his own; if one was right the other was wrong.

The words of Christ to the penitent thief, "To-day thou shalt be with me in Paradise," imply a life of conscious fellowship beyond, and because it was such, having all the elements of a perfect condition.

There are indeed words of Christ that seem to imply a resurrection from the grave, as, "The hour cometh in which all that are in the tombs shall hear his voice." If we read these words literally we must believe that the entire man, body and soul, is in the grave, which is more than can be claimed by any. The very absurdity drives us to another conception, — that of Christ's assertion of his power over both worlds, the living and the dead.

Again Christ said repeatedly: "I will raise him up at the last day," but we must not read these words as an endorsement of a far-off resurrection but rather as a pledge of help to the end, and of final victory. He adopted a current phrase because any other would have diverted the mind from the main thought.

Christ's own resurrection yields a proof of the immediate resurrection of all. He was the Son of Man, and as He fulfilled all the righteousness of humanity, so He illustrated the life of humanity. He lived and died as a man, He rose and ascended into heaven as a man. Why should we assert a part of this and not the whole? Why die as a man, but rise as God? We have no authority for drawing such a line of demarcation between these two phases of his career. Instead, the whole significance of his relation to humanity demands that no such line shall be drawn. He would not be the Son of man, nor the Saviour of mankind, if his resurrection had been immediate, and mankind's were to be delayed for ages. To every believer who closes his eyes in death trusting in Him, He says "*To-day thou shalt be with me.*"

We cannot enter upon a full examination of St. Paul's great chapter on the subject, but will only say, read it, with the points already discussed in view, and you will find verse after verse ranging itself naturally under them. "Flesh and blood cannot inherit the kingdom of God, neither doth corruption inherit incorruption." "If there is a natural body, there is also a spiritual body," — one succeeding the other. We have borne the image of the earthly, we shall bear the image of the heavenly; but there is no hint that countless ages intervene between them. The whole drift of the triumphant words is towards an immediate exchange of one image for the other. There are words in this chapter that are hard to understand. It is not easy to get a clear conception of what St. Paul means when he says: "We shall not all sleep, but we shall all be changed." There is often an element of futurity in his references to the resurrection seemingly at variance with other references. But St. Paul used all his great words — faith, justification, death, resurrection — in different senses. Thus he says: "If ye then be risen with Christ," — meaning a spiritual resurrection already accomplished. But the great fifteenth chapter is aimed directly at those who held this view of it; the difference being that St. Paul held both views, and his opponents but one. Doubtless in some sense the resurrection will be future and far off, and perhaps simultaneous for all, but it will not be the resurrection from the dead. The death of man, and his assumption of a spiritual body, is not the whole of the resurrection. It stands for "the finished condition of humanity," and its final presentation to God as the work of Christ. "What mysteries lie beyond the mark" of death we know not. St. Paul may have had glimpses that he could not wholly express. But when he said that he was willing to be absent from the body and to be present with the Lord; and that he desired to depart and to be with Christ, he had no thought of a resurrection that would put a moment between the death of his body and his presence with the Lord.

And this may be our faith. Having life in its abundance, there is no break in its current at death; there is no waste of even endless ages. If joined to the divine Life, every change must be to more life. If one with Christ, how can it be that we shall not share his destiny, and go from world to world in his company? Because we are one with the Life, death has no more any dominion over us. With such hopes let us await our time of departure. With such hopes let us lay our dead in the grave, — not dead, not here, for they are risen.

THE METHOD OF PENALTY.

> "But in these cases,
> We still have judgment here; that we but teach
> Bloody instructions, which, being taught, return
> To plague the inventor; this even-handed justice
> Commends the ingredients of our poison'd chalice
> To our own lips."
> *Macbeth*, I. 7.

"You reap what you sow — not something else — but that. An act of love makes the soul more loving. A deed of humbleness deepens humbleness. The thing reaped is the very thing sown multiplied a hundred-fold. You have sown a seed of life — you reap life." — ROBERTSON'S *Sermons*, Vol. I., No. XIV.

"Oh! that my lot may lead me in the path of holy innocence of word and deed, the path which august laws ordain, laws that in the highest empyrean had their birth, of which heaven is the father alone, neither did the race of mortal man beget them, nor shall oblivion ever put them to sleep. The power of God is mighty in them, and groweth not old." — SOPHOCLES, *Œd. Tyr.*

THE METHOD OF PENALTY.

"Some men's sins are evident, going before unto judgment; and some men also they follow after." — 1 Timothy v. 24.

I do not claim to be wholly correct in my use of these much-disputed words, when I connect them with God's judgment of sin. I presume they simply mean that some men's characters are open, and anticipate the verdict of more thorough knowledge; others are more reticent, and become known only after a longer trial of them. They are simply an injunction of carefulness, made by St. Paul to Timothy, in regard to ordination; as though he had said, "Be careful whom you ordain; some men are transparent, easily understood; others reveal themselves more slowly." They are the words of age and wisdom addressed to youth and inexperience, with perhaps some special vindication in the not over-robust nature of Timothy.

Still they contain the principle I wish to bring out, namely, men's sins manifest themselves variously as to time, some reaping their penalty soon, others late; some in this world, others in the next world. I am certainly within the spirit of the text when I say that some sins anticipate judgment; they invoke it, and receive its sentence, and experience its penalty, apparently before the time; they run their course quickly, and incur their doom in this life. There are other sins that meet with little check; they are slow to overtake their consequences; they come upon little in this life that can be called penalty. Speaking from daily observation, we may say that the retribution of some sins begins in this world; while there are other sins that await their punishment in the next world.

I am well aware of a distinction often made by which the consequences of sin are divided into chastisement and penalty; one being reformatory, and having the good of the sufferer in view; the other penal, and looking towards governmental ends. But the distinction is confusing to practical thought; we cannot be sure that it is true; and if it were, who shall draw the line of demarcation? I prefer, for practical purposes, to regard both elements as present in all penalty, to see in it always a reformatory design, and also a purpose to vindicate the law, — two inseparable things, however.

Both elements are present in every actual case of natural penalty. No man suffers the painful consequences of vice without knowing that the pain calls for reformation, and also that it is a vindication of the excellence of the law. Why should we discriminate between what God has so closely united? Neither in nature nor in the Scriptures do we find a warrant for drawing a line through the consequences of sin, and saying, "This is disciplinary, and that is penal." The suffering involved in sin utters but one voice, but it utters it in various notes, and with an undertone. It first sounds a

THE METHOD OF PENALTY. 319

note of warning: "Do not sin; you will suffer if you do." When sin is committed it says: "Do not sin again." And if the sin is repeated, and settles down into a habit, it says: "You will suffer so long as you sin." At the same time there may be heard the deep under-tone of conscience declaring the punishment to be just. This is all that penalty says to the sinner; that sin begets suffering; and that the suffering is divinely just; and it says the latter in order to make the lesson of the former effective. When a man suffers in consequence of sin, and, at the same time, sees it to be just, connecting it of course with the Maker of the law, he is feeling the two strongest motives adverse to sin that are possible to his nature. Penalty says this first and last and always; and it never says anything else. What authority have we for intruding upon this profound operation of God's law with our arbitrary distinction, saying: "Up to this point the suffering is chastisement, but beyond it is hopeless penalty.; hitherto it is for man's good; henceforth it is for the glory of God and the maintenance of his government." I protest against this distinction, because it is practically mischievous and weakening in the everyday experience of men. I would not have one think, when he is feeling the painful consequences of sin, that he is simply undergoing chastisement with a view to the correction of his fault, but I would have him also feel that he is enduring the wrath of God against sin. In other words, I would not withhold the grandest element of penalty from any stage of its action, but would secure the action of its entire meaning upon the earliest as well as the latest phase of sin. The natural conscience makes no such distinction. As the body withers under the pain engendered by its sin, the conscience confesses that it is undergoing the just punishment of God. To thrust the distinction between chastisement and punishment into this indivisible experience, is to weaken and undo its saving work.

It is never well to make distinctions in moral operations that are not plainly indicated in those operations. Human ingenuity may not only make this distinction in regard to penalty, but many more; they are possible to thought; but if you would have the penalty of sin effective, do not lay the finger of analysis upon it; let it stand in the singleness of its awful grandeur, warning the sinner and showing forth the wrath of God upon sin. It would augment public virtue if men were taught that the painful consequences of their sins and crimes are even now the veritable judgments of God; if already they could be made to feel that the pains that have hold of them are the pains of hell. The Gehenna of which Christ spoke, lay just outside the walls of Jerusalem. The smoke of its never-quenched fires rose before the eyes of his audience. There, close at hand, was the pit into which their whole bodies would speedily be cast if they did not cut off their offending hands and feet, and pluck out their offending eyes. He did not say, "The pains in your offending members are simply admonitory, — merely corrective of your faults; soon you are to be punished in some other way and for another purpose." Not thus does a great moral teacher warn men of their sins. The thunderbolt of retribution is not divided into sections, according to a theological note-book; it does not flash two lights upon the guilty soul. When punishment overtakes sin, be it sooner or later, it contains its whole meaning.

There is a distinction, however, as to the time in which the consequences of sin assert themselves as punishment; a distinction simply of sooner or later, here or hereafter, based upon the kind of sin.

We shall best come to an understanding of this truth by looking a little into the method of retribution.

It is, as its definition implies, a return of disobedience, or payment, when, in due time, it returns again. It is the natural and inevitable consequence of broken law. If we seek for an explanation of this law, we find none, except that it is so. We perceive its fitness and beneficence, but farther back we cannot go. The law is wrought into our moral nature, and also into our consciousness; certainly, it commands early and universal assent.

We notice also that the penalty is akin to the sin; it is under the seed-law, — like yielding like. The elements of one pass on into the other, merely changing their form and relation to the man, like the little book of the Apocalypse, sweet in the mouth but bitter in the belly. We pay out sin; it is repaid as penalty, — the same metal coined with a new inscription, or molten to flow a burning stream through all our bones. We receive back the things we have done, changed only as mist is changed to water, and heat to flame. The law of cause and effect, a necessary relation, the most generally recognized principle known to the human mind, covers the whole matter. And the effect often bears so absolute resemblance to the cause as to arrest the imagination, and is called poetic justice; the murderer drinking the poison he had prepared for another.

In human government it is not so, but only because of its imperfection. When we reason from the human to the divine government, and infer that God governs as man does, we reason from imperfection to perfection; we infer from the sick what the well man will do; from the ignorant what the wise will think, — a species of logic it is time to have done with. If there is any special feature of the divine government, it is that it is not like any human government yet set in operation. The latter cannot use the seed-principle, the law of cause and effect, except in a limited degree, because it has not the creating of its subjects. It is an increated principle, and cannot be superinduced to any great extent. When a man steals, all that human law has yet learned to do is to imprison, or otherwise injure him, inflicting an arbitrary, deterrent suffering. Society merely defends itself. It is seldom skillful enough to establish a *natural* relation between the crime and the penalty.

But that part of human society which is not organized into government, the social relationship of men, is more skillful to connect evil with its natural punishment. If one sins against the conventional laws, or moral instincts, of society, he meets with exclusion or disgrace according to the nature of the offense. Treachery is punished with scorn; cowardice with its own branding name of contempt; a liar by the loss of trust; pride fails at last of sympathy; selfishness reaps its own isolation. Dante, with finest perception, illustrates the principle by placing upon the heads of hypocrites crowns of lead, thus forcing them to look where before they had looked in mock humility. Society, because it is a spontaneous relation, thus attains somewhat to the divine method; but only in God's moral kingdom do we find the principle perfectly observed. Planned for self-regulation, and in analogy with the laws of growth, it hides the fruit of punishment within the seed of disobedience. There is no arbitrary and artificial arrangement of prisons, and stripes, and fiery chains; but whatever there is of these is the inevitable outgrowth of sin.

There is a most significant recognition of this principle underlying all of Christ's references to the subject. In no case does He touch the matter of penalty, but He recognizes it as flowing naturally out of sin. The unforgiving debtor goes himself to prison; the sleeping virgins find a closed door; the guest without a wedding garment is excluded from the feast; they who make excuse, go without; the prodigal comes to want; the slothful servant loses that which he had; they who will not minister to humanity are sent away from the presence of the Son of Man, who is the head of humanity; they who will not cut off offending members must suffer the corruption of their whole body, and be cast into the Gehenna whose flame is evermore burning up corruption; Dives, living in selfish ease, and giving the hungry Lazarus but the crumbs that fell from his table, comes at last into torment, and thirsts for one cooling drop of water; for selfish ease works surely towards tormenting want.

Cause and effect; natural order; congruity between the sin and its penalty; — these are the unfailing marks that the great teacher put upon the subject. What wisdom, what truth, what justice, is the voice of universal reason and conscience.

It is the weakness of human government that it does not employ this principle in the punishment of crime, so far as it might. It was a doubtful policy that abolished the whipping-post and pillory. If a brutal husband whips his wife at home, he can have no better punishment than a whipping in public; or, if this be corrupting to the people, then in private. No punishment is so effective as that which makes a man feel in himself what he inflicts upon another. And if men who in secret do shameful deeds, who follow shameful callings behind screened doors and windows, could be exposed in humiliating ways to public contempt, they would not only be justly but effectively punished. For many shameful occupations need only to have the stamp of shame put upon them, to be driven out of existence. If the keepers of brothels were to be exposed to public view at noonday, with appropriate inscriptions above their heads, their business and numbers might shrink within an endurable compass.

If these suggestions be thought to imply a retrograding civilization, let me answer, they harmonize with the divine order. This is exactly what God does with offenders; it is his way of punishing, and so of preventing sin, bringing hidden things to light, giving back to men what they have done whether it be good or evil. It were wise to be slow in pronouncing barbarous a principle and method so plainly a part of God's eternal order.

Christ did not reject this law, technically known as the *Lex talionis*, when He said: "Ye have heard that it hath been said, an eye for an eye, and a tooth for a tooth; but I say unto you, resist not him that is evil." He merely took away from it the element of revenge. The Scribes had lost sight of the rule as a principle of judicial action, and made it one of retaliation. As such He condemned it, but He left the principle intact, and used it over and over in his moral teachings. It is a part of that older law which He said was to be fulfilled to the uttermost, — not however as a spirit of revenge, the "wild justice" of the savage, — but of that even-handed justice which Plato declares to be the very essence of the state.

There is but one sound, effective method of punishing wrong-doing, and that is to make the offender feel the evil he has inflicted. God has wrought it into the nature of man, and the order of the universe. We have no intimation in the Scriptures or in nature that sin is punished in any other way. And it is altogether probable that God's ways are sufficient for their ends. Let us not then go about to concoct other schemes of penalty, and thrust them into God's plans, because they correspond to our systems. It is one thing to reason from nature up to God, but quite another to reason from human institutions that are full of human imperfection.

This divine method of punishment does not exclude from it a sense of the feelings of the Lawgiver. This, too, is bound up in a natural way with the sin. Hence it is not necessary to make a distinction between punishment and penalty, on the ground that one expresses the feeling of a personal Lawgiver, while the other is the natural consequence of sin. This distinction is the fruit of a mechanical, extra-mundane conception of God; it is not necessary in order to secure the presence of such personal feeling. A proper conception of God as immanent in the order of nature avoids the necessity of the distinction; the operations of nature are expressions of God's personal feelings. When a man breaks a law of God, a sense of the wrath of God at once asserts itself, if the conscience is natural; if it is hardened, it slumbers, but sooner or later it awakes. The painters set forth a universal truth when they depict Cain as fleeing from the dead body of Abel with downcast head; there was an eye above whose glance he felt, but could not face. And thus the wrath of God against sin is wrought into the very automatism of the body.

We do not know that there is any other way in which God can lay hold of a sinner to punish him. I do not mean that God is limited in Himself, but in the offender. The pain must reflect the sin, or the sinner is not punished; he will not feel the justice of the punishment, or get to hate the sin, until he has tasted its bitterness, and felt its discord as an agony in his own soul. God sustains all relations through law; even love and grace are by law — the law of love and grace. There is even a "law of liberty." But the special feature of the sinner's relation to God is a relation of law, — *broken* law, and his punishment consists in the fact that he is shut up with it. And out of the fragments of broken law rise barriers, built by nature, that shut the sinner away from everything but the broken law: away from God, away from all true fellowship with men, away from himself, till at last he finds himself in the outer darkness of utter disorder, a prison whose bolts will never draw back unless Eternal Love without hears the voice of penitence within.

As we thus look at retribution in the mingled light of revelation and reason, we are prepared to understand why it is that some sins are punished in this world, while other sins await punishment in a future world.

If we were to classify the sins that reap their painful consequences here, and those that do not, we would find that the former are offenses that pertain to the body, and the order of this world; and that the latter pertain more directly to the spiritual nature. The classification is not sharp; the parts shade into one another; but it is as accurate as is the distinction between the two departments of our nature. In his physical and social nature man was made under the laws of this world. If he breaks these laws, the penalty is inflicted here. It may continue hereafter, for the grave feature of penalty is that it does not tend to end, but continues to act, like force imparted to an object in a vacuum, until arrested by some outside power. But man is also under spiritual laws, — reverence, humility, love, self-denial, purity, and all that are commonly known as moral duties. If he offends against these, he may incur but little of painful consequence. There may be much of *evil* consequence, but the phase of suffering lies farther on. The soil and atmosphere of this world are not adapted to bring it to full fruitage.

Stating our distinction again: punishment in this world follows the sins of the grosser part of our nature, — that part which more specially belongs to this world, — sins against the order of nature, against the body; sins of self-indulgence and sins against society. The punishment that awaits the next world is of sins pertaining to the higher nature, sins against the mind, the affections, and the spirit. The seed of evil sown in the soil of this world comes to judgment here. The seed of evil sown in the hidden places of the spirit, does not bear full fruit till the spiritual world is reached. Man is coördinated to two worlds. They overlap and reach far into one another; the spiritual inter-penetrates the physical; and the physical sends unceasing influences into the spiritual. Still, each is a field whereon evil reaps its appropriate harvest.

Illustrations of the first confront us on every side; judgment pronounced and executed here; sin punished here. Take the commonest but most instructive example — drunkenness. As soon as desire becomes stronger than the will, it begins to act retributively. When appetite dictates to the moral nature, the man's feet touch the threshold of hell. The shame, the conscious weakness, the unsatisfied desire rising at last to torment, — what are these but the pains of hell? But the full cycle of sin and penalty is not completed except in his body. Bloated and distorted in countenance, senses benumbed, powers enfeebled, blood fevered, nerves tremulous as the aspen, haunted by visions, consumed by inward fires; but every pain, every thrill of weakened nerves, every enfeebled sense, each tottering step of the debased flesh towards the dust, is the proper penalty of this kind of sin. Having sown to the flesh, he reaps of the flesh corruption. His sin works out its penalty on its own ground. I do not say that it ends here, because it is also linked with an order more enduring than this world. For, as one standing over against a mountain may fill the whole valley with the clamor of shouting, but hears at length an echo as if from another world, so these sins, having yielded their first fruits here, may stir up vaster penalties hereafter. The terrible feature of penalty, so far as any light is thrown upon it from its own nature, is that it cannot anticipate an end. It is a cause, and cause always works. It is seed, and the law of seed is endless growth. Penalty, by its own nature, must go on forever unless it meets a stronger opposing power.

The subject finds various illustration: indolence eating the scant bread of poverty; willful youthhood begetting a fretful and sour old age; selfishness leading to isolation; ambition overreaching itself and falling into contempt; ignorance yielding endless mistake; worldly content turning first into apathy, then into disgust; these every-day facts show that if we sin against the order of this world, we are punished in this world. If we sin against the body we are punished in the body. If we break the laws of human society, it has immediate and appropriate penalties. Each after its own kind, and in its own time, is the universal law.

We turn now to the other point, namely, that sins against the spiritual nature do not incur full punishment here, but await it in the spiritual world.

We constantly see men going through life with little pain or misfortune, perhaps with less than the ordinary share of human suffering, yet we term them sinners. They do not love nor fear God; they have no true love for man; they reject the law of self-denial and the duty of ministration; they stand off from any direct relations to God; they do not pray; their motives are selfish; their temper is worldly; they are devoid of what are called *graces* except as mere germs or chance outgrowths, and make no recognition of them as forming the substance of true character. Such men break the laws of God, and of their own nature, as really as does the drunkard, but they meet with little apparent punishment. There may be inward discomfort, pangs of conscience at times, a painful sense of wrongness, a dim sense of lack, but nothing that bears the stamp of penalty. These discomforts grow less, and at last leave the man quite at ease. The petty and inevitable troubles of life are not the punishments of such sin; they do not awaken a conviction that they proceed from sin. But the drunkard, the sluggard, the voluptuary, know that their sufferings are the penalties of their sins. These men seem to be sinning without punishment, and often infer that they do not deserve it. The reason of the difference is plain. They keep the laws that pertain to this world, and so do not come in the way of their penalties. They are temperate, and are blessed with health. They are shrewd and economical, and amass wealth. They are prudent and avoid calamities. They are worldly wise, and thus secure worldly advantages. Courteous in manners, understanding well the intricacies of life, careful in device and action, they secure the good and avoid the evil of the world. If there were no other world, they would be the wisest men, because they best obey the laws of their condition. But man covers two worlds, and he must settle with each before his destiny is decided: he may pass the judgment seat of one acquitted, but stand convicted before the other. It is as truly a law of our nature that we shall worship as that we shall eat. If one starves his body he reaps the fruit of emaciation and disease. But one may starve his soul and none remark it. This world is not the background upon which such processes appear, or they appear but dimly; but when the spiritual world is reached, this spiritual crime will show itself.

When, a half century ago, the famous Kaspar Hauser appeared in the streets of Nuremberg, having been released from a dungeon in which he had been confined from infancy, having never seen the face or heard the voice of man, nor gone without the walls of his prison, nor seen the full light of day, a distinguished lawyer in Germany wrote a legal history of the case which he entitled, "A Crime against the Life of the Soul." It was well named. There is something unspeakably horrible in that mysterious page of history. To exclude a child not only from the light, but from its kind; to seal up the avenues of knowledge that are open to the most degraded savage; to force back upon itself every outgoing of the nature till the poor victim becomes a mockery before its Creator, is an unmeasurable crime; it is an attempt to undo God's work. But it is no worse than the treatment some men bestow upon their own souls. If reverence is repressed, and the eternal heavens are walled out from view; if the sense of immortality is smothered; if the spirit is not taught to clothe itself in spiritual garments, and to walk in spiritual ways:

such conduct can hardly be classed except as a crime against the life of the soul.

But one thing is certain. As the poor German youth was at length thrust out into the world for which he was so unfitted, with untrained senses in a world of sense, without speech in a world of language, with a dormant mind in a world of thought, — so many go out of this world, — with no preparation in that part of their nature that will most be called into use. There the soul will be in its own realm; it will live unto itself, a spirit unto spiritual things. What darkness, what confusion, what bewilderment, what harrowing perplexity must the unspiritual soul feel when it enters the spiritual world! A spiritual air to breathe; spiritual works to do; a spiritual life to live, but the spirit impotent! If there has been absolute perversion of the moral nature here, it must assert itself there in the sharpest forms, but the natural penalty of the greater part of human sin is darkness. For the greater part of sin consists in withholding from the soul what it needs; in low contentedness with this world, in refusing to look into the heavens that insphere us. This is the condemnation, that men have loved darkness. And the penalty of loving darkness, is *darkness*: a soul out of keeping with its condition, and therefore bewildered, dazzled by light it cannot endure, or blind from the disused sense, it matters not which; it is equally in darkness. A true life in this world is indeed the best preparation for the world to come; but it must not be forgotten that the chief duties in this world are spiritual, and that spiritual heavens overarch this world as well as the next.

I hope this discourse will awaken within us a living sense of the certainty of the punishment of sins here and hereafter. It is not strange that the world of thinking men reject it when it is taught as some far off, arbitrary, outside infliction by God in vindication of his government, the issue of some special sentence after special inquisition. This is unlike God, it has no analogy, no vindication in the Scriptures; it is artificial, coarse, unreasonable. It is just now the special scoff of the world, but the scoff is the echo of unreasoning words reiterated till the world was weary of them. Carry the subject over into the field of cause and effect and we find it irradiated by the double light of reason and revelation. It takes on a necessary aspect. Penalty is seen to be a natural thing, like the growing of seed. It is not a matter that God, in his sovereignty, will take up after a time, but is a part of his ever-acting law.

The question of penalty is not to be settled by yea or nay count; it cannot be set aside by a sneer of fine oratory; nor is it the pliant tool of system-building theology on either side; it is not a question to be settled with men, nor with revelation only, but with the order of nature, with the soul under law, with God as the author of nature and the framer of law. The pain that now attends disobedience is a proof and pledge that all broken law will reap its appropriate pain: each offense after its kind, and in its own time. It is not a matter of text or decree, but of *law* which is also text and decree, even all texts and all decrees.

Does any one, turning aside from the certainty and fitness of future punishment, ask how long, or how brief, are God's penalties? — questions needless under the principles laid down. How long? So long as sin reaps its consequences. How brief? Not till the uttermost farthing of defrauded order and wronged justice is paid back to the ordainer of order and justice; not till the darkness-loving eyes open to the light, and the self-centered affections turn to God. Will this happen "at last — far off — at last, to all?" The answer is hidden in the mystery of personality. The logic of the gospel is salvation, and the secret of the universe is joy; "so runs my dream;" so we read with our finite eyes, but these same eyes discern also a shadow they cannot pierce.

The worthier question is, How shall I avoid the sin? Or, having sinned, how shall I be rid of it? How shall I turn back its stream of fatal tendency, which, if not checked by some all-powerful hand, must flow on, so far as the sinner can see, forever?

THE JUDGMENT.

"When the future life begins, every man will see Christ as He is, and the sight of Him may of itself bring a finality to his character and destiny, as it discovers each man fully to himself." — PRESIDENT PORTER, *New-Englander*, 1878.

"It only requires a different and apportioned organization — the body celestial instead of the body terrestrial — to bring before every human soul the collective experience of his whole past experience. And this, — this, perchance, is the dread Book of Judgment, in whose mysterious hieroglyphics every idle word is recorded. Yea, in the very nature of a living spirit it may be more possible that heaven and earth should pass away, than that a single act, a single thought, should be loosened or lost from that living chain of causes, to all whose links, conscious or unconscious, the free will, our absolute self, is coextensive and co-present." — COLERIDGE.

"We are to think of the Judgment not as an *event*, limited to a specific 'day,' but as a *process*, which runs its course throughout the whole existence of the responsible subjects of law." — WHITON, *Gospel of the Resurrection*, page 144.

"Death, if I am right, is, in the first place, the separation from one another of two things, soul and body, nothing else. And after they are separated they retain their several characteristics, which are much the same as in life. . . . When a man is stripped of his body, all the natural and acquired affections of the soul are laid open to view." — PLATO, *Georgias*.

THE JUDGMENT.[1]

"And I saw the dead, the small and the great, standing before the throne; and the books were opened; and another book was opened, which is the book of life; and the dead were judged out of those things which were written in the books, according to their works." — REVELATION xx. 12.

It is related of Daniel Webster, the regality of whose moral endowment no one disputes, that when once asked what was the greatest thought that had ever occupied his mind, he replied, "The fact of my personal accountability to God."

A common definition of man is that he is an accountable being. The epithet carries a world of meaning. It differentiates man from the rest of creation. Consciously accountable for conduct, —

[1] It is not within the proper scope of a sermon to treat this subject with that close criticism it is now receiving from theological scholars; for this I refer my readers to such works as Dr. Mulford's *Republic of God*, and Dr. Whiton's *Gospel of the Resurrection*, — two notable additions of the day to theology. While I fully accept their teaching that Judgment is a constantly recurring crisis, I also recognize the fact that it has an objective basis in the changes that attend man's personal history. Thus, a change of worlds is followed by judgment, — the change evokes judgment; thus, "it is appointed unto men once to die, and after this cometh judgment." But the Scriptures do not indicate that this judgment involves finality as distinguished from previous judgments; it *may* involve it, but not necessarily, and only as successive judgments or crises point towards finality. Finality is to be found in character, and not in judgment, except as a crisis tends to develop and fix character. The true substance of judgment is to be sought in subjective moral conditions, and not in external governmental arrangements.

this makes man *man*. Eliminate accountability, and he drops into the category of instinct and natural desire; if he is a savage, he becomes a beast; if he is civilized, he becomes virtually a criminal. The great leading question in government, in society, in religion, in individual life, is how to awaken and render active a sense of accountability. It is the factor that stands between freedom and law; free to obey law; an inwrought sense demanding this use of freedom.

Freedom and conscience imply accountability; accountability implies rendering account, and this implies a judgment; such is the logic that covers human life, few and simple in its links, but strong as adamant, and inexorable as fate. It underlies and binds together the twofold kingdom of time and eternity, — one chain, whether it binds things in heaven, or things on the earth.

No one of these coördinate facts is widely separated from the others. The sense of accountability is all the while acting; we are constantly rendering account; we are all the while undergoing judgment and receiving its awards.

It is the weakness of formulated theology that it arbitrarily transfers the most august and moving features of God's moral government to a future world, thus placing the wide and mysterious gulf of time and death between actions and their motives. It is an axiom in morals that the nearer motive commonly determines the conduct; hence it should be as close as possible. The wisdom of this is hinted in the speed with which suffering overtakes any infringement of the laws of existence. That which threatens to end life quickly, causes quick suffering. The moment we touch fire we are burned; the sentence of broken law is executed at once. And all broken law begins at once to incur judgment; the quick pang of conscience that follows sin is the first stroke of judgment; while undergoing it, the soul is passing a crisis, and turns to the right or the left hand of eternal righteousness.

Thus we are all the while rendering account to the laws without and within; we are all the while undergoing judgment and receiving sentence of acquittal or condemnation. It does not follow, however, that because judgment is drawn forward into this world from the next, that it is confined to this world. Great moral laws have universal sweep. As gravitation is the same here and in Sirius, and as righteousness is the same in this life and in the life to come, so the great leading operations of our moral nature are the same in all worlds and in all times. Instead of confining judgment to the future, we take it out of time-relations, and make it a fact of eternity. It is an ever on-going process. Conduct is always reaching crises and entering upon its consequences. It may be cumulative in degree, and reach crises more and more marked; it may at last reach a special crisis which shall be *the* judgment when the soul shall turn to the right or left of eternal destiny.

But while this latter phase of the great truth may well be allowed to breathe over us an august and solemn influence, it should no less be remembered that the throne of judgment is now set, and that the Judge is all the while judging men and nations in righteousness. The powers and solemnities of eternity already enfold us. There is no grandeur or awfulness of future pageant that is not now enacting, if we had eyes to see it. It is a part of our moral blindness that we do not see it. It is the fault of theology that it does not teach men, as Christ taught them, that the generations do not pass away till the divine judgments pronounced on them are fulfilled. The most imperative moral need of the age is a belief that the sanctions of God's eternal laws are now in full force and action about us, asserting their majesty and glory in the blessings and inflictions that all the while flow out of them; sure to act hereafter because they are acting now. The kingdom of heaven is at hand, complete, king and sceptre, law and sanction; its reign is begun, it commands, and judges, and rewards, and condemns. It is the recognition of this great moral fact, unseen by the world, and but half seen by theology, that is needed to put us where Christ stood, and to unfold to us the divine order as it appeared to Him. We simply misread — we fail of correct intellectual conception, — when we interpret his words upon the coming of the Son of Man, and his separating work, taking one and leaving another, as referring to some world-end event. In no one of his discourses does He declare more plainly his coming and judgment than in that on the destruction of the temple, but the generation was not to pass away before his words were to be fulfilled.

Let us not belittle this life. There is no moment of time grander than the present. The ages of eternity will usher in no day more momentous than those that are now passing; for already his fan is in his hand, and He is separating the wheat from the chaff, taking one and leaving another. Already and evermore are we passing through crises or judgments that turn us into right or left hand paths. The providential event, or the moral conviction that tests our character and gives it tendency, is a coming and judgment of the Son of Man. For judgment does not consist in assigning the reward or penalty — that is done by the laws, but in discerning between right and wrong, and separating them. It consists in making manifest, as St. Paul says: "We shall all" — not appear — but "*be made manifest* before the judgment seat of Christ." But while recognizing the need of holding to the perpetual coming of the Son of Man for judgment, thus making this life the full theatre for the action of his eternal kingdom, we also recognize the truth that judgment is a fact of the life to come.

A profound view of judgment as a test or crisis entailing separation, shows us that it attends *change;* for it is through change that the moral nature is aroused to special action. It is a law that catastrophes awaken conscience. Indeed, all great outward changes, of whatever character, appeal to the moral faculties. They are God's opportunities for getting access to the soul. It is also a peculiarity of the action of the moral nature under great outward changes, that man is disclosed to himself.

Recall the most joyful event of your lives, and you will find it to have been also a period of great self-knowledge. Recall your deepest sorrow and you will still more vividly recognize it as an experience in which there was a deep, interior measurement of yourself. Recall the chief catastrophe of your life, the loss by fire, the failure in business, and you will confess that the manner in which you bore it has become a sort of test by which you estimate your character. You got a fair look at yourself, that had much to do with your future.

If change has this revealing and judging power, the change of worlds must have it in a superlative degree. There are no moral laws and forces there that are not also here, for the kingdom of heaven is upon earth, but they may act with greater intensity because of our own changed relation to them. Another world, another body, other senses, other relations, the dimness of earth gone, the clear unrefracting light of eternity shining around us; here is a change that the Judge may well use and name as the judgment of all. It is appointed unto men once to die, and after that cometh judgment; the testing and unveiling of character and conduct. Preëminently, far beyond anything that has preceded, man is then judged and assigned his true place and direction.

I do not claim to understand and harmonize the many symbolical references to future judgment in the Bible. But any attempt to harmonize them under a conception of one general assize, one event, one day, one assembly of the vast humanity, is vain and useless; it is too incongruous, too difficult of conception to justify itself. The fact that all the Biblical references are symbolical, indicates that the bare method and procedure of judgment do not easily come within the range of human thought. Revelation wisely dresses its great moral operations in objective forms — parables, and visions, and symbols, — a drapery that we may throw aside as soon as we have eyes to see the bare and simple truth it unfolds. Thus Christ taught, first the parable, then its interpretation.

I think the central truth of the judgment can nowhere more easily be got at than in the passage before us. No other symbol than that of *books* could so vividly convey the fact that the whole life comes into judgment. Nothing is left out or forgotten; there can be no mistake. The books are the unerring transcript of the life. The simplicity of the symbol is marred by the introduction of " another book " than those recording the works. Why is there "another book which is the book of life; " and what does it mean? All exegesis of the Apocalypse is doubtful, involving as it does, facts that transcend conception. Here and there are rifts in the surging clouds of symbolism through which we seem to get some clear glimpses of " things to come," but we must not be too confident. Perhaps we are interpreting best, when we bow before the mysterious words and say, " Thou, O Lord, knowest, we do not." Still let us humbly venture a reply.

Mankind do not go up to the throne of God to be

judged simply by their works. Parallel with humanity is the Kingdom of Heaven. Parallel with men's deeds are the purposes of God. Over and above what humanity does of itself is a plan of redemption, the working out of which enters into human destiny. It may be that the other book represents that other power, and the influences that flow out of the life of Christ. It is a book of life, and He is the life of the world. Men are judged by the records of their works, but it may be that the sentence pronounced is affected by what is written in the book of life. I am aware that this complicates the thought, but we must remember that the problem of spiritual destiny is not absolutely simple. It has other elements than mere goodness and badness. It involves the divine will, a reconciliation, a work wrought upon humanity as well as by it; it has a God-ward as well as a man-ward side. Nor is it strange that a question involving such a mystery as evil should be hard to answer. With an unknowable element in the problem, who shall solve it? And when this or that is asserted about eternal destiny on either side, as though it were a matter of alphabetic plainness, we say, "Explain evil, before you assert its consequences." While the way of life is plain, so that even a little child may walk in it, it is overhung by mysteries whose shadows deepen as it leads into the future.

But we will leave this side issue and turn to the main thought: the books out of which men are judged. We say at once, "Books, records, items of conduct written down in order! how can there be such things in a spiritual world? — earthly things after the earth itself has vanished?" There can indeed be no books, but there may be something that corresponds to books; no records, items of conduct, engraved or engrossed, but there may be something that answers the purpose of records. There may be no reading of charges, or rehearsal of deeds, but there may be something that shall make everything known and evident. Where shall we look, to what shall we turn, for such a solution? I do not think we are permitted to go outside of nature and its divine laws for answer. The books must be found in God, or nature, or man. The mind of God must indeed be a tablet whereon are written all the works of men, but let us not touch that ineffable mystery without warrant. Science, in the person of some of its high priests, has suggested that all the deeds of men are conserved as distinct forces in the ether that fills the spaces of heaven, and may be brought together again in true form, in some new cosmos, as light traversing space as motion, is turned to heat when arrested by the earth. But we can find no link between such a fact, if it be a fact, and the moral process of judgment. We must search man himself for the elements of his great account.

There is more in man than we have yet compassed. He is a deep down which the plummet of science has not yet sunk. We look at ourselves, and say: "Here I am, a body with five senses; a mind that thinks and chooses; a soul that enjoys and suffers and loves and worships; a grand category of faculties, something worthy of immortality?" but we have not reached the bottom of our nature. A closer analysis, or chance revelations as in dreams or abnormal conditions, indicate faculties that slumber, or exist in germ, that may awaken, or grow into fullness. We do not yet know the capacity or reach of our most evident powers. Let a fit of anger or the delirium of disease, or some great excitement like that of battle, possess the body, and resources of physical strength are developed not common to it. Horatius holds the bridge against an army. Achilles in his wrath slays the mighty Hector. The sick, in the delirium of fever, pass from utter weakness to herculean strength; even the body is an unmeasured force.

Take the mind: at first it is merely a set of faculties, without even self-consciousness, but contact with the world brings them into action, — first observation, then memory; soon the imagination spreads its folded wings; then comes the process of comparison and combination, and thus the full process of thinking is developed, — a process to which there is no end, and the capacities of which are immeasurable. When we reach the limit of our own powers, we open the pages of some great master of thought, and there find new realms that reveal corresponding powers.

Take the soul: there are faculties that exist only in germ till certain periods of life arise. The child knows nothing of the love that breaks in upon the youth with its rapturous pain and yearning of insatiable desire, flooding the heights of his being, but the capacity was in the child. The soft touch of a babe's hand unlocks new rooms in the heart of the mother. New relations, new stages of life, disclose new powers and reveal the mysteries of our being. We are all the while finding out new agencies in nature; even its component parts are not yet all discovered, while the forces developed by combination are doubtless immeasurable in number and degree. It is a most suggestive fact that the bringing together of two or three simple substances develops that prodigious force seen in the stronger explosives. If mere combination of material things yields such results, what may new scenes and new contact not do for the soul; what new powers, what new experiences may not follow when the spirit breathes ethereal air, and the eyes look on the whiteness of God's throne! It is the specialty of man that his nature is an unsounded deep. A handful of acorns covers a mountain-side with forest, — a sufficient mystery when we think of it, — but there it ends, in simple immense reproduction. But man, being made in the image of God, is stored with endless capacities, for he has a long journey before him down the endless ages, and new powers will be needed, — fresh wings as he mounts into higher atmospheres. Such a theme must be touched reverently, but I know nothing to forbid us regarding the soul of man as a seed dropped from God's own self into this earthy soil, here to begin its endless growth back towards its source, — an end never to be attained, because limiting conditions have been assumed, but still at an ever lessening distance. What other dream can cover so well the majesty and mystery of our nature?

But we need not let our thought travel so wide from absolute knowledge in order to find a capacity that shall uphold the fact of future judgment. Take the memory, the faculty through which the consciousness of identity is preserved. With so important a function to fulfill, it is altogether probable that its action is absolute, that is, it never forgets. We cannot understand its action, but probably we speak accurately when we say that an *impression* is made upon the mind. The theory that memory is a physical act, and therefore cannot outlast death, is untenable. Matter, having no real identity, cannot uphold a sense of identity, which is the real office of memory. The impression of what we do, say, hear, see, feel, and think, is stamped upon the mind. An enduring matrix receives the impression; is it probable that it is ever lost? We think we forget, but our thought is corrected by everyday experience. The recalling of what was lost, shows that the forgotten impression remains true. The mind wearied by toil forgets at night, but remembers when sleep has refreshed the body. The *body* forgot; the *mind* retained its knowledge. How significant! If death is sleep, with what freshness will the mind resume its offices when its new morning dawns upon it! We forget the faces we have seen, but on the first fresh glimpse we remember them. We revisit scenes that long since had faded from memory, but the new sight uncovers the old impression. Even so slight a thing as a note of music, or a perfume, will bring up scenes long ago forgotten; a strain of music, and a face that had grown dim to memory, comes back from the dead in all its freshness. I never hear a certain hymn but a scene of my childhood plants itself before me with such vividness that all else fades out, and I can see nothing beside: a little country school-house dimly lighted for evening service, and a small company of neighbors and kindred assembled for prayer and praise. I have heard the symphonies of the great masters, and choruses sung by vast multitudes, but above them all I can hear the hymn that bore up the supplicating praise of that little assembly, and I doubt not I shall hear it when I hear the song of Moses and the Lamb, for it mingled with the foundations of my beginning. And who has not by chance taken in the perfume of new-mown hay, and by that subtle breath been borne back to the early home, the hill-side, the winding river, and the dear companionship of the past? It is a most significant fact that so slight a thing can thus stir and uncover the depths of memory. You are all familiar with the common fact that persons resuscitated from drowning uniformly speak of that flash of inner light by which their entire lives pass in order before them. What can this be but a prelude to what follows every death — the beginning of a revelation that only fails of completion through chance? How plainly does it suggest that nothing is forgotten, and that death unlocks the chambers of memory, revealing all the deeds done in the body. If so, it must be for a purpose; there must be some special intent in this divine ordinance by which revelation attends great change. You are also familiar with the often quoted incident, — commented on by Coleridge, — of the servant-maid of a German professor, who, while ill of fever, repeated long phrases of Greek and Hebrew, having by chance, when well, heard her master utter them aloud. How delicate the tablet that receives such impressions, how tenacious in its keeping, and yet how sure to render them up! DeQuincey, a profound observer upon the subject, says that when under the influences of opium, the most trifling incidents of his early life would pass again and again before his distempered vision, varying their form, but the same in substance. These incidents, which were originally somewhat painful, would swell into vast proportions of agony, and rise into the most appalling catastrophes. This was the action of a diseased nature, but it indicates what shape our lives may assume if viewed at last through the medium of a sin-diseased soul. The body may be a clog upon the soul, but it keeps down what is evil as well as what is good. There is no doubt but that all the nobleness and excellence of our nature will spring into full sight and action when this clog is taken off; and there is like certainty that the evil within us will stand forth in equal clearness of light. Death is simply the removal of conditions, the unveiling and making manifest of the whole man.

Not only does the memory retain conduct, but all impressions upon the soul remain imbedded within it. Nothing is lost that has once happened to it. Nature is a wonderful conserver of what takes place in its realm. Science has been showing us of late something of the force residing in the actinic rays of light, by which it transfers impressions from one object to another. Wherever light goes, it carries and leaves images. The trees mirror one another, and opposing mountains wear each the likeness of the other upon their rocky breasts. These fine properties in nature suggest corresponding probabilities in man. It is poor logic to accept these fresh miracles of nature that are being so often revealed, and hold that we have compassed man and his possibilities. If such a process as this is going on in the dull substances without, how much more surely is it going on in the soul. All contact leaves its mark. We are taking into ourselves the world about us, the society in which we move, the impress of every sympathetic contact with good or evil, and we shall carry them with us forever. We do not pass through a world for nought,—it follows us because it has become a part of us.

It may be said that these impressions are so numerous and conflicting that they can yield no distinct picture hereafter. But we must not limit the capacity of the soul in this respect, in the presence of greater mysteries. In some sense, it may present, as it were, a continually fresh surface. A most apt illustration waits upon our thought drawn from the palimpsests found in the monasteries of Italy; parchments that, centuries ago, were inscribed with the history or laws of heathen Rome, the edicts of persecuting emperors, or the annals of conquest. When the church arose, the same parchments were used again to record the legends and prayers of the saints. Later still, they were put to further use in rehearsing the speculations of the school-men, or the revival of letters, yet presenting but one written surface. But modern science has learned to uncover these overlaid writings one after another, finding upon one surface the speculations of learning, the prayers of the church, and the blasphemies of paganism. And so it may be with the tablets of the soul, written over and over again, but no writing ever effaced, they wait for the master-hand that shall uncover them to be read of all. What are these Apocalyptic books but records of our works printed upon our hearts? What are the books opened but man opened to himself?

This is a view of the judgment that men cannot scoff at. Its elements are provided; its forces are at work; it lies within the scope of every man's knowledge. It is but the whole of what we already know in part. Even now sin draws off by itself, shunning the light of day and the gaze of good men; hereafter the separation will be complete. Even now good and evil stamp their works upon the face, configuring the whole body to their likeness; there the soul will stand forth in all its actual proportions, and this standing forth is that opening of the books which goes before judgment. It is man opened to himself; opened also to the universe of intelligent beings.

As there are powers in man that render judgment possible, so there are conditions on the other side that coöperate. One cannot be judged except there be one who judges. Man is judged by man; nothing else were fit. The deflections from perfect humanity cannot be measured except by the standard of perfect humanity. Hence it is the Son of Man, the humanity of God, who judges. When man meets Him, all is plain. His perfection is the test; He furnishes the contrast that repels, or the likeness that draws. This then is judgment: man revealed by the unveiling of his life, and tested by the Son of Man.

I have striven so to present it that we shall feel its certainty. It is not an arbitrary arrangement of the future, dissociated from the laws of our nature, but it is their inevitable outworking. Its preliminary process, its foreshadowings, are part of present experience. Just in the degree in which character discloses itself, does the judgment of separation take place. Possibly there may be one here whose heart and life are vile, whose mind is the nest of evil thoughts, whose desires run unchecked into baseness; and by the side of such a one may sit another, pure in heart and life. They sit side by side, and may go hence together, may even dwell under the same roof, and break bread together, but if they were suddenly revealed to one another, soul to soul, with no veil of flesh between, one all fair and pure, the other dark and foul, they would by instinct separate and fly apart. And the judgment is this only, — a separation. There will be no need that the judge shall point to the right or the left. Each will go to his own place, is all the while going thither, by the law of his own nature.

The theme has one lesson for us all, — a lesson of preparation.

Prepare by repentance for sin, by faith in Christ, by fellowship with the Spirit.

Prepare by honest thought, by self-denial, by unending struggle after righteousness, by spiritual aspiration.

Thus prepared, the opening of the book of our life will bring no shock or shame, and the judgment will but conduct us a step nearer to that throne from which heaven and earth have fled away.

LIFE A GAIN.

"Though nothing can bring back the hour
Of splendor in the grass, of glory in the flower —
We will grieve not, rather find
Strength in what remains behind;
In the primal sympathy
Which, having been, must ever be;
In the soothing thoughts that spring
Out of human suffering;
In the faith that looks through death,
In the years that bring the philosophic mind."
WORDSWORTH, *Ode on Immortality.*

"The web of our life is of a mingled yarn, good and ill together: our virtues would be proud if our faults whipped them not; and our crimes would despair if they were not cherished by our virtues." —*All's Well That Ends Well*, iv. 3.

"Silent rushes the swift Lord
Through ruined systems still restored,
Broadsowing, bleak and void to bless,
Plants with worlds the wilderness;
Waters with tears of ancient sorrow
Apples of Eden ripe to-morrow.
House and tenant go to ground,
Lost in God, in Godhead found."
EMERSON, *Threnody.*

"Draw, Holy Ghost, Thy seven-fold veil
Between us and the fires of youth;
Breathe, Holy Ghost, Thy freshening gale,
Our fever'd brow in age to soothe."
Christian Year; Confirmation.

LIFE A GAIN.

"I came that they may have life, and may have it abundantly." — St. John, x. 10.

THERE is a strange question that has come under discussion of late, — a question symbolizing the audacity of the age and something of its lack of reverence, — namely, "Is life worth living?" The book that made it a title is nearly forgotten, but the question still enters into the speculations of the schools and into the common talk of men. It seems strange that any one should ask the question in soberness and sincerity, and as though it were debatable, until we recollect that a philosophy has won for itself recognition that has for its main thesis that life is *not* worth living because this is not only a bad world, but the worst possible world. It is not difficult to detect the genesis of this brave philosophy. So soon as one begins to doubt the goodness of God, or to suspect ever so vaguely that God is not infinitely good, one begins to doubt if life has much value. So soon as there is a suspicion that there is not an eternal goodness behind and under life, it changes color and grows cheap and poor.

It happens just now that in several directions the goodness of God, or, at least, the proofs of it are being questioned. The philosopher is still stumbling over the problem of the ages, the existence of evil, with partial but not entire relief in the doctrine of evolution; the *why* is simply carried farther back. The scientists, many of them, are saying that for their part they see no clear evidence of a creating goodness; see much indeed that looks in an opposite direction, or simple indifference to happiness. The reactions of an intense age, and the revelations of motives in a state of society in which there is no secrecy, an age strong in analysis but weak in synthesis, favor the same tendency. Suddenly, the world seems to have discovered that it suffers, and that man is selfish; it can dissect life with alarming accuracy, but it has not yet learned to put it together. When there is doubt as to the source, there will be doubt of the value of whatever flows from it. If God is not good, his greatest gift may not be good. If the infinite force does not act beneficently, no inferior force can evolve any good. If the eternal tide flows with indifference to happiness, happiness will be a matter of chance. The more impatient overleap all reasoning on either side, and ask, If man was made to be happy, why is he not happy? — not an easy question to answer nor a good one to ask. The questioner has no advantage because answer is difficult, and he has the disadvantage of being forced to answer it himself; if he is presumptuous he will attempt it; if he is wise, he will say, I have not the data, and will "trust the larger hope."

The question with which we started involves an

audacity that almost forbids its utterance. We might perhaps question a *feature* of life, but to turn face to face upon existence itself and doubt its worth, to point life with an interrogation,—thought can go no farther in audacity,—a thing not identical with courage, but rather with that folly which dares the sphinx that slays if the riddle is unsolved. If we get an answer in the negative, we cannot avoid the wish that the earth were shorn of life and swinging once more on its round, a mute, dead world, and the farther wish that creation itself were blotted out, and if creation, also the Creator. This is logical, but to sweep infinite space and eternal duration clean of matter and being, to empty and then annihilate the universe,—such audacity reaches beyond sublimity, and sinks into the ridiculous. The Puritan mother of Samuel Mills, who, when her son, under the stress of morbid religious feeling, cried out, "Oh, that I had never been born," said to him, "My son, you *are* born, and you cannot help it," was more philosophical than he who says, "I am, but I wish I were not." A philosophy that flies in the face of the existing and the inevitable, forfeits its name. And a philosophy which, having found out that life is undesirable, proposes to get rid of it,—the position of the pessimist-school, namely, to educate the race to the wisdom of universal and simultaneous suicide,—has, at least, a difficult matter in hand, the end of which need not awaken concern. There is some other issue before mankind than self-extinction. Life may get to appear very poor and worthless, but the greater part will prefer to live it out to the end. Great nature has us in hand, and, while allowing us a certain liberty, and even wildness of conduct, has barriers beyond which we cannot go. "You may rail at existence," she says, "but you cannot escape it." It may be impossible to escape by what is termed self-destruction. We were not consulted as to the beginning of existence; it may be that we can have no voice as to its end. We may throw ourselves over the battlements of the life that now holds us, but who can say that we may not be seized by the mysterious force that first sent us here, and be thrust back into this world, or some other no better, to complete an existence over which we have no power? If a malignant or indifferent force evolved human existence, it is probable that, by reason of these very qualities, it will continue this existence; were it to permit extinction it would violate its own nature. A being made or evolved cannot outmaster or outwit the being or force from which it sprang?

"'T is not within the force of fate,
The fate conjoined to separate."

If existence is so wretched that extinction is desirable, it is necessary to suppose a good God in order to be certain of attaining it; no other would permit it. But will He not rather deliver from the misery and preserve the life? Whether the pessimist is aware of it or not, he wears the cap and bells, and his doleful doctrines, however soberly uttered, will be heard as jests. Still it is not amiss that the question has come up; it has the use of turning the thought of the age to human life with careful scrutiny and measurement. Men have always been ready enough to see the evil in life; that side of existence has been well attended to, but the other side, the good wrought into it, has not been fairly estimated. And especially we have been too ready to conclude that life is a waning process, a game of inevitable loss, a glory that fades away into dullness and night. The weight of uttered testimony leans to this side, for there is a strange property in human ill that draws thought to it. The great masters write tragedies and comedies, one in seriousness, the other in jest. "Vanity of vanities, all is vanity;" "Few and evil have been the days of my life;" so reiterates the moralist and sage of all ages, uttering, however, his feeling rather than his thought, pitying rather than scrutinizing himself. But now that men are rising up and calmly asserting that these estimates are a true and final verdict drawn from all the facts of life, that life is a fading glory, a vanishing process, a deception ending in total loss, we are forced to consider if these representations have even the color of truth. For life must not be suspected. If not held as of supreme value it loses all value, and sinks out of all use; it is the beginning and the sure prognostic of utter demoralization. When the glory of life is tarnished, it does not need to be cast away, it is gone already. One who holds existence cheap, destroys the basis of achievement; character is graduated by the estimate put upon that which holds character. One may die cheerfully at God's bidding, but only at his; or gladly for a cause, but the cause must be worthy of the sacrifice.

The subject is so large that only one phase of it will now be taken up, namely, a comparison between what is gained and what is lost in life as it goes on.

That there are gains and losses, wrought even into the texture of life, there is no question, but which are in excess, is a matter of debate. That multitudes make life a waning process through evil, there is no doubt. The real question is, Is life so organized that it is a process of gain rather than loss, with the further question if the loss does not subserve the gain?

In making this comparison we start with the fact that there seems to be possible but one kind of excellence at a time. We never see a person simultaneously at the height of personal beauty, of energy, and of wisdom; one excellence follows another. Hence we must not infer that, because one phase passes away and another comes on, there is actual loss; it is possible that there may be a succession characterized by an ascending grade. In childhood there is a grace and symmetry, a certain divineness in movement and play of feature, that quickly disappear, but are nearer perfection than anything of any sort that comes after. I can see God in the patience and ecstasy of the saints, but not so clearly as in the features and movements of a little child. St. Sebastian holds no comparison with the sacred Babe in the discerning eye of art. Their angels behold the face of the Father, and we behold God in them. If this divine beauty could live on, we say, how much richer and more glorious life would be! But it vanishes, and something less ethereal and more substantial comes in. We still have beauty, but the suggestion of divineness is gone. The physical is shot through with the bright flame of human passion, and made glorious by the kindling light of thought. The child shone with a beauty reflected from the creating Hand; the youth is beautiful with his own feeling and thought, an advance in kind, but not in degree. The excellence is higher in kind than that of childhood, but its ineffable charm, the utter grace, the eye that looks from measureless depths into yours, unabashed because it knows no evil, — being gazing upon being, as the angels may, — these are gone. But the downcast eye and mounting color of youthhood are higher because they speak of the personality that is coming on: the divine withdraws to make room for the human. And then, as beauty loses its freshness, there is a transfer of excellence from the physical to the intellectual and moral. A certain external glory passes, but now comes on courage, strength, imagination, and thought. And now for the first, life begins to yield fruit self-grown. Up to this point it has seemed a reflection of the world out of which it came; it slowly fades as in a dissolving picture, leaving less pleasing forms, but as we touch them, we find they are not images but realities. But after a long period of full personality marked by strength and achievement, a change comes on that seems to be one of absolute loss. Energy, courage, hope, fade out by slow degrees, — the down-hill of life, we call it. And loss indeed it is; a fine glory, the rarest excellence yet realized, has passed, but it is a question if the repose of feeling, the calmness of thought, the charity of disposition that follow, are not higher. They do not count so high in the ordinary estimate, for there is nothing men so admire as the resistless energy and unconquerable spirit of the middle period of life. Out of them spring the main achievements of society, and it is natural to value highest that which seems greatest. But we should hesitate before deciding that life culminates in the middle, and that half of it is given up to its own decay. Here is a great improbability, at least. It may be, as in preceding periods, that one kind of excellence has yielded to another and higher; that life is not like crossing a mountain, a climb to the summit, and an equal descent to the foot. It may be that life is not the exhaustion of a certain amount of vitality, not a ripening and a decay, but is a process quite different. It may be that it has in it a law of endless ascent, that life represents an unquenchable force, and can never be less than it is. If we take one view, it leaves life a sad mystery; if the other, it makes it explicable, for so long as life is on the gain, it explains and indorses itself, — like Emerson's flower, "it is its own excuse for being." But a life that mounts only to sink back to the same level, confounds thought. Now, as between these theories, one of which has some color of external facts to support it, yet leaves life sad and inexplicable, and the other of which explains it and puts it in harmony with other truth, we are bound to choose the latter by every principle of reason. It is a false logic that makes us content with mystery when there is any possible explanation of it. Being itself may be involved in eternal mystery, and may forever deepen as existence goes on, but the adjuncts of being, its end and its relations, are solvable and not parts of the "unending, endless quest." And if I find myself shut within a dark cave, as Plato pictured, I will welcome the faintest glimmer that seems to play about a possible opening into the world of light. Enough comes through to assure us that life, as ordained by God, if undisturbed by sin, is throughout a steady gain through a succession of excellences, each higher in kind than the preceding. Just here the text has force. Sin, without doubt, breaks up this order of growth and succession of higher qualities, and the Christ is here to restore it and to secure for it that growing abundance of which it is capable. But we are now speaking rather of the natural, inwrought order of life, than of rescue from its perversions.

Let us, if we can, make a comparative estimate of the loss and gain as we pass our allotted years.

1. We lose the perfection of physical life, its grace and exuberance. The divineness of childhood, the exultation in mere existence, the splendor of youth, the innocence that knows no guile, the faith that never questions, the hope that never doubts, the joy that knows no bounds because the limitations of life are not yet reached, — these all pass away. "But are not these immense losses?" we say. "What can be better or greater than these?" In

a certain sense there is nothing better or higher, but these qualities are not properly our own; they are colors laid on us, divine instincts temporarily wrought into us, but not actual parts of us; they fall away from us because they are not. Yet they are not wholly and forever lost; they recede in order that we may go after and get firmer hold of them. The child is guileless by nature, — the man because he has learned to hate a lie. The child is joyous, it knows not why, — God made it so; it is Nature's joy rather than its own; but a man's joy is the outcome of his nature reduced to harmony, — thought, feeling, and habit working under personality to the same end. One is necessarily ephemeral, the other is lasting, because it is the product of his own nature; it may not be so complete and divine of aspect, but it has become an integral and permanent factor of the man. The loss, therefore, is not so great as it seems; it is rather a transformation.

2. We lose, in time, the forceful, executive qualities. We no longer undertake enterprises of pith and moment, or take on heavy responsibilities. Old men do not explore unknown continents, or learn new languages, or found new institutions, or head reforms, or undertake afresh the solid works of the world; the needed energy is gone, but not necessarily lost; it may have been transmuted, as motion is changed into heat and light.

3. When we come to mental qualities, there is smaller loss. It is sometimes thought that the imagination decays with years, but it rather changes

its character. In youth it is more erratic, and may better be named as fancy; in age it is steadier and more subservient to the other faculties, entering into them, making the judgment broader, the sense of truth keener, and bringing the possibilities of truth within reach of thought. In the greater minds the imagination rather grows than lessens. Sophocles, Milton, Goethe, lead a vast host of poets and philosophers who never waned in the exercise of this grandest faculty. It is to be doubted if there is such a thing as decay of mental power. When one is tired one cannot think, words come slowly, the thread of discourse is easily lost, memory is dull, the judgment loses its breadth, the perception its acuteness; but a few hours of sleep restore the seeming loss. So what seems decay may pertain only to the age-wearied flesh; the mind is still there, as it was in weariness and sleep, with all its strength and stores. It is true that in the years of middle life, there is a certain thoroughness and intensity in all things done or thought, that comes from strength, but the judgment is not so sure, the grasp is not so comprehensive, and the taste so correct, as later on.

This, then, seems to be the sum of the losses sustained in life: a certain natural or elemental divineness of early childhood not to be kept as such, but to be lost as a divine gift, and reproduced as a human achievement; the bloom and zest of youth; the energy and force of maturity, and certain features or sides of our mental qualities. But we detect no loss of moral qualities, and but little of mental.

The order is significant: the physical changes utterly, the mental partially, the moral not at all, if the life is normal.

What now do we gain as life goes on?

1. This evident progress from the lower to the higher must be accounted a gain. It does not matter how this progress is made, whether by actual loss of inferior qualities supplanted by higher, or by a transformation of forces, though the latter is more in accord with natural science, which asserts that force is indestructible, — an assertion of tremendous scope of inference; for if force is indestructible, it must have a like basis or medium through which it acts; thus it becomes a potent argument for an unending life. However this be, each phase of existence is so beautiful that we are loath to see it yield to the next; still it is a richer stage that comes on. A mother, enraptured with the perfect beauty of her babe, wishes, with foolish fondness, that she might keep it a babe forever, yet is content to see it unfold its larger life, and "round to a separate mind." None of us would choose, if we might, to go back to any previous phase, and stay there. We may long for the innocence of youth, but who would take it with its ignorance, — for the zest of youth, but not at the expense of immaturity; for the energy of mid-life, but not at the cost of the repose and wide wisdom of age.

2. Though we lose energy and courage and present hope, we gain in patience, and, upon the whole, suffer less. It is glorious to defy fortune with strength, but it is better to be able to bear fortune

with patience. We are under illusion while we are pitting our energy against the forces of the world, but when at last we can say, "I cannot conquer but I can endure," we are no longer acting under illusion but in true accord with the might and majesty of our nature. Ulysses could not contend against the tempest, but he was superior to it when

> "He beat his breast, and thus reproached his heart;
> Endure, my heart; far worse hast thou endured."

"Man is but a reed," says Pascal, "but he is a thinking reed; were the universe to crush him he would still be more noble than that which kills him, for he knows that he dies, and the universe knows nothing of the advantage it has over him." This elaborated patience, and knowledge of one's relations to life, is an immeasurable gain over the untested strength and false measurements of our earlier years.

3. We make another gain as thought grows calm, and the judgment is rounded to its full strength. Knowledge becomes wisdom. Passion and prejudice pass away from our estimates. And especially we gain in comprehensiveness and so lose the spirit of partisanship. This not only renders age valuable to the world, but it is a comfortable possession; it is a deliverance from the small tempests that fret the surface of life. Then only, truth feeds the mind with its unalloyed sweetness.

4. There is a great gain in the later years of life, in certain forms of love and sympathy. The passion of early love, its semi-selfishness, and the restriction and prejudice of early sympathy, pass away, but

love itself remains in all its strength, purer, calmer, more universal. It takes on a yearning quality, it pities, it forgives and overlooks, it bears and hopes and forgets, and so is like God's own love. Early love is intense but it is without knowledge, but that of age is calm and broad because it is wise. Especially does the grace of charity belong to full years. The old are more merciful than the young; they judge more kindly and forgive more readily. Hence they are poor disciplinarians, but their fault is rather their virtue; they are not called to that duty. This changing and expanding form of the supreme principle of our nature has great significance in the question before us. At no time are we let from under its power; at first an instinct, then a conscious passion for one, but blind; then a down-reaching tenderness for children, wiser and more patient; then an out-reaching to humanity, moved by conscience and guided by knowledge; and at last a pitiful, universal sympathy that allies itself to the Eternal Love. Here is a gain that is simply immeasurable, spanning the breadth between the unconscious instinct of the child and the method of God's own heart.

There is also in advanced years a mingling and merging of the faculties, one in another. Thought has more faith in it and faith more thought; reason more feeling and feeling more reason; logic and sentiment melt into each other; courage is tempered with prudence, and prudence gets strength and courage from wisdom; joys have in them more sorrow and sorrows more joy; if it has less zest it touches the mind at more points, while sorrows lose their keenness by falling under the whole range of faculties. An old man does not feel the same rapture before a landscape as one younger, but he sees it with more eyes, so to speak; his whole nature sees it, while the youth regards it with only the one eye of beauty. This united action of the mind, this coöperation of all the faculties, is something far higher than the disjointed experiences of early life. It is like the action of the Divine Mind in which every faculty interpenetrates every other, making God one and perfect. And in man, it is an intimation that he is approaching the Divine Mind, and getting ready, as it were, for the company of God.

Life is a fire, yet not to blast and reduce to ashes, but to fuse. It takes a vast assemblage of qualities and faculties most unlike and often discordant, and reduces them first to harmony and then to oneness. Consider how man is made up; under a simple bond of self-consciousness a set of qualities not otherwise related, warring against each other; good and evil passions, selfishness and love, pride and humility, prudence and folly, mental faculties so unlike at first as to antagonize each other; the logical faculty opposed to imagination, reason to sentiment, the senses demanding one verdict and the conscience another, — such a world is man at the outset. Life is the reconciliation of these diversities and antagonisms; the process may be attended by apparent loss, but only apparent. The law of the conservation of forces holds here as in the physical world. In the fire of life, the form is melted away from each quality, but only that their forces may flow together and be fused into one general force that shall set towards the Eternal Righteousness. Thus there comes on that process and condition of life which is called a *mellowing*. When the growth is normal and is unhindered by gross or deep-seated sin, a change or development takes place in nearly all that is well described by this word. The man ripens, his heart grows soft, he speaks more kindly. A rich autumnal tint overspreads his thoughts and acts. He looks into the faces of little children with a brooding tenderness. He finds it hard to distinguish between the faults and the vices of the young. He hates no longer anything except a lie, and that because it contradicts the order into which he has come. He draws no sharp, condemnatory lines about conduct, but says to all offenders, "Go and sin no more." His pride dies away; he no longer cherishes distinctions, but talks freely with the humble and has no awe before the great; he forgets his old notions of dignity, and is a companion with his gardener or with the President. This state is sometimes regarded as weakness, and as though it sprang from dulled faculties, but it is simply the moral qualities come into preponderance, or rather the equilibrium of all the forces. Life has ripened its fruits, and the man begins to feel and act like God. Something of the divine patience and charity and wisdom begin to show in him, and we now see why God made him in his own image, and gave him his life to live. If life can start at the point of mere existence, and thence grow up into likeness to God, it is worth living. And if life reaches so far, we may be sure it will go on. If it gets to the point of laying hold of God, and begins to feel and act like God, it will never relax its hold, it will never cease from action so essentially and eternally valuable. There is the same reason for the continued existence of such a being as of God Himself; that which is like the Best must, for that very reason. live on with the Best. We can no more conceive of God suffering such a one to go out of existence than that a good father would put to death his child most like himself because of the likeness.

This line of thought has force only in the degree in which life is normal, but the fact that it is not wholly such does not break up or foil the divine intention wrought into it. For there is a provision in humanity against its own failures. Life of itself may not reach its proper fullness, but One is in humanity who is redeeming it from its failures and filling its cup even to overflow. Nor is the sadness of age an indication of real loss; it may have another meaning: —

> "The clouds that gather round the setting sun,
> Do take a sober coloring from an eye
> That hath kept watch o'er man's mortality."

It may be a wise provision for attenuating the thread that holds us to this world. The main feature of life is not its sorrow or its joy, nor even its right or wrong doing. Its main feature is that, starting at the bare point of existence, it grows with such stride and rapidity that it yields first a person, and then reaches up to God, into whose affinities and likeness it enters as a partaker. The space between the infant and a mind walking in conscious oneness with God marks a gain so immense, so rich and wonderful, that we cannot measure it. It is from such a stand-point that the value of life is to be estimated, and not from the amount of sorrow and happiness, nor from any failure through evil. What is evil when there is a soul of goodness in all things? What is sin when it is redeemable? What is a little more or a little less of suffering when such gain is possible? What are toils and what are storms, when such a port is to be reached? The plan seems almost indifferent to happiness and to evil, utilizing one and contending against the other, while it presses steadily towards this gigantic gain, the growth of a soul from simple consciousness into God-likeness.

It is somewhat the fashion now to derogate from the dignity and glory of life. There is doubt that it leads to anything besides its own end; a weakened sense of God suggests a poor and low estimate of it. "Let us eat and drink, for to-morrow we die," is a sentiment that hovers in the air. There is no way to prevent it from becoming the watchword of society, but by a fresh incoming of faith in God as the Father of men and the Ordainer of life with its laws and ends, — facts not left to the waywardness of our human reason, but revealed in a true Son of God who incarnated the full glory and perfection of life, and makes it abundant for every other child of God.

THINGS TO BE AWAITED.

"Man is, properly speaking, based upon Hope, he has no other possession but Hope; this world of his is emphatically the Place of Hope."
— *Sartor Resartus*, ii. 7.

"Sleep after toil, port after stormy seas,
Ease after war, death after life, does greatly please."
Faërie Queen, i. 9.

"The preliminary step to following Christ is the leaving the dead to bury the dead, not clamoring on his doctrine for an especial solution of difficulties which are referable to the general problem of the Universe."
ROBERT BROWNING'S *Essay on Shelley.*

THINGS TO BE AWAITED.

"Until the day break, and the shadows flee away."—THE SONG OF SOLOMON, ii. 17.

I DO not know the nature of the feeling out of which these words sprang. It may be hard to determine whether it was a human or a divine rapture, whether it enfolded only some Jewish lover, or whether, under such chaste and tender symbols, it uttered the yearning delight of God in his church. It hardly matters which; a true love is as sacred as a holy church, for the church is but the Lamb's wife. They stand on the sacred page, in their tender beauty, like a golden sunset which to one may be only a "promise of a fair to-morrow," to another a simple refraction of light, to another a symbol of eternal repose and glory. The meaning of words lies not wholly in the words themselves, but also in us. Whatever the first use and intent of this phrase, it describes a waiting, and a joy to come, a waiting under darkness and shadow, and a joy to come with the light. And so they answer well the purpose of suggesting the truth of which I shall speak, namely, that there are many things in life and destiny that are to be awaited.

Man, in his inmost being, is not keyed to the temporal, but to the eternal. The final solution of life is not to be found in the past, the present, or the future, but in a state named eternity, in which "time shall be no longer," — a state unconditioned by a material body and by cycles of time, — a state of absolute freedom and of unfettered existence; whatever the man *is*, that he is perfectly, whether good or bad. I do not mean that he will be perfectly good or bad, but that there will remain on him no condition nor limitation of his character. At present, there are weights and checks on the expression of character; in the eternal state there are none; it has absolute expression, and works in perfect freedom to its proper end, whether it be good or evil. But here and now man is put into relations of time, and, while character is always mounting towards this eternal state as into a native ether, it is shaped in and by time. Past, present, and future, are realities that we cannot escape. As Carlyle says: "The curtains of yesterday drop down; the curtains of to-morrow roll up, but yesterday and to-morrow both are." The maxims that bid us forget the past, and trust the future, and live in the present, while they contain a half truth, hold also an insidious error. We cannot forget the past, and we ought not to forget it; we can be insensible to the future, but we ought not to be insensible to it. It is by the forfeiture of our greatness and essential nature, that we put the main emphasis of life upon the present. All the past is shut up within us, and is a sort of perpetual present. All the future is before us, and though duty is a present thing, it is constructed out of the past, and runs endlessly into the future. We thus have the past with its memories, the present with its duties, and the future with its anticipations, — one for wisdom, one for action, and one for hope, — a trinity of temporal environment holding man until he is ready to be let into eternity. Eternity now is, but we enter its fullness by the path of futurity, and so, in common speech, we treat as one the eternal and the future worlds.

Despite the brave assertion of the present as the only field of action, and so, by narrow inference, of thought, the future plays a large part in life and character. "One world at a time," is a motto for a brute and not for a man. To stand before the future world as before a dead wall, is an attitude to which we are not called; we are not made after that fashion, but are keyed to anticipation and hope; and if so, then we are keyed to a world in which hope has fulfillment, and not to a world in which it is a steadily dissolving illusion. Anticipation and hope are not mere features of a religious faith, but essential conditions of true living, hands and feet by which we travel towards, and lay hold of, our destiny. Hence there are many things that belong to us which are put into the future, and are therefore to be *awaited;* and since we are put into this relation of *waiting,* we must not fret because we do not have them, nor strive to get them before they are due.

We can speak confidently of such things only as we now know in part, beginnings that here have no completion, germs that come to leaf and bud, but not to fruit, in the soil of this world; processes that have promise of great results but are cut short of them, desires and aspirations that now have no full satisfaction.

1. We wait for *rest*. If the question were raised: is man made for toil or for rest? the answer would be a mixed and qualified one. He is appointed to toil, he is destined to rest; one is his condition, the other is his end. If man is made in God's image, he is made to share in God's condition; and both Christian revelation and heathen conjecture unite in conceiving of Deity as in repose, eternally acting yet in eternal rest. This is no contradiction, but a simple necessity when the powers are infinite and harmonious. Ruskin, in one of his most thoughtful passages, has aptly touched the truth: "As opposed to passion, changefulness, and laborious exertion, repose is the especial and separating characteristic of the eternal mind and power; it is the 'I am' of the Creator opposed to the 'I become' of all creatures. The desire of rest planted in the heart is no sensual nor unworthy one, but a longing for renovation, and for escape from a state whose every phase is a mere preparation for another equally transitory, to one in which permanence shall have become possible through perfection." As we grow in this image and pass beyond its early limitations, we approach this eternal rest; it remains for the children of God. If it be said that man can never attain this repose because he can never reach the eternal perfection and power, it may be answered that it does not depend upon the propor-

tions of the being, but upon the harmony of his powers and upon his adjustment to his external condition. One whose nature has been reduced to perfect harmony may have perfect peace within, and also without, if also he is in a world entirely adapted to him. But we have not this rest at present except in some foretaste of it in our spirit. Unceasing toil is the largest feature of human life. It is divinely appointed, but it is painful; it is a blessing, but also a suffering; an evil thing, but with a soul of goodness in it. It is wise, for, if remitted, vice creeps in, but it is no less a bond that chafes, a burden that weighs down, a trial that wearies the spirit. It walls in virtue and undergirds character, yet it is the most pathetic feature of human society. As the sun journeys about the earth, it summons the greater part of those it shines on to hard and heavy toil till its setting dismisses them to brief rest. And this rest is chiefly found in sleep, the nightly death to life, as though rest were no part of man's conscious life. Let us not regard as fancy this hint thrown out by the order of nature. When man would rest, he is taken out of this conscious world into one, how unlike! but because unlike to this, like to some other in which rest is the main feature. If we die, in a sense, to this daily life of toil, to get rest, and thus go off into a world of freedom that is revealed to us by fragments of chance-remembered dreams, how surely is it an intimation that the other death ushers us into a world of absolute freedom and repose; for freedom and repose are correlatives. Weariness does not come from action but from restraints put on action. There is a spiritual *vis inertiæ*. As a world moves with tireless motion in a void, so the mind may act in perpetual vigor and freshness when the resistances of time are taken off. Hence "there is no night there;" hence He "neither slumbers nor sleeps." To all else, to bird and to beast, the sun brings joy, but to man only toil. How much weariness, how much ache of body and disease, how much lethargy of mind and cramping of powers, how much vain longing and bitter complaint and sullen endurance and despair, it yields, it were impossible to tell. But no feeling heart can dwell on it a moment, and not break with unavailing sympathy. And yet, in itself, it is the great blessing of this life. "Thank God for work," is the cry of every wise heart. As society goes on, it will lessen its severity and take away some of its sharpest stings, but it will never eliminate the fact. The moment toil is exchanged for leisure, a gate is opened to vice. When wealth takes off the necessity of labor and invites to idleness, nature executes her sharpest revenge upon such infraction of the present order; the idle rich live next door to ruin. How strange a condition! Made for rest; made in the image of Him who dwells in eternal repose, yet when we stretch out our hand for the likeness, the fiery sword that guards this tree of life scorches us with deadly flame! How shall we explain it? Here is toil, our lot, our necessity, wrought into the human order, our safeguard against evil, but full of essential pain, uncongenial, out of keeping with what is deepest in us, at odds with conscious destiny; how shall we carry the conflicting elements in our mind? I answer, that rest is something to be awaited in God's own time. To unduly seize it, is ruin; it breaks the mould in which our life is cast. To patiently wait for it makes toil endurable, and assures us that our external lives are not a mockery of the hopes wrought into us. Some morning, this shadow will flee away. In the church of St. Nazaro in Florence is an epitaph upon the tomb of a soldier, as fit for the whole toiling race as for his own restless life: "Johannes Divultius, who never rested, rests, — hush!" We say of our dead, "they rest from their labors." Whatever the future world may be to us or require of us, it is not clothed in the guise of toil, but offers seats of eternal rest; it is the contrast of earth, the other side of mortal existence as spirit is the other side of matter.

2. We wait for the renewal of lost powers.

However we answer the question, if life is a process of loss or gain, it cannot be denied that real or apparent loss is one of its largest features, even when life is at its best. Is this loss absolute, or do we regain that which seems to pass? If the former, it puts a hard and almost despairing look upon existence. We come into life dowered with good, — high instincts, noble emotions, graces of person and spirit, faculties divine in their freedom, — imprints that testify to our divine creation. Surely God made us, and his work justifies Him! But all this glory and grace that invest us at the outset, — these divine touches left on us by the creative hand, — pass away. The freshness, the beauty, the glory, the innocence, the boundless vitality, the native hope, the instinctive faith, the high purpose, fade out. Something better, or something that better serves a present purpose, may take their place: still they are good, — glories put on us by God's own hand. And if any say they are but natural, only so much the more are they divine. Shall I never, — so we are forced to ask ourselves, — shall I never have again the buoyancy of youth, the zest, the innocence, the unquestioning faith, the ardent desire and unconquerable will, the bounding vigor of body and mind, with which I began life? We do not get half way through our allotted years before these riches are gone from us. If they are gone forever, one half of life, at least, is spent under an ever-deepening shadow. It is difficult to believe that existence is so ordered; that God's increated gifts are annihilated; that the impress of his hands, the similitudes of Himself, are blotted out forever. It were unendurable for us, it were like a waste on the part of God, if these first riches of our being are to perish. It is easier to conceive of this mysterious soul that we are, as a garner in which whatever is good is preserved; that it hives the sweetness of life for future use, as bees hive honey for winter's need; that, as a flower folds its beauty and perfume in the husk-clad seed, and will produce them again, so these first excellences are hidden in the enfoldings of this life, to reappear when the spiritual body shall blossom into its eternal state. St. Paul speaks of the redemption of the body as something that is waited for. He means no narrow doctrine of a physical resurrection, but a renewal of existence, — a restoration of lost powers.

It changes the whole color of life, and its character also, if we take the one view or the other, — if we regard existence as a dying-out process, or as passing into temporary eclipse, to emerge with all its past glories when the shadows of death flee away.

3. We wait for the full perfecting of character.

I do not mean, of course, that we are to wait in the sense of relaxing effort after perfection, — such waiting may end in an eternal failure of character, but rather that the effort that now only partially succeeds will finally reach success.

There is nothing that weighs more heavily upon a right-minded man than the slow progress he makes in overcoming his faults. Here we are at twenty, with the faults of childhood upon us: peevish, ungoverned, insatiable; at thirty, with the faults of youth: vain, inconsiderate, pleasure-loving; at forty, still wearing the badges of early folly: proud, passionate, sensual; at fifty or sixty, but not yet wise with the experience of life: selfish still, unsympathetic, ambitious, full of conscious weaknesses, and perhaps with an ill-repressed brood of evil habits, and the characteristic vice of age, — avarice. Yet all the while we may have been striving after the good, curbing the evil, keeping our faces heavenward, all the while aiming to fear

God and keep his commandments, never at any time wholly giving up the strife after ideal excellence. This, after all, is the tragical feature of life, that it is linked with so much failure in character; that it is given for wisdom, and yet we are not wise; for goodness, and we are not good; for overcoming evil, and evil remains; for patience and sympathy and self-command and love, and yet we are fretful and hard and weak and selfish. This makes the bitterness of death, and calls out the cry, Vanity of vanities, all is vanity! There is nothing a right-minded man desires so much as entire right-mindedness. Will it never come? Yes, — but it must be awaited. Entireness is nowhere a feature of present existence, else it could not be a world of hope and promise. On no thing can we lay our hand and say, Here is finality and perfection. The adamant is crumbling to dust; the orderly heavens oscillate towards final dissolution, and foretell "new heavens;" in every soul is weakness and fault. We are keyed not to attainment, but to the hope of it by struggle towards it. And it is the struggle, and not the attainment, that measures character and foreshadows destiny. Character is not determined by faults and weaknesses, and periodic phases of life, nor by the limitations and accidents of present existence, but by the central purpose, the inmost desire of the heart. If that be turned towards God and his righteousness, it must at last bring us thither.

4. We await the renewal of sundered love.

When love loses its object its charm is interrupted, for love is oneness and cannot brook separation. It is impossible to believe that God has organized into life an incurable sorrow; that He has made love, which is the best conceivable thing, — being the substance of Himself, — the necessary condition of the greatest misery. If man willfully perverts love so that it becomes this, it were another matter, but that God has so ordered existence that love is thwarted into unquenchable sorrow, it is impossible to believe. If this were so, we no longer have a good God. But what is infinite sorrow, what is greatest misery, but love sundered by hopeless death? There is but one gate that leads out of this labyrinth of mortal perplexity, one thing and one only will make life other than a curse, namely, a belief that love, being eternal in its nature, will have an eternal realization. Hence, we do not believe that death is an end of love's oneness. Love may suffer an eclipse, but it is not sent wailing into eternal shadows. It is as sure as God Himself that human love shall again claim its own. Will He have his, and not give us ours? Will the Father of men keep his children forever in his conscious heart, and not let me have mine? There is nothing in this universe of mingled light and shadow so sure as this. But this eternal union must be awaited. It begins here, springing out of mysterious oneness; it grows up amidst unspeakable tenderness, rising from an instinctive thing to an intellectual and moral union, losing nothing, and weaving into itself every strand of human sympathy till it stands for the whole substance of life, and so vanishes from the scene. If this prime reality is an illusion, then all else is. If it does not outlast death, then all may go. But love is not a vain thing, and God does not mock Himself and us when He makes us partakers of his nature.

> "What is excellent,
> As God lives, is permanent;
> Hearts are dust, hearts' loves remain,
> Heart's love will meet thee again."

5. We wait for the mystery to be taken off from life.

The crucial test of a thoughtful mind is a sense of the mystery of life in this world. The mind that regards everything as common, as a matter of course, has not begun to think. One who has even once put the question, *Why?* before life, its origin, its relation to matter, its purpose, may be accounted thoughtful. The main feature of the highest intellectuality is that of awe and question before the mystery of being and destiny. This is the reason that such names as Plato, Shakespeare, Goethe, Shelley, Pascal, Emerson, Hawthorne, and "Geo. Eliot," are placed so high in the list of greatness; whatever their treatment of the mystery of life, they have the deepest sense of it. It is this that makes Hamlet greater than Macbeth: one is a plain picture of a human passion; the other depicts a man who is brooding on the mystery of life. The critics cannot explain the drama; nor could Shakespeare himself have explained it; the difficulty lies in the subject. It is this that takes such a man as Robertson out of the ranks of ordinary preachers

and puts him by himself. This highest order of
mind is not antagonistic to faith; it is simply conscious of the incomprehensible range of truth.
None but an inferior mind has a plan of the universe; it is to the thoughtless that all things are
plain. What is life? What is matter? What is
the relation between them? What is creation?
Granting evolution, what started the evolving process? Assuming God, what is the relation of creation to Him? What the relation of man? What
is this that thinks and wills and loves — this *I?*
And then, what is it all for? Is there a final purpose and an order tending to it, or is it but the
whirl of molecules, the dust of the universe circling
for a moment in space, of which we are but some
atoms? Is there a bridge between consciousness
and the external world, or a gulf that cannot be
spanned or fathomed? Is life a reality, or is it a
dream from which we may awake in some world of
reality to find that this world was but the vision of
a night? We are born out of sleep; we die into
sleep. Are we truly awake between? What certainty is there that these senses convey true reports
of the outer world, and that it may not be a phantasm, a projected play of our own consciousness that
may vanish some moment like a dissolving cloud?
These are questions that are never absent from the
great minds; they send their color into the sonnets
and plays of Shakespeare; they prompt the philosophies from Pythagoras down; they tinge the
great poems; they rise in every thoughtful mind
whenever he looks into the heavens at night, or

listens to the endless murmur of the sea, or considers the mystery involved in touch and sight and sound, or takes in the sweep of the generations, one coming and another going, forcing the question — Whence? Whither?

It is useless to deny that this mystery carries with it a sense of pain. It is alien to mind, a condition foreign to our nature. And the more thoroughly mind is true to itself, the more painfully does it feel the darkness. When Goethe, dying, said, "Let the light enter," he uttered, not the highest and best hope of the heart, but the dearest satisfaction of the intellect. He felt that he was going where the shadows that hang over this world would flee away, and he could find some answer to the questions that had vexed him here.

So, too, those commoner questions, Why does evil exist? Why do the innocent suffer? Why does one suffer on account of another? Why does life end untimely? Why is man so subject to nature? Why is the experience of life so long in ripening the fruit of wisdom? Why are the chances so against man that he spends his days in sorrow and evil? Why is there not more help from God? Why does life gradually assume the appearance of a doom, spent in vanity and ending in death? We get no full answer to these questions in this life. We make some petty syllogisms about freedom as the necessary condition of good, and evil as incidental to the best possible system, and the like, — true enough they are, perchance, but they are not answers: they simply throw the questions a little farther back. Our faith teaches us submission and trust, but it does not tell us *why* these things are so. And because they are not explained, some blaspheme, and some despair, and some make the mystery an excuse for sin : " it is all a tangle — let us eat and drink."

Shall these questions never be answered? It is not easy to believe that mind will forever be harassed by an alien element; it may always require something other than itself to stand upon, or as a foil like that which the jewel-merchant puts under precious stones to reflect their color, but it will not forever wear this *other* as a clog and burden. It is the function of mind to know, its proper element is knowledge and certainty. Insolvable mystery, especially such as involves pain, cannot well be a permanent and final feature of existence. Being itself may forever remain a mystery, and may deepen as existence goes on, but it involves no suffering, it is simply inexplicable wonder at self. But these other shadows that cloud life, these questions that tire and fret us with their importunity, yet admit of no sure answer ; these problems that often render faith well-nigh impossible, and prompt us to " curse God and die ; " these slowly vanish when the great light of eternity dawns on us. That were a poor world if it did not do this for us. Mystery may remain, but it will be harmonious mystery. The accusing doubt, the seeming contradiction, the painful uncertainty, will pass away, and we shall see " face to face " and know even as we have been known.

If the grounds of this expectation are asked for, we find them in these words of St. Paul: we shall know *as* God knows. The mystery of the present life is due to the fact that it is so heavily conditioned by its material environment; matter contends against spirit. But as existence goes on, if it is normal, it throws off these conditions and presses towards absolute action and full freedom. This is the eternal state, and this action is eternal life, and the world where it is achieved is the eternal world. The whole process and condition is illustrated in the Christ. His peace was perfect, his joy was full, He knew that God heard Him, He saw the Father, He dwelt in light, and so his whole life had the freedom and certainty and perfection of eternity. One with Christ by faith here and now, yet overshadowed by clouds and beset with struggles, we await the hour, not "troubled" nor "comfortless," when we shall be with Him where He is, in the light of the shadowless "eternal noon."

6. We wait for full restoration to the presence of God.

I do not forget that through Christ we come to the Father; that the obedience of the Son is the path that leads to the Father's house. There is no truth but that truth, no way but that way, no life but that life; there is no other name under heaven by which men can be saved, because that name carries with it the elements and methods of salvation. All this is true, but it is an unfulfilled process. There is a knowledge and presence of God

for which we long that is not met even in Christ,
for He Himself was as one who waited for a joy set
before Him; He Himself was about to go to the
Father's house, not yet having come to it. The
perfection of Christ's revelation of God does not
consist in an entire uncovering of God, but in
showing a way that leads to God. Much indeed
He reveals, his heart of love, his righteous will,
but we demand more than knowledge of those we
love: we demand presence, sight, contact. When
Christ was teaching the people, He had all knowledge of God, but when the weary day was past, He
climbed the mountain — alone — if, in the remote
and solitary height, and in the deeper solitude of
darkness, He might get some closer sight of God.
Jacob, on his way to meet Esau, well enough knew
there was a God above him, but that was not
enough, and so he wrestled till daybreak for a revelation that should be more than knowledge. "Tell
me thy name," show me thy very self, is the cry of
his needy heart.

Whether we have come to the hour of conscious
need or not, it is the demand of every one of us.
There are hours when the whole world, and all it
contains, shrivels to nothingness, and God alone
fills the mind; hours of human desolation, seasons
of strange, mysterious exaltation, times of earthly
despair, or of joy; the height and excess of any
emotion bears us away into a region where God
Himself dwells. But even if we have taught ourselves to make the impression of these hours constant, there is still an unsatisfied element in the

knowledge. We long for more, for nearness, for sight or something that stands for sight, for the Father at hand, and the home of the soul. I know that in many and many of God's children there is a longing for God that is not satisfied, because they are children and are away from the Father's house. And I know still better that the unrest of this weary world is its unvoiced cry after God.

This full, satisfying presence of God, must be awaited. It is contended against by sense, by the world of things, by the limits that shut out the infinite, and by our own slow and hesitating departure from the evil and the sensual,—a muddy vesture of decay doth grossly close us in; but when this falls off, and these earthly shadows flee away, we shall see face to face, and know as we are known.

In showing that there are many things that are to be awaited, even till another life, I am aware how perilously near we run to the suggestion that, if these things are so, strife after the best, and most we can get in this world, may be relaxed. But we must not forget that all truth is double; we strive, we wait. There is no doubt but this life and world are mainly keyed to struggle, that man is a doer and not a waiter. The main purpose of life should be to get all the good out of it possible. Force from nature all the sweetness you can; wring from the earth all her richness; get all the joy possible from sight and sense and sound; test to the utmost the ministering power of everything and relation; wait for nothing that you may have by proper effort. This is our great, human privilege, but when we have used it to the utmost, there will be many things we want that we have not gained. The greatest things, the most vital, do not lie within the scope of our powers, yet as they belong to us they may be confidently awaited. We are free, but we are also bound; but our life and nature reach beyond our limitations, and lay claim to what is beyond our present reach.

This is a great truth; it uncovers the divine part of us. To live with only a recognition of our present possibilities, to draw all our joy and comfort from such things as we can now get under our touch and sight. as so many are telling us, — this, I conceive, to be thoroughly brutish. It makes man but another bird among the trees, or another insect humming in the evening air. But to hope and wait for the highest and best we can conceive, this expands life, this stretches out its short span. This affords a field for the solution of its mysteries, for the cure of its ills, for regaining what is lost, for recomposing the "sweet societies" of earth, for that realized oneness with God which is the unceasing cry of the God-created spirit.

Hence the last look at destiny is that of a seat in the eternal throne: all limitations ended, all heights surmounted, all things hoped and waited for gained!

Important Religious Books
Published by
HOUGHTON, MIFFLIN & COMPANY
BOSTON
The Riverside Press, Cambridge

A. Barth.

THE RELIGIONS OF INDIA. Translated from the French by REV. J WOOD. 8vo, gilt top, $5.00.

A masterly treatise on the religious thought, worship, and history of one of the most interesting people on the face of the earth. — *Advertiser* (Boston).

E. E. Beardsley, D. D.

THE HISTORY OF THE EPISCOPAL CHURCH IN CONNECTICUT, from the Settlement of the Colony to the Present Time. 2 vols. 8vo, $6.00.

Buddhist Birth Stories.

BUDDHIST BIRTH STORIES; or, Jataka Tales. Translated by T. W. RHYS DAVIDS. 8vo, gilt top, $5.00.

Many a wonder-story with which the little inmates of American nurseries are charmed to sleep was told, long centuries ago, under the shadows of the Himalayas. They present a nearly complete picture, quiet, unaffected by European intercourse, of the social life and customs and popular beliefs of the common people of Aryan tribes closely related to ourselves, just as they were passing through the first stages of civilization, a priceless record of the childhood of our race. — *Tribune* (New York).

John Bunyan.

THE PILGRIM'S PROGRESS. 16 full-page illustrations. 16mo, 75 cents.

THE SAME. New *Popular Edition*, from new plates. With Archdeacon Allen's Life of Bunyan (illustrated), and Macaulay's Essay on Bunyan. 62 wood-cuts. 12mo, $1.00.

THE SAME. *Holiday Edition*, comprising, in addition to the Popular Edition, a Steel Portrait of Bunyan, and Eight Colored Plates. 8vo, full gilt, $2.50.

James Freeman Clarke, D. D.

TEN GREAT RELIGIONS. An Essay in Comparative Theology. With an Index. 8vo, $3.00; half calf, $5.50.

CONTENTS: Ethnic and Catholic Religions; Confucius and the Chinese; Brahmanism; Buddhism, or the Protestantism of the East; Zoroaster and the Zend Avesta; The Gods of Egypt; The Gods of Greece; The Religion of Rome; The Teutonic and Scandinavian Religion; The Jewish Religion; Mohammed and Islam; The Ten Religions and Christianity.

He treats the ten condemned faiths in a spirit of the fullest reverence, anxious to bring to light whatever of good is contained in them, regarding each as in reality a religion, an essay toward the truth, even if only a partially successful one. . . . A great body of valuable and not generally or easily accessible information. — *The Nation* (New York).

Nothing has come to our knowledge which furnishes evidence of such voluminous reading, such thorough study and research, and such masterly grasp of the real elements of these religions, as does the volume before us. James Freeman Clarke has accomplished a work here of solid worth. — *Missionary Review* (Princeton).

TEN GREAT RELIGIONS. Part II. A Comparison of all Religions. 8vo, $3.00; half calf, $5.50.

CONTENTS: Description and Classification; Special Types, Law of Development; Origin and Development of all Religions; The Idea of God in all Religions: Animism, Polytheism, Pantheism, Ditheism, Tritheism, and Monotheism; The Soul and its Transmigrations in all Religions; The Origin of the World in all Religions; Evolution, Emanation, and Creation; Prayer and Worship in all Religions; Inspiration and Art in all Religions; Ethics in all Religions; Idea of a Future State in all Religions; The Future Religion of Mankind.

COMMON-SENSE IN RELIGION. A Series of Essays. 12mo, $2.00.

CONTENTS: Common Sense and Mystery; Common-Sense View of Human Nature; On the Doctrine Concerning God; The Bible and Inspiration; The True Meaning of Evangelical Christianity; The Truth about Sin; Common-Sense and Scripture Views of Heaven and Hell; Satan, according to Common-Sense and the Bible; Concerning the Future Life; The Nature of Our Condition Hereafter; Common-Sense View of the Christian Church; Five Kinds of Piety; Jesus a Mediator; The Expectations and Disappointments of Jesus; Common-Sense View of Salvation by Faith; On not being Afraid; Hope; The Patience of Hope; Love; The Brotherhood of Men.

As the common-sense of religion is the most certain reality of all life, the title of these essays is admirably chosen. It must arrest attention in face of the conservative determination to relegate religion to the domain of darkness, dreams, disease, myths, and other uncertainties. — *Advertiser* (Boston).

He writes, not for the learned, but for the simple; and there is hardly a child but might follow his course of thought, and take delight in his fresh and striking illustrations. — *Atlantic Monthly.*

Joseph Cook.

BOSTON MONDAY LECTURES.

These wonderful lectures stand forth alone amidst the contemporary literature of the class to which they belong. — London Quarterly Review.

BIOLOGY. With Preludes on Current Events. Seventeenth edition. 3 colored illustrations. 12mo, $1.50.

TRANSCENDENTALISM. With Preludes on Current Events. 12mo, $1.50.

ORTHODOXY. With Preludes on Current Events. 12mo, $1.50.

CONSCIENCE. With Preludes on Current Events. 12mo, $1.50.

HEREDITY. With Preludes on Current Events. 12mo, $1.50.

MARRIAGE. With Preludes on Current Events. 12mo, $1.50.

Mr. Cook did not take up the work he has accomplished as a trade, or by accident, or from impulse; but for years he had been preparing for it, and prepared for it by an overruling guidance. . . . He lightens and thunders, throwing a vivid light on a topic by an expression or comparison, or striking a presumptuous error as by a bolt from heaven. — JAMES MCCOSH, D. D.

Professor J. L. Diman.

THE THEISTIC ARGUMENT AS AFFECTED BY RECENT THEORIES. Edited by Professor GEORGE P. FISHER. 8vo, $2.00.

The author has succeeded in making it clear that recent science impels us to a point where the necessity of admitting the existence of God is irresistible; that its most elevated conceptions and widest generalizations render it necessary to accept the presence and constant efficient energy of God as realities, and that the modes of operation which science discloses are in harmony with the fundamental principles and postulates of Christianity. — *British Quarterly Review.*

Dr. Diman concedes to his opponents every advantage of debate, adopts their phraseology, follows their methods of reasoning, grants to them every principle that they have established wholly or approximately, and, indeed, a great deal that is scarcely more than conjecture; and yet he is able to present a defense of theistic doctrine that will seem most admirable and most consolatory to its adherents and most embarrassing to some of its enemies. He has conducted the whole discussion with rare ability, and has furnished sound reasoning at every successive step. — *Times* (New York).

ORATIONS AND ESSAYS, WITH SELECTED PARISH SERMONS.
A Memorial Volume, with a Portrait. 8vo, gilt top, $2.50.

CONTENTS: A Commemorative Discourse. J. Lewis Diman. By the Rev. James O. Murray. — *Literary and Historical Addresses:* The Alienation of the Educated Class from Politics; The Method of Academic Culture; Address at the Unveiling of the Monument to Roger Williams in Providence; The Settlement of Mount Hope; Sir Henry Vane. — *Reviews:* Religion in America, 1776-1876; University Corporations. — *Sermons:* The Son of Man; Christ, the Way, the Truth, and the Life; Christ, the Bread of Life; Christ in the Power of His Resurrection; The Holy Spirit, the Guide to Truth; The Baptism of the Holy Ghost; The Kingdom of Heaven and the Kingdom of Nature.

I think it is not the partiality of personal friendship which leads me to regard these productions of Professor Diman as not surpassed by any other writings of the same class in our literature. — Professor GEORGE P. FISHER.

One cannot read these pages without becoming conscious of contact with the workings of a strong and an earnest mind. The words betoken culture, scholarship, and, what is more important, they show that he who wrote them lived near to God. — *The Churchman* (New York).

The rich contents of this volume assure his place among our noblest teachers and scholars. — *Christian Register* (Boston).

The Dhammapada.

TEXTS FROM THE BUDDHIST CANON, commonly known as Dhammapada, with accompanying Narratives. Translated from the Chinese, by SAMUEL BEAL, Professor of Chinese, University College, London. 8vo, gilt top, $2.50.

This is a most important addition to our knowledge, as the Pali texts of this work, hitherto available to scholars, and translated by Professor Max Müller and others, contain only two thirds of the matter which has survived in the Chinese version. — *The Athenæum* (London).

Joseph Edkins, D. D.

RELIGION IN CHINA. Containing a brief account of the Three Religions of the Chinese, with Observations on the Prospects of Christian Conversion among that People. 8vo, gilt top, $2.50.

Dr. Edkins writes with the firmness and clearness of a mind that has mastered its subject; and few scholars will require a completer statement of the principles of the Chinese theologies, their development, present phase, and contrasted character, than he furnishes. — *Tribune* (New York).

CHINESE BUDDHISM. A volume of Sketches, Historical, Descriptive, and Critical. 8vo, gilt top, $4.50.

With the purpose constantly in mind to speak for the advancement, the civilization, and the Christianization of the Chinese, Dr.

Edkins has here written a work fit to serve, for ordinary readers at least, the double purpose of a history of Buddhism and a critical examination of its effects upon the intellect and life of China. It is a work of great interest and of permanent value. — *Evening Post* (New York).

Ludwig Feuerbach.

THE ESSENCE OF CHRISTIANITY. Translated from the Second German Edition by MARIAN EVANS (George Eliot). 8vo, gilt top, $3.00.

I confess that to Feuerbach I owe a debt of inestimable gratitude. Feeling about in uncertainty for the ground, and finding everywhere shifting sands, Feuerbach cast a sudden blaze into the darkness, and disclosed to me the way. — S. BARING-GOULD, in *The Origin and Development of Religious Belief.*

Washington Gladden.

THE LORD'S PRAYER. Seven Essays on the Meaning and Spirit of this universal Prayer. 16mo, gilt top, $1.00.

Often as we offer this prayer, and much as we have studied over it to give proper expositions of it from the pulpit and in the catechism, we shall henceforth pray it more intelligently than we ever have before; nay, we have learned, we think, to pray better in all our supplications, and to comprehend more in them than has been our wont. — *Lutheran Quarterly* (Philadelphia).

W. R. Greg.

THE CREED OF CHRISTENDOM. Its Foundations contrasted with the Superstructure. 2 vols. 8vo, gilt top, $5.00.

A model of honest investigation and clear exposition, conceived in the true spirit of serious and faithful research. — *Westminster Review* (London).

Dr. Martin Haug.

ESSAYS ON THE SACRED LANGUAGE, WRITINGS, AND RELIGION OF THE PARSIS. Second Revised Edition, by Dr. E. W. WEST. 8vo, gilt top, $4.50.

It supplies the most accurate knowledge now accessible of one of the noblest forms of historic religion, and is the product of genuine and thorough scholarship. — *Christian Register* (Boston).

Hindu Pantheism (A Manual of).

THE VEDANTASARA. Translated, with Annotations, by Major G. A. JACOB, Bombay Staff Corps. With Preface by E. B. COWELL, M. A., Professor of Sanskrit in the University of Cambridge. 8vo, gilt top, $2.50.

The Vedântasâra, acknowledged to be the best presentation of the modern phase of these tenets, is in this little book translated, and its fourteen sections are explained, one by one, with large critical annotation. The notes show wide research in the realm of curious speculation, while the translation may be accepted as accurate and faithful. — *Christian Union* (New York).

Hymns of the Ages.

HYMNS OF THE AGES. First, Second, and Third Series. Each in one volume, illustrated with steel vignettes, after TURNER. 12mo, $1.50 each; half calf, $9.00 a set; morocco, $12.00.

They date all the way from the sixth century to-day. But, oldest and newest, they deal with that which is older than the ancientest, and newer than the latest of them. And this is the ground of their excellence, and of the esteem in which they are held, — that worthily and sincerely they deal with that truth in souls whose infinite variety age cannot wither and custom cannot stale, and with which every heart, as it is pure, finds itself at home in a dear and sacred kinship. — *Christian Examiner.*

Henry James.

THE SECRET OF SWEDENBORG. Being an Elucidation of his Doctrine of the Divine Natural Humanity. 8vo, tinted paper, $2.50.

We admire the metaphysical acuteness, the logical power, and the singular literary force of the book, which is also remarkable as carrying into theological writing something besides the hard words of secular dispute, and as presenting to the world the great questions of theology in something beside a Sabbath-day dress. — *Atlantic Monthly.*

SOCIETY THE REDEEMED FORM OF MAN, AND THE EARNEST OF GOD'S OMNIPOTENCE IN HUMAN NATURE. Affirmed in Letters to a Friend. Crown 8vo, $2.00.

Samuel Johnson.

ORIENTAL RELIGIONS, AND THEIR RELATION TO UNIVERSAL RELIGION. By SAMUEL JOHNSON.

INDIA. 8vo, 802 pages, $5.00; half calf, $8.00.

Samuel Johnson's remarkable work is devoted wholly to the religions and civilization of India; is the result of twenty years' study and reflection by one of the soundest scholars and most acute thinkers of New England, and must be treated with all respect, whether we consider its thoroughness, its logical reasoning, or the conclusion, unacceptable to the majority, no doubt, at which it arrives. — *Republican* (Springfield).

CHINA. 8vo, 1,000 pages, $5.00; half calf, $8.00.

Altogether the work of Mr. Johnson is an extraordinarily rich mine of reliable and far-reaching information on all literary subjects connected with China. . . . He decidedly impresses us as an authority on Chinese subjects. — E. J. EITEL, Ph. D., Editor of *The China Review* (Hong Kong).

Thomas Starr King.

CHRISTIANITY AND HUMANITY. Sermons. Edited, with a Memoir, by EDWIN P. WHIPPLE. Fine steel portrait, 12mo, $2.00; half calf, $4.00.

CONTENTS: The Experimental Evidence of Christianity; Cries from the Depth; The Supremacy of Jesus; Christian Thought of the Future Life; True Spiritual Communications; Life more Abundantly; Lessons of the Drought; The Christian and the Heathen Dollar; The Divine Estimate of Death; Distribution of Sorrows; Deliverance from the Fear of Death; The Two Harvests; The Organ and its Symbolism; The Supreme Court Decision and our Duties; Living for Ideas and Principles; The Heart and the Issues of Life; Salt that has lost its Savor, or Religion Corrupted; Lessons from the Sierra Nevada; Living Waters from Lake Tahoe; The Comet of July, 1861; Religious Lessons from Metallurgy; Christian Worship.

The Koran.
SELECTIONS FROM THE KORAN. By EDWARD WILLIAM LANE. A new edition, revised and enlarged, with an introduction by STANLEY LANE POOLE. 8vo, gilt top, $3.50.

Alvan Lamson, D. D.
THE CHURCH OF THE FIRST THREE CENTURIES; or, Notices of the Lives and Opinions of the Early Fathers, with special reference to the Doctrine of the Trinity; illustrating its late origin and gradual formation. Revised and enlarged edition. 8vo, $2.50.

Dr. Lamson was a Unitarian in opinion, but in this book he does not advocate his views except by showing how they are supported by history.

Rev. J. Long.
EASTERN PROVERBS AND EMBLEMS ILLUSTRATING OLD TRUTHS. 8vo, $3.50.

This curious collection of proverbs, gleaned principally from among the Eastern peoples, illustrates the analogy of the old truths of Scripture with the common sayings in every-day use in the East.

Samuel Longfellow and Samuel Johnson.
HYMNS OF THE SPIRIT. 16mo, $1.25.

A collection of remarkable excellence.

W. A. McVickar, D. D.
LIFE OF THE REV. JOHN McVICKAR, S. T. D. With portrait, crown 8vo, $2.00.

Hundreds of scholars in all professions and vocations, now living, will be delighted with this admirable biography of their revered master, who for fifty years stood foremost among the eminent men who filled the professors' chairs in Columbia College. — *Journal* (Albany).

William Mountford.
EUTHANASY; or, Happy Talk towards the End of Life. New edition, 12mo, $2.00.

It is the product of a mind cultivated, gentle, and reverent, appealing to the subtle intuitions of the spirit, and aiming to persuade the soul to rest in the peace of confidence in the goodness of God. — *Advertiser* (Boston).

Elisha Mulford, L L. D.

THE REPUBLIC OF GOD. 8vo, $2.00.

It is the mirror of the age, the gospel of the age, the embodiment of the thought of the age, and yet, for the most part, it is the statement of the truth of all ages as it concerns the spiritual life of man. The prime thought of the book can no more be shaken than the eternal hills, and whether men accept or dispute different points in its development, it is one of the few books that sooner or later create a new world for men to live in. — *Times* (New York).

No book on the statement of the great truths of Christianity at once so fresh, so clear, so fundamental, and so fully grasping and solving the religious problems of our time, has yet been written by any American. — *Advertiser* (Boston).

It is the most important contribution to theological literature thus far made by any American writer. — *The Churchman* (New York).

A book which will not be mastered by hasty reading, nor by a cool, scientific dissection. We do not remember that this country has lately produced a speculative work of more originality and force. ... The book is a noble one — broad-minded, deep, breathing forth an ever-present consciousness of things unseen. It is a mental and moral tonic which might do us all good. — *The Critic* (New York).

Rev. T. T. Munger.

ON THE THRESHOLD. Familiar Lectures to Young People on Purpose, Friends and Companions, Manners, Thrift, Self-Reliance and Courage, Health, Reading and Intellectual Life, Amusements, and Faith. 16mo, gilt top, $1.00.

This book touches acts, habits, character, destiny; it deals with the present and vital thought in literature, society, life; it is the hand-book to possible careers; it stimulates one with the idea that life is worth living; there are no dead words in it. The production of a book of this sort is not an every-day occurrence: it is an event; it will work a revolution among young men who read it; it has the manly ring from cover to cover. — *Times* (New York).

THE FREEDOM OF FAITH. Sermons. 16mo, $1.50.

CONTENTS: Prefatory Essay: The New Theology; On Reception of New Truth; God our Shield; God our Reward; Love to the Christ as a Person; The Christ's Pity; The Christ as a Preacher; Land-Tenure; Moral Environment; Immortality and Science; Immortality and Nature; Immortality as Taught by the Christ; The Christ's Treatment of Death; The Resurrection from the Dead; The Method of Penalty; Judgment; Life a Gain; Things to be Awaited.

J. A. W. Neander.

GENERAL HISTORY OF THE CHRISTIAN RELIGION AND CHURCH. Translated from the German by Rev. JOSEPH TORREY, Professor in the University of Vermont. With an Index volume. The set, with Index, 6 vols., $20.00. Index volume, separate, $3.00.

"Neander's Church History" is one of the most profound, carefully considered, deeply philosophized, candid, truly liberal, and independent historical works that have ever been written. In all these respects it stands head and shoulders above almost any other church history in existence. . . . Professor Torrey has executed admirably his part of the task; and I can say of his translation (what I can say about no other that I have ever seen), I now use the translation constantly in preference to the original.— Professor CALVIN E. STOWE, Andover, Mass.

Peep of Day Series.

PEEP OF DAY SERIES. Comprising "The Peep of Day," "Precept upon Precept," and "Line upon Line.". 3 vols. 16mo, each 50 cents; the set, $1.50.

Elizabeth Stuart Phelps.

THE GATES AJAR. 16mo, $1.50.

Of all the books which we ever read, calculated to shed light upon the utter darkness of sudden sorrow, and to bring peace to the bereaved and solitary, we give, in many important respects, the preference to "The Gates Ajar."— *The Congregationalist* (Boston).

Physicus.

A CANDID EXAMINATION OF THEISM. By PHYSICUS. 8vo, gilt top, $2.50.

Prayers of the Ages.

PRAYERS OF THE AGES. Compiled by CAROLINE S. WHITMARSH, one of the editors of "Hymns of the Ages." $1.50.

I have long wished for something of the kind, a broad, liberal, catholic presentation of what must be regarded as the flower of the world's piety and devotion. The "Hymns of the Ages" are favorite volumes with me, and I have comforted the sick and sorrowing with them. But this last volume, it seems to me, I shall value highest.— JOHN G. WHITTIER.

George Putnam, D. D.

SERMONS BY GEORGE PUTNAM, D. D., late Pastor of the First Religious Society in Roxbury, Massachusetts. With fine steel portrait. 16mo, gilt top, $1.75.

CONTENTS: If Thou hadst been here; I have Trodden the Wine-Press alone; Life a Voyage; Jesus and Solomon; Almost and Altogether; Tekel; Christian Manliness — Doing and Standing; Go Quickly; True Religion; Unitarianism; Infidelity; One Faith; The Windows towards Jerusalem; Oh, that I knew! The One Foundation; The Offense of the Cross; Science and Theology; Hath God said it? Righteousness First; Hindrances; Anthropomorphism; Thou shalt say, No; The Miracle of Cana; Introductory I. and II.; Ordaining Address.

Rev. James Reed.

SWEDENBORG AND THE NEW CHURCH. 16mo, $1.25.

While the work is definite and positive in its affirmations, it is written in an admirable spirit, and is quite free from every taint of that narrow sectarianism or supercilious dogmatism which too often disfigures professedly religious works, and may be cordially recommended to any one who desires to acquaint himself with the principles of Biblical interpretation and the theological views of the Swedenborgians or New Church. — *Christian Union* (New York).

Edward Robinson, D.D., LL.D.

HARMONY OF THE FOUR GOSPELS, in Greek. 8vo, $1.50.

THE SAME, in English, 12mo, 75 cents.

BIBLICAL RESEARCHES IN PALESTINE. 3 vols. 8vo, with maps, $10.00. Price of the maps alone, $1.00.

Dean Stanley said of these volumes: "They are amongst the very few books of modern literature of which I can truly say that I have read every word. I have read them under circumstances which riveted my attention upon them while riding on the back of a camel; while traveling on horseback through the hills of Palestine; under the shadow of my tent, when I came in weary from the day's journey. These were the scenes in which I first became acquainted with the work of Dr. Robinson. But to that work I have felt that I and all students of Biblical literature owe a debt that can never be effaced."

It lays open, unquestionably, one of the richest discoveries, one of the most important scientific conquests, which has been made for a long time in the field of geography and Biblical archæology. — CARL RITTER.

PHYSICAL GEOGRAPHY OF THE HOLY LAND. A Supplement to "Biblical Researches in Palestine." 8vo, $3.50.

A capital summary of our present knowledge. — *London Athenæum.*

HEBREW AND ENGLISH LEXICON OF THE OLD TESTAMENT, including the Biblical Chaldee. From the Latin of WILLIAM GESENIUS, by EDWARD ROBINSON. *Twenty-second Edition.* 8vo, half russia, $6.00.

Gesenius is indispensable. No one has yet arisen who, with the same comprehensive mastery of the lexical material, can lay claim to the uniform sobriety of philological judgment and the all but absolute freedom from bondage to the trammels of theory which characterize Gesenius. He is still the "prince of Hebrew lexicographers." — Professor P. H. STEENSTRA, *Cambridge Episcopal Theological School.*

ENGLISH-HEBREW LEXICON: Being a complete Verbal Index to Gesenius' Hebrew Lexicon. By JOSEPH LEWIS POTTER, A. M. 8vo, $2.00.

Rev. Thomas Scott.

THE BIBLE, WITH EXPLANATORY NOTES, PRACTICAL OBSERVATIONS, AND COPIOUS MARGINAL REFERENCES. By Rev. THOMAS SCOTT. 6 vols. royal 8vo, sheep, $15.00.

I believe it exhibits more of the mind of the Spirit in the Scriptures than any other work of the kind extant. — Rev. ANDREW FULLER.

William Smith.
DICTIONARY OF THE BIBLE, comprising its Antiquities, Biography, Geography, and Natural History. By WILLIAM SMITH. Edited by Professor HORATIO BALCH HACKETT and EZRA ABBOT, LL. D. In four volumes, 8vo, 3,667 pages, with 596 illustrations. Cloth, beveled edges, strongly bound, $20.00; full sheep, $25.00; half morocco, $30.00; half calf, extra, $30.00; half russia, $35.00; full calf, or full morocco, gilt, $40.00; russia, or levant, $45.00.

There are several American editions of Smith's Dictionary of the Bible, but this edition comprises not only the contents of the original English edition, unabridged, but very considerable and important additions by the editors, Professors Hackett and Abbot, and twenty-six other eminent American scholars.

This edition has 500 more pages than the English, and 100 more illustrations; more than a thousand errors of reference in the English edition are corrected in this; and an Index of Scripture Illustrated is added. In view of the improvements made in this edition, Professor ROSWELL D. HITCHCOCK, of New York, said: "There cannot well be two opinions about the merits of Smith's Bible Dictionary. What was, to begin with, the best book of its kind in our language, is now still better." The *London Bookseller* remarked: "It seems that we have to thank America for the most complete work of the kind in the English, or, indeed, in any other language."

No similar work in our own or in any other language is for a moment to be compared with it. — *Quarterly Review* (London).

Robert South, D. D.
SERMONS PREACHED UPON SEVERAL OCCASIONS. With a Memoir of the author. 5 vols. 8vo, $15.00; sheep, $20.00; half calf, $25.00.

We doubt if, in the single quality of freshness and force of expression, of rapid and rushing life, any writer of English prose, from Milton to Burke, equaled South. — E. P. WHIPPLE, in *North American Review.*

South's sermons are adapted to all readers and all days. — *Retrospective Review* (London).

Harriet Beecher Stowe.
RELIGIOUS POEMS. Illustrated. 16mo, gilt, $1.50.

The poems are all characterized by the genius of Mrs. Stowe. . . . There is a profound appreciation of the *inner life* of religion, — a wrestling for nearness to God. — *American Christian Review.*

A Talmudic Miscellany.
A TALMUDIC MISCELLANY; or, A Thousand and One Extracts from the Talmud, the Midrashim, and the Kabbalah. Compiled and translated by P. I. HERSHON. With Introductory Preface by Rev. F. W. FARRAR. 8vo, gilt top, $4.50.

A scholarly and painstaking book — the volume has a solid value. —*Tribune* (New York).

It will interest theologians, historians, and thinkers. — *Advertiser* (Boston).

Henry Thornton.

FAMILY PRAYERS, AND PRAYERS ON THE TEN COMMANDMENTS, with a Commentary on the Sermon on the Mount, etc. By HENRY THORNTON. Edited by the late Bishop EASTBURN, of Massachusetts. 12mo, $1.50.

Probably no published volume of family prayers has ever been the vehicle of so much heart-felt devotion as these. They are what prayers should be — fervent, and yet perfectly simple. — *Christian Witness.*

Professor C. P. Tiele.

OUTLINES OF THE HISTORY OF RELIGION TO THE SPREAD OF THE UNIVERSAL RELIGIONS. 8vo, gilt top, $2.50.

His main object is to show how that one great psychological phenomenon which we call religion has developed and manifested itself in such various shapes among the different races and peoples of the world. By this outline sketch of the author we see how all religions, even those of highly civilized nations, have grown up from the same simple germs, and we also learn the causes why these germs have in some cases attained such a rich and admirable development, and in others have scarcely grown at all. — *Transcript* (Boston).

The book is one of uncommon and curious interest. — *Courant* (Hartford).

James M. Whiton.

THE GOSPEL OF THE RESURRECTION. 16mo, gilt top, $1.25.

A thoughtful and reverent study of one of the fundamental doctrines of Christianity. To those who are capable of rightly apprehending the spiritual conceptions which Dr. Whiton embodies in this volume, they will serve to clear away many mistaken and material ideas, and will help to make the sublime and inspiring truth of a life beyond the grave more intensely and vitally real. — *Journal* (Boston).

John Woolman.

THE JOURNAL OF JOHN WOOLMAN. With an Introduction by JOHN G. WHITTIER. 16mo, $1.50.

Get the writings of John Woolman by heart. — CHARLES LAMB.

A perfect gem. His is a beautiful soul. An illiterate tailor, he writes in a style of the most exquisite purity and grace. His moral qualities are transferred to his writings. His religion is love. His Christianity is most inviting: it is fascinating. — H. CRABB ROBINSON, in his *Diary.*

N. B. A Catalogue of all the publications of HOUGHTON, MIFFLIN & Co., *containing portraits of many distinguished authors, will be sent to any address on application.*

HOUGHTON, MIFFLIN & CO., BOSTON, MASS.
11 EAST SEVENTEENTH STREET, NEW YORK.

www.ingramcontent.com/pod-product-compliance
Lightning Source LLC
Chambersburg PA
CBHW022110290426
44112CB00008B/615